OpenStack Swift

Joe Arnold and members of the SwiftStack team

Lynn Stewart
SwiftStack
lstewart@swiftstack.com
678-485-4058

Beijing • Cambridge • Farnham • Köln • Sebastopol • Tokyo

OpenStack Swift

by Joe Arnold and members of the SwiftStack team

Printed in the United States of America.

Published by O'Reilly Media, Inc., 1005 Gravenstein Highway North, Sebastopol, CA 95472.

O'Reilly books may be purchased for educational, business, or sales promotional use. Online editions are also available for most titles (*http://safaribooksonline.com*). For more information, contact our corporate/institutional sales department: 800-998-9938 or *corporate@oreilly.com*.

Editor: Andy Oram
Production Editor: Nicole Shelby
Copyeditor: Charles Roumeliotis
Proofreader: Carla Thornton
Indexer: Judy McConville
Cover Designer: Ellie Volckhausen
Interior Designer: David Futato
Illustrator: Rebecca Demarest

October 2014: First Edition

Revision History for the First Edition:

2014-10-08: First release

See *http://oreilly.com/catalog/errata.csp?isbn=9781491900826* for release details.

ISBN: 978-1-491-90082-6

[LSI]

Table of Contents

Part IV. Planning a Swift Deployment

Part V. Debugging and Troubleshooting

Preface

Modern object storage began when applications started to store and serve up assets for web and mobile users. More and more applications needed to deliver content directly to users regardless of whether they were using a laptop, tablet, or smartphone. Object storage is powerful because it can speak the language of the web: HTTP. Additionally, because of its adeptness at storing non-transactional data, it is perfect for archives, backups, file sharing, scientific and research data, and digital media.

This book covers both the Swift object storage project (referred to simply as Swift) and SwiftStack, an object storage software company and platform. SwiftStack offers user-friendly ways of accessing, deploying, and managing Swift clusters. Our goal is to show you how to use Swift on your own, present SwiftStack's main features, and help you decide whether SwiftStack makes sense for you. We believe SwiftStack is a terrific product suitable for many uses, but rest assured that the Swift ecosystem is rich and growing, so there are plenty of options for service providers if SwiftStack turns out not to be a good fit. In the end we want to sell you on Swift object storage, not necessarily on SwiftStack.

Now, six years out from having first used object storage for my applications, I want to share my experiences dealing with the dramatic growth of data. I was fortunate to have a front-row seat as part of the team building one of the first widely used Platform-as-a Service (PaaS) environments running on top of Amazon Web Services. This helped the industry see how powerful an HTTP-based object storage system could be. Personally, I have seen how object storage delivers more flexibility, less lock-in, better control, and lower costs than what traditional storage systems could provide. I have also heard similar things from other organizations. With data (but not IT budgets) growing exponentially, there is absolute certainty that data storage challenges will persist and grow, affecting pretty much everyone who stores and serves data at scale.

The catalyst for this book was the pain I experienced firsthand deploying and managing object storage systems at scale. As a deployer, I often found myself wanting additional practical information. I also wanted to understand more fully the fundamentals of how these systems work, and why and how they should be used. Now it's my hope that this book can deliver both practical and theoretical insights about an important and rapidly evolving topic: object storage with Swift.

Before proceeding further, I'd like to share John Dickinson's memories of working on the original Swift development team. John explains why and how Swift was developed and captures the collaborative and innovative spirit of OpenStack and the development of Swift.

The Origins of Swift: From the Small to the Open

Recalled fondly by John Dickinson, OpenStack Swift Project Technical Lead, Director of Technology at SwiftStack.

In 2008, Rackspace developed its Rackspace Cloud Files cloud storage service as a response to customer demands and as an answer to Amazon's Simple Storage Service (S3). The underlying technology developed for the first iteration of Rackspace Cloud Files was great up to a point, but frankly required a lot of time, effort, and money to scale. With unstructured data growing so rapidly, we knew we needed something better. So in August 2009, Rackspace set a team to work developing a complete, ground up replacement for their initial cloud storage platform. I was fortunate to be on the original project team, code-named "Swift."

A team of about nine of us set to work. None of us had specific roles. Mostly, we sat around in a small, often hot room, on the fourth floor in downtown San Antonio, identifying the hard problems we needed to solve. We were trying to figure out how we would deploy Swift, what the network would look like, what the infrastructure to support it was going to look like—all that good stuff. We were very collaborative, but we would also compete to arrive at the best solution. We'd think about a problem and then go home. Two people would come back the next day with implementations for it and we'd choose the one we thought was better. There was a really great team dynamic and it was an awesome experience. Ideas were always flying around that room and some of them were crazy. But some of them worked out really well.

We worked on this for about a year and in July 2010, as part of the OpenStack project that Rackspace cofounded with NASA, we released the source code for Swift under the Apache 2 license. We contributed the Cloud Files Swift Code, which became OpenStack Object Storage. In October 2010, a subsequent release of Swift, named "Austin," which included the compute orchestration framework contributed by NASA, was made public. The first commercial deployments of Swift outside Rackspace were at Korea Telecom and Internap, which used Swift to provide public cloud storage services. (That's how I came to know Joe Arnold, and ultimately join SwiftStack.) Swift is now used by web companies, businesses of all sizes, life sciences companies, research organizations, and service providers worldwide.

In the end, I think we created the kernel of a great cloud storage platform and I am proud to have been part of that. But it is also very gratifying to be part of something larger. When Rackspace Hosting made a short video about how Swift was made, we chose to end with a shot of text receding into star-filled outer space. Our invocation of *Star Wars* was partly tongue in cheek and partly serious. We really did and still do feel that we're part of a growing rebel force fighting the emergence of proprietary cloud stacks and creating a standard way to deploy applications and connect clouds. We're still part of the minority, but our forces and capacities are growing, in large part because more and more companies and developers are working with OpenStack Swift.

Why This Book?

At SwiftStack, a company that I cofounded in 2011, our big idea was to provide Swift object storage with a management system so our customers could achieve (1) flexibility in how (and where) they deployed their storage, (2) control of their data without being locked in to a vendor, and (3) extremely economical private cloud storage.

These features are the essence of software-defined storage (SDS), a new term that is still evolving. We think the term perfectly illustrates the fundamental change that Swift represents. Key aspects of SDS are scalability, adaptability, and the ability to use most any hardware. Operators can now make choices concerning how their storage is scaled and managed, and how users can store and access data—all driven programmatically for the entire storage tier, regardless of where the storage resources are deployed. SwiftStack was very early in this trend and was one of the first to offer an SDS storage controller to manage commodity storage hardware.

SwiftStack is dedicated to delivering and improving Swift solutions because we believe that data storage should scale globally, without technical constraints, limits, or lock-in. When data-centric organizations and data-centric applications can grow unconstrained, they will be able to discover and take advantage of new opportunities and innovations in their industries.

This book was started as a way to voice those beliefs. We are highlighting SDS, which is a fundamental change that is happening in the storage sector. Of course, we will shine the spotlight brightly on understanding the Swift object storage project and we will introduce SwiftStack. We bring not just our ideas—but the experience of the entire SwiftStack team. SwiftStack is fortunate to include some of the founders of Swift and top contributing Swift developers. Together, we have learned much from real-world deployments, large and small, which we will share with you throughout this book.

Who Should Read This Book?

OpenStack Swift is written for deployers, operators, and developers interested in using Swift. Although it's not necessary to read this book cover to cover, we make an attempt to provide the topics in a logical order.

This book attempts to explain Swift in clear and simple terms so that anyone can understand the basic concepts and principles, though a few skills will be useful to get the most out of this book. We assume some familiarity with Linux administration, networking, and storage. Additionally, basic programming skills will come in handy for the chapters covering the Swift API. We offer programming overviews on Python, Ruby, PHP, and Java.

This book aims to help newcomers learn from our experiences. Our goal is to get you up and running more quickly and easily, making your successful conversion to Swift, well, swifter!

What's in This Book?

This book has three major components. Part I (Chapters 1 through 4) covers the fundamentals of Swift in a way we hope is accessible to all our readers. Think of it as a Swift boot camp. We aim to familiarize you with the architecture, history, use cases, and basic operation of Swift.

Part II (Chapters 5 through 8) is geared to developers who want to get the most out of their Swift cluster. A big shift has happened with the transition from filesystems to objects, and these chapters will provide a foundation on how to use an HTTP-addressable object storage system. How to use Swift—and how *not* to use Swift—will be covered in gruesome detail.

The next major component of the book is for storage operators, architects, and systems administrators. We break this section into three parts—installation, planning a deployment, and ongoing operations. Part III (Chapters 9 and 10) covers Swift installation options. Part IV (Chapters 11 through 14) offers guidance on deployment considerations: hardware, networking, and Swift features of interest to operators. Finally, Part V (Chapters 15 through 17) covers what to do when (not if) something goes wrong.

Depending on your interests, here are a few possible itineraries through the book:

- If you're responsible for designing and architecting a Swift cluster, read Part I, then check out Part IV.
- If you're a developer, after reading Part I, continue with Part II to learn about Swift and its API.

- If you're a systems administrator or in operations, read Part I, then head straight to Part III, then Part IV.

Conventions Used in This Book

The following typographical conventions are used in this book:

Italic
: Indicates new terms, special emphasis, URLs, email addresses, filenames, and extensions.

`Constant width`
: Used for program listings, as well as within paragraphs to refer to program elements such as variable or function names, databases, data types, environment variables, statements, and keywords.

`Constant width bold`
: Highlights key parts of examples.

Angle brackets (<>)
: Shows text that should be replaced with user-supplied values or values determined by context.

The following terms are used in this book:

Drive, disk, device
: A *drive* refers to a storage medium, generally a hard disk drive (HDD) or solid-state drive (SSD). The term *disk* can also be used. A *device* is a drive as it is seen by the system.

OpenStack Object Storage, OpenStack Swift, Swift Object Storage, Swift
: OpenStack Object Storage is commonly called OpenStack Swift or Swift Object Storage, or simply referred to as Swift within the OpenStack community. All these terms are used in the book and all references to Swift should be understood as referring to the OpenStack Swift project.

Multi-region cluster
: Sometimes referred to as global cluster or geo-cluster. We prefer the term *multi-region cluster* (MRC) as it best fits with the actual tiering name (regions) and indicates that regions need not be separated by vast geographic distances.

Swift node
: A machine running Swift processes is referred to as a node.

Using Code Examples

This book aims to help you work effectively with Swift. In general, you may use the code in this book in your programs and documentation. You do not need to contact us for permission unless you're reproducing a significant portion of the code. For example, writing a program that uses several chunks of code from this book does not require permission. Selling or distributing a CD-ROM of examples does require permission. Answering a question by citing this book and quoting example code does not require permission. Incorporating a significant amount of example code from this book into your product's documentation does require permission.

We appreciate, but do not require, attribution. An attribution usually includes the title, author, and publication year. For example: "*OpenStack Swift*, by Joe Arnold and members of the SwiftStack team (O'Reilly). Copyright 2015 SwiftStack, Inc., 978-1-491-90082-6."

If you feel your use of code examples falls outside fair use or the permission given here, feel free to contact us via email (*contact@swiftstack.com*).

Examples will be maintained at *http://swiftstack.com/book/*.

Safari® Books Online

Safari Books Online is an on-demand digital library that delivers expert content in both book and video form from the world's leading authors in technology and business.

Technology professionals, software developers, web designers, and business and creative professionals use Safari Books Online as their primary resource for research, problem solving, learning, and certification training.

Safari Books Online offers a range of plans and pricing for enterprise, government, education, and individuals.

Members have access to thousands of books, training videos, and prepublication manuscripts in one fully searchable database from publishers like O'Reilly Media, Prentice Hall Professional, Addison-Wesley Professional, Microsoft Press, Sams, Que, Peachpit Press, Focal Press, Cisco Press, John Wiley & Sons, Syngress, Morgan Kaufmann, IBM Redbooks, Packt, Adobe Press, FT Press, Apress, Manning, New Riders, McGraw-Hill, Jones & Bartlett, Course Technology, and hundreds more. For more information about Safari Books Online, please visit us online.

How to Contact Us

SwiftStack provides an SDS system for object storage. Our solution combines a unique, decoupled storage controller with Swift, which gives our customers cost-effective, scale-out storage running on standard server hardware.

The company was founded in 2011 to help operations teams implement and manage an easy-to-use, multitenant, and highly scalable cloud storage platform. Our product is compatible with Red Hat Enterprise Linux, CentOS, and Ubuntu, and can run on a wide range of hardware.

SwiftStack is headquartered in San Francisco, CA, with support operations covering Asian and European time zones. To contact us, you can email *contact@swiftstack.com*. If you have specific questions for me, you can email me at *joe@swiftstack.com*.

As you use this book and work with Swift and SwiftStack, we invite your comments and feedback. From the very start, Swift has benefited from the contributions of hundreds of developers and users. And we hope that doesn't stop.

This book was a collaborative effort. We're proud of what we've put together. But we also know there will be future editions and we invite your comments, feedback, and suggestions. Please let us know what we need to correct or add; share your insights; and help us create a resource that will serve you and the broader community better. You can do so by visiting *http://swiftstack.com/book/*.

Please address comments and questions concerning this book to the publisher:

> O'Reilly Media, Inc.
> 1005 Gravenstein Highway North
> Sebastopol, CA 95472
> 800-998-9938 (in the United States or Canada)
> 707-829-0515 (international or local)
> 707-829-0104 (fax)

We have a web page for this book, where we list errata, examples, and any additional information. You can access this page at *http://bit.ly/openstack_swift*.

To comment or ask technical questions about this book, send email to *bookquestions@oreilly.com*.

For more information about our books, courses, conferences, and news, see our website at *http://www.oreilly.com*.

Find us on Facebook: *http://facebook.com/oreilly*

Follow us on Twitter: *http://twitter.com/oreillymedia*

Watch us on YouTube: *http://www.youtube.com/oreillymedia*

Acknowledgments

Over a hundred developers have contributed to Swift. I'd like to thank each one of them for their ongoing contributions. There are also hundreds of operators of Swift who count on a stable, reliable storage system. Without them, Swift would just be an interesting idea. So, I would like to thank all of the Swift operators for trusting us with your data.

This book is the collaborative work of several authors. Amanda Plimpton served as a linchpin for this project. In addition to the chapters she wrote, she was able to dream up, assemble, and pull out of us the many pieces of content needed to form a cohesive whole. Jon Solera authored five crucial chapters on how to architect and develop Swift applications, how to use and develop Swift middleware, and options for authentication and authorization. Martin Lanner contributed several chapters on building, managing, and benchmarking Swift clusters.

This project couldn't have come together without the support of a large cast. Many at SwiftStack have contributed to writing this book. Thanks to Hugo Kuo for his expert knowledge of configuring Swift, and to Alexander Corwin, Darrell Bishop, John Dickinson, Clay Gerrard, Sam Merritt, Zack M. Davis, and everyone else on the team who provided feedback. Thanks to Anders Tjernlund for thinking we should write this book in the first place.

Thanks to our technical reviewers, Paul Luse, Peter Portante, and Rodney Peck, who took time from their busy schedules to help us make a better book. Thanks to Christina Marcet for technical editing. Finally, many thanks to Mark Feldman for providing his craft of writing to this project and for advocating for the reader.

—Joe Arnold

PART I
Fundamentals and Architecture

This part covers the fundamentals of Swift—think of it as a Swift boot camp. It aims to give you useful information about the architecture and purpose of Swift that will guide you to administering and programming it correctly. This section also discusses some history, use cases, major Swift components, and the basic operation of Swift.

CHAPTER 1
The Evolution of Storage

Joe Arnold

In 2011, OpenStack Object Storage, code-named Swift, was launched as an inaugural project within the OpenStack cloud computing project. OpenStack Swift was a thoughtful and creative response to the unprecedented and precipitous growth in data. It introduced the world to an open-source storage system proven to run at extremely large scale.

The timing couldn't have been more perfect. Just as the growth in online data was taking off, software-defined storage (SDS) with systems such as Swift was being developed. Object storage and SDS are logical next steps in the evolution of storage.

But before getting into Swift (in Chapter 2), we should examine the boom in unstructured data, its particular storage requirements, and how storage has evolved to include object storage and SDS. We will also explain how object storage compares to the more familiar block and file storage.

Storage Needs for Today's Data

In this era of connected devices, demands on storage systems are increasing exponentially. Users are producing and consuming more data than ever, with social media, online video, user-uploaded content, gaming, and Software-as-a-Service applications all contributing to the vast need for easily accessible storage systems that can grow without bounds. A wide spectrum of companies and institutions are facing greater and greater storage demands. In the geological and life sciences, machine-generated data is much more valuable when it is accessible. Video productions are taping more hours at higher resolution than ever before. Enterprises are capturing more data about their projects and employees expect instant access and collaboration.

What is all this data? The majority is "unstructured" data. This means that the data does not have a predefined data model and is typically stored as a file as opposed to an entry in a database (which would be structured data). Much of this unstructured data is the ever-proliferating images, videos, emails, documents, and files of all types. This data is generated by consumers on billions of devices with more coming online each year. Data is also being generated by the many Internet-connected devices such as sensors and cameras across all types of industry.

The Growth of Data: Exabytes, Hellabytes, and Beyond

To understand the scale of this growth in data, consider that according to research conducted by the International Data Corporation (IDC) in 2013, worldwide installed raw storage capacity (byte density) will climb from 2,596 exabytes (EB) in 2012 to a staggering 7,235 EB in 2017.[1] Stored data is continuing to grow at ever faster rates, leading IDC to estimate that by 2020 the amount of data in the world will reach 35,840 exabytes. Divided by the world's population, that is roughly 4 terabytes per person.

By now you might be wondering just how big an exabyte is. It's an almost unimaginably large quantity, but let's try. It's equivalent to about one thousand petabytes (PB), one million terabytes (TB), or one billion gigabytes (GB). These figures will be meaningful to some, but if they're not, we'll contextualize this a bit more. An average book takes up about 1 megabyte. The largest library in the world, the Library of Congress, has about 23 million volumes, which total approximately 23 TB of data. So it would take over 43,000 libraries the size of the Library of Congress to generate an exabyte. Another example would be high-resolution photos, which are roughly 2 MB in size; an exabyte would be almost 537 billion high-resolution photos.

Storage capacity continues to grow, necessitating new labels for ever larger quantities of data. Beyond an exabyte (10^{18} bytes), we have the zettabyte (10^{21} bytes) and yottabyte (10^{24} bytes), which follow the prefixes offered by the International System of Units (SI). In response both to the rapid growth of data and the proliferation of terms, some have suggested that we simply use "hellabyte," for "hell of a lot of bytes."

Requirements for Storing Unstructured Data

Unstructured data often needs to be stored in a way that ensures durability, availability, and manageability—all at low cost.

Durability
: Durability is the extent to which a storage system can guarantee that data will never be permanently lost or corrupted, in spite of individual component failures (such as the loss of a drive or a computer). Data is arguably the most critical (and often irreplaceable) thing we create. Many types of data must be stored forever. In a data

1. Press release for *IDC's Outlook for Data Byte Density Across the Globe Has Big Implications for the Future*, October 2013. (*http://bit.ly/idc_press*)

center, most unstructured data needs to be kept for a very long time to meet customer expectations, legal and regulatory requirements, or both.

Availability
: Availability refers to a storage system's uptime and responsiveness in the face of individual component failures or heavy system load. Unstructured data usually needs to be available in an instant across a variety of devices regardless of location; users want to access their data on their mobile devices, laptops at home, and desktops at work. Although some data can be archived, many users expect most of their data to be immediately available.

Manageability
: Manageability—the level of effort and resources required to keep the system functioning smoothly in the long term—can easily be an issue with small storage systems, or even with a personal computer. The concept can include personnel, time, risk, flexibility, and many other considerations that are difficult to quantify. With larger storage systems coming online, manageability becomes critical. Storage should be easy to manage. A small number of administrators should be able to support a large number of storage servers.

Low cost
: Unstructured data needs to be stored at low cost. With enough money, any storage problem can be solved. However, we live in a world of constraints. Business models and available budgets require low-cost data storage solutions. There are many factors that need to be accounted for in a systems' overall costs. This includes initial up-front expenses, such as the cost of acquiring hardware. But there are also ongoing costs that might need to be factored in. These costs might include additional software licenses, personnel costs to manage the system, and data center costs such as power and bandwidth.

No One-Size-Fits-All Storage System

Although it would be great if there was a one-size-fits-all solution for the large amounts of mostly unstructured data the world is generating, there isn't. Storage systems entail trade-offs that we can think of as responses to their particular requirements and circumstances.

The CAP theorem, first advanced by Eric Brewster (University of California at Berkeley professor, Computer Science Division) in 2000, succinctly frames the problem. It states that distributed computer systems cannot simultaneously provide:

Consistency
: All clients see the same version of the data at the same time.

Availability
: When you read or write to the system, you are guaranteed to get a response.

Partition tolerance
: The system works when the network isn't perfect.

Because these are incompatible, you have to choose the two that are most important for your particular circumstances when implementing a distributed computer system.[2] Because partition tolerance isn't really optional in a distributed system, this means partition tolerance will be paired with either consistency or availability. If the system demands consistency (for example, a bank that records account balances), then availability needs to suffer. This is typically what is needed for transactional workloads such as supporting databases. On the other hand, if you want partition tolerance and availability, then you must tolerate the system being occasionally inconsistent. Although purpose-built storage systems offer an operator more reliability for a particular workload than a general-purpose storage system designed to support all workloads, if a system purports to do all three equally well you should take a closer look. There are always trade-offs and sacrifices.

Following the CAP theorem, Swift trades consistency for *eventual* consistency to gain availability and partition tolerance. This means Swift is up to the task of handling the workloads required to store large amounts of unstructured data. The term "eventual consistency" refers to a popular way of handling distributed storage. It doesn't meet the ideal of providing every update to every reader before the writer is notified that a write was successful, but it guarantees that all readers will see the update in a reasonably short amount of time.

This allows Swift to be very durable and highly available. These trade-offs and the CAP theorem are explored in greater depth in Chapter 5.

Object Storage Compared with Other Storage Types

Different types of data have different access patterns and therefore can be best stored on different types of storage systems. There are three broad categories of data storage: block storage, file storage, and object storage.

Block storage
: This stores structured data, which is represented as equal-size blocks (say, 2^{12} bits per block) without putting any interpretation on the bits. Often, this kind of storage is useful when the application needs to tightly control the structure of the data. A common use for block storage is databases, which can use a raw block device to efficiently read and write structured data. Additionally, filesystems are used to ab-

2. This principle is similar to the adage that says you can only pick two: fast, cheap, or good.

stract a block device, which then does everything from running operating systems to storing files.

File storage
: This is what we're most used to seeing as desktop users. In its simplest form, file storage takes a hard drive (like the one on your computer) and exposes a filesystem on it for storing unstructured data. You see the filesystem when you open and close documents on your computer. A data center contains systems that expose a filesystem over a network. Although file storage provides a useful abstraction on top of a storage device, there are challenges as the system scales. File storage needs strong consistency, which creates constraints as the system grows and is put under high demand. In addition, filesystems often require other features (such as file locking) that create a barrier for working well with large amounts of data.

Object storage
: This will be familiar to those who regularly access the Internet or use mobile devices. Object storage doesn't provide access to raw blocks of data; nor does it offer file-based access. Instead, it provides access to whole objects or blobs of data—generally through an API specific to that system. Objects are accessible via URLs using HTTP protocols, similar to how websites are accessible in web browsers. Object storage abstracts these locations as URLs so that the storage system can grow and scale independently from the underlying storage mechanisms. This makes object storage ideal for systems that need to grow and scale for capacity, concurrency, or both.

One of the main advantages of object storage is its ability to distribute requests for objects across a large number of storage servers. This provides reliable, scaleable storage for large amounts of data at a relatively low cost.

As the system scales, it can continue to present a single namespace. This means an application or user doesn't need to—and some would say shouldn't—know which storage system is going to be used. This reduces operator burden, unlike a filesystem where operators might have to manage multiple storage volumes. Because an object storage system provides a single namespace, there is no need to break data up and send it to different storage locations, which can increase complexity and confusion.

A New Storage Architecture: Software-Defined Storage

The history of data storage began with hard drives connected to a mainframe. Then storage migrated off the mainframe to separate, dedicated storage systems with in-line controllers. However, the world keeps changing. Applications are now much larger. This means their storage needs have pushed beyond what the architecture of an in-line storage controller can accommodate.

Older generations of storage often ran on custom hardware and used closed software. Typically, there were expensive maintenance contracts, difficult data migration, and a tightly controlled ecosystem. These systems needed tight controls to predict and prevent failures.

The scale of unstructured data storage is forcing a sea change in storage architecture, and this is where SDS enters our story. It represents a huge shift in how data is stored. With SDS, the entire storage stack is recast to best meet the criteria of durability, availability, low cost, and manageability.

SDS places responsibility for the system in the software, not in specific hardware components. Rather than trying to prevent failures, SDS accepts failures in the system as inevitable. This is a big change. It means that rather than predicting failures, the system simply works through or around those failures.

Unstructured data is starting to rapidly outpace structured data in both total storage and revenue. SDS solutions offer the best way to store unstructured data. By providing a way to deal with failures, it becomes possible to run your system on standard and open-server hardware—the kind that might fail occasionally. If you're willing to accept this, you can easily add components to scale the system in increments that make sense for your specific needs. When whole systems can be run across mix-and-match hardware from multiple vendors—perhaps purchased years apart from each other—then migration becomes less of an issue.

This means that you can create storage that spans not just one rack, one networking switch, or even just one data center, but serves as a single system over large-scale, private, corporate networks or even the Internet. That is a powerful defense against the deluge of data that many businesses are experiencing.

Software-Defined Storage Components

An SDS system separates the intelligence and access from the underlying physical hardware. There are four components of an SDS system:

Storage routing

The storage routing layer acts as a gateway to the storage system. Pools of routers and services to access the routers can be distributed across multiple data centers and geographical locations. The router layer scales out with each additional node, allowing for more capacity for data access.

The routers in an SDS system can route storage requests around hardware and networking faults. When there is a hardware failure, the system applies simple rules to service the request by assembling the necessary data chunks or retrieving copies of the data from non-failed locations.

The processes in an SDS system account for access control, enable supported protocols, and respond to API requests.

Storage resilience
: In an SDS system, the ability to recover from failures is the responsibility of the software, not the hardware. Various data protection schemes are used to ensure that data is not corrupted or lost.

  There can be separate processes running on the system to continuously audit the existing data and measure how well the data is protected across multiple storage nodes. If data is found to be corrupt or not protected enough, proactive measures can be taken by the system.

Physical hardware
: Within an SDS system, the physical hardware stores the bits on disk. However, nodes storing data are not individually responsible for ensuring durability of their own data, as that is the responsibility of the storage resilience systems. Likewise, when a node is down, the storage routing systems will route around it.

Out-of-band controller
: SDS systems should be efficient to manage and scale. These distributed storage systems need an alternative form of management rather than a traditional storage controller, which intercepts each storage request. Therefore, an out-of-band, external storage controller is used by operators to orchestrate members of a distributed SDS system.

  A controller can dynamically tune the system to optimize performance, perform upgrades, and manage capacity. A controller can also allow faster recoveries when hardware fails and allow an operator to respond to operational events. In this way, an SDS controller can orchestrate available resources–storage, networking, routing, and services–for the entire cluster.

Benefits of Software-Defined Storage

SDS systems can effectively manage scale and drive operational efficiencies in the infrastructure. Capacity management is a lot simpler with an SDS system, because each component is a member of a distributed system. Because of this arrangement, upgrades, expansions, and decommissions can be achieved without any downtime and with no need for forklift (physical) data migration.

The separation of physical hardware from the software allows for mix-and-match hardware configurations within the same storage system. Drives of varying capacity or performance can be used in the same system, enabling incremental capacity increases. This allows for just-in-time purchasing, which lets you take advantage of the technology innovation curve and avoid deploying too much storage.

SDS solutions are also often open source, which means better standards, more tools, and the ability to avoid lock-in to a single vendor. Open source encourages a large thriving ecosystem, where the diversity of the community members drives standards and tools. Now that we're building applications that need to be compatible with more and more devices, creating and refining standards becomes more and more important.

Why OpenStack Swift?

Swift allows for a wide spectrum of uses, including supporting web/mobile applications, backups, and active archiving. Layers of additional services let users access the storage system via its native HTTP interface, or use command-line tools, filesystem gateways, or easy-to-use applications to store and sync data with their desktops, tablets, and mobile devices.

Swift is an object storage system, which, as we have discussed, means it trades immediate consistency for eventual consistency. This allows Swift to achieve high availability, redundancy, throughput, and capacity. With a focus on availability over consistency, Swift has no transaction or locking delays. Large numbers of simultaneous reads are fast, as are simultaneous writes. This means that Swift is capable of scaling to an extremely large number of concurrent connections and extremely large sets of data. Since its launch, Swift has gained a community of hundreds of contributors, gotten even more stable, become faster, and added many great new features.

Swift can also be installed on what is often referred to as *commodity hardware*. This means that standard, low-cost server components can be used to build the storage system. By relying on Swift to provide the logical software management of data rather than a specialized vendor hardware, you gain incredible flexibility in the features, deployment, and scaling of your storage system. This, in essence, is what software-defined storage is all about.

But what might be most interesting is what happens "under the hood." Swift is a fundamentally new sort of storage system. It isn't a single, monolithic system, but rather a distributed system that easily scales out and tolerates failure without compromising data availability. Swift doesn't attempt to be like other storage systems and mimic their interfaces, and as a result it is changing how storage works.

This comes with some constraints, to be sure, but it is a perfect match for many of today's applications. Swift is more and more widespread and is evolving into a standard way to store and distribute large amounts of data.

Conclusion

In recent years, two major changes to storage have come about in very short order. First, the emergence of web and mobile applications have fundamentally changed data consumption and production. This first started with the consumer web and has grown quickly with increasing numbers of enterprise applications.

The second major change has been the emergence of SDS, which enables large, distributed storage systems to be built with standards-based, commodity storage servers. This has dramatically reduced the costs of deploying data-intensive applications, as there is no reliance on individual hardware components to be durable.

In the next chapter we introduce OpenStack Swift. We will more fully discuss the features and benefits of Swift. After that you'll get to dive into the particulars of the architecture of Swift.

CHAPTER 2
Meet Swift

Joe Arnold

In this chapter you will meet Swift, learning about some of its key features and benefits. This conceptual overview will prepare you for later chapters that go into much greater detail, including Chapter 9, where we cover installing a Swift cluster from source. You will also meet SwiftStack the company, which provides software and support to install and operate Swift. You won't see much of SwiftStack again until Chapter 10 when we cover installing SwiftStack software.

Swift is a multi-tenant, highly scalable, and durable object storage system designed to store large amounts of unstructured data at low cost. Swift is used by businesses of all sizes, service providers, and research organizations worldwide. It is typically used to store unstructured data such as documents, web content, backups, images, and virtual machine snapshots. Originally developed as the engine behind RackSpace Cloud Files in 2010, it was open-sourced as part of the OpenStack project. With hundreds of companies and thousands of developers now participating in the OpenStack project, the usage of Swift is increasing rapidly.

Swift is not a traditional filesystem or a raw block device. Instead, it lets you store, retrieve, and delete objects along with their associated metadata in containers ("buckets" in Amazon S3 terminology) via a RESTful HTTP API. Developers can either write directly to the Swift API or use one of the many client libraries that exist for popular programming languages, such as Java, Python, Ruby, and C#.

Swift's key characteristics include:

Scalablity
: Swift is designed to scale linearly based on how much data needs to be stored and how many users need to be served. This means that it can scale from a few nodes with a handful of drives to thousands of machines with dozens, even hundreds, of petabytes of storage. As the system grows in usage and the number of requests increase, performance doesn't degrade, in part because Swift is designed to be scal-

able with no single point of failure. To scale up, the system grows where needed—by adding storage nodes to increase storage capacity, adding proxy nodes as requests increase, and growing network capacity where bottlenecks are detected.

Durability
: Swift's innovative distributed architecture means that it provides extremely durable storage. The essence of durability is that stored objects will always be available and have data integrity. To ensure an object is persistently available, Swift copies it and distributes the copies across the cluster. Auditing processes run, verifying that data is still good. Replicators run to ensure that the correct number of copies are in the cluster. In the event that a device fails, missing data copies are replicated and placed throughout the cluster to ensure that durability levels are maintained.

Multi-regional capability
: Swift can distribute data across multiple data centers, which may have high latency between them. Distribution can be done for a number of reasons. One would be to provide high availability of data by allowing it to be accessed from each region. Another reason would be to designate one region as a disaster recovery site.

  Swift does this by allowing operators to define *regions* and *zones* within a cluster. Regions generally specify geographic boundaries, such as data centers in different cities. Zones are portions of regions that define points of failure for groups of machines, such as a rack where all the nodes are on one power source going to the same switch. The use of regions and zones ensures that Swift places copies across the cluster in a way that allows for failures. It enables a cluster to survive even if a zone is unavailable. This provides additional guarantees of durability and availability of data.

High concurrency
: Swift is architected to distribute requests across multiple servers. By using a shared-nothing approach, Swift can take advantage of all the available server capacity to handle many requests simultaneously. This increases the system's concurrency and total throughput available. This is a great advantage to those who need to satisfy the storage needs of large-scale web workloads.

Flexible storage
: Swift offers great flexibility in data architecture and hardware, allowing operators to tailor their storage to meet the specific needs of their users. In addition to the ability to mix and match commodity hardware, Swift has storage polices that allow operators to use hardware in a way that best handles the constraints of various situations. For example, need higher performance for some data? Create a storage policy that only uses the SSDs in the cluster. Need data to be available across the globe? Create a storage policy that encompasses data centers across the world. Need data to be in a particular country? Create a policy that will place data only in that region.

Swift's underlying storage methods are also very flexible. Its pluggable architecture allows the incorporation of new storage systems. Typically, direct-attached storage devices are used to build a cluster, but emerging technology (such as key/value Ethernet drives from Seagate) and other open source and commercial storage systems that have adaptors can become storage targets in a Swift cluster.

Open source
: Swift is open-sourced under the Apache 2 license as part of the OpenStack project. With more than 150 participating developers as of early 2014, the Swift community is growing every quarter. As with other open source projects, source code can be reviewed by many more developers than is the case with proprietary software. This means potential bugs tend to be more visible and are more rapidly corrected than with proprietary software. In the long term, "open" generally wins.

Large ecosystem
: The Swift ecosystem is powered by open source code, but unlike some open source projects, it is a large ecosystem with multiple companies that test and develop Swift at scale. Having so many vendors participating greatly reduces the risk of vendor lock-in for users. The large number of organizations and developers participating in the OpenStack project means that the development velocity and breadth of tools, utilities, and services for Swift is great and will only increase over time. Many tools, libraries, clients, and applications already support Swift's API and many more are in the works. With such a vibrant and engaged ecosystem, it is easy to obtain tools, best practices, and deployment know-how from other organizations and community members who are using Swift.

Runs on commodity hardware
: Swift is designed from the ground up to handle failures, so reliability of individual components is less critical. Swift installations can run robustly on commodity hardware, and even on regular desktop drives rather than more expensive enterprise drives. Companies can choose hardware quality and configuration to suit the tolerances of the application and their ability to replace failed equipment.

  Swift's ability to use commodity hardware means there is no lock-in with any particular hardware vendor. As a result, deployments can continually take advantage of decreasing hardware prices and increasing drive capacity. It also allows data to be moved from one media to another to address constraints such as IO rate or latency.

Developer-friendliness
: Developers benefit from the rich and growing body of Swift tools and libraries. Beyond the core functionality to store and serve data durably at large scale, Swift has many built-in features that make it easy for application developers and users. Features that developers might find useful include:

Static website hosting
: Users can host static websites, which support client-side JavaScript and CSS scripting, directly from Swift. Swift also supports custom error pages and auto-generated listings.

Automatically expiring objects
: Objects can be given an expiration time after which they are no longer available and will be deleted. This is very useful for preventing stale data from circulating and to comply with data retention policies.

Time-limited URLs
: URLs can be generated that are valid for only a limited period of time. These URLs can prevent hotlinking or enable temporary write permissions without needing to hand out full credentials to an untrusted party.

Quotas
: Storage limits can be set on containers and accounts.

Upload directly from HTML forms
: Users can generate web forms that upload data directly into Swift so that it doesn't have to be proxied through another server.

Versioned writes
: Users can write a new version of an object to Swift while keeping all older versions.

Support for chunked transfer encoding
: Users can upload data to Swift without knowing ahead of time how large the object is.

Multirange reads
: Users can read one or more sections of an object with a single read request.

Access control lists
: Users can configure access to their data to give or deny others the ability to read or write the data.

Programmatic access to data locality
: Deployers can integrate Swift with systems such as Hadoop and take advantage of locality information to lower network requirements when processing data.

Customizability
: Middleware can be developed and run directly on the storage system. For further details on these features, see Part II.

Operator-friendly
: Swift is appealing to IT operators for a number of reasons. It lets you use low-cost, industry-standard servers and disks. With Swift, you can manage more data and use cases with ease. Because an API is used to store and serve data, you do not spend time managing volumes for individual projects. Enabling new applications is easy and quick. Finally, Swift's durable architecture with no single point of failure lets you avoid catastrophic failure and rest a bit easier. The chapters in this book on deploying and operating Swift clusters will provide you with an overview of how easy it really is.

Upcoming features
: The Swift developer community is working on many additional features that will be added to upcoming releases of Swift, such as storage policies and support for erasure coding. Storage policies will allow deployers and users to choose what hardware data is on, how the data is stored across that hardware, and in which region the data resides. The erasure coding support in Swift will enable deployers to store data with erasure coding instead of (or in addition to) Swift's standard replica model. The design goal is to be able to have erasure-coded storage plus replicas coexisting in a single Swift cluster. This will allow a choice in how to store data and will allow applications to make the right trade-offs based on their use.

Meet SwiftStack

SwiftStack is a company that provides highly available and scalable object storage software based on OpenStack Swift and is one of your alternatives to installing, integrating, and operating Swift directly from source.

Several of the core contributors who are part of the approval process for code contributions to the Swift repositories work at SwiftStack. This, in combination with the company's real-world experience in deploying Swift, allows SwiftStack to contribute heavily upstream and often lead many of the major initiatives for Swift in collaboration with the rest of the Swift developer community.

The SwiftStack software package includes an unmodified, 100% open source version of OpenStack Swift and adds software components for deployment, integration (with authentication and billing systems), monitoring, and management of Swift clusters. SwiftStack also provides training, consulting, and 24×7 support for SwiftStack software, including Swift. The SwiftStack product is composed of two parts:

SwiftStack Node
: This runs OpenStack Swift. SwiftStack Node software automates the installation of the latest, stable version of Swift via a package-based installer. At this writing, there are installers for CentOS/Red Hat Server 6.3, 6.4, or 6.5 (64-bit), or Ubuntu 12.04 LTS Precise Server (64-bit). Additionally, the SwiftStack Node software provides

preconfigured runtime elements, additional integrations, and access methods described below.

SwiftStack Controller
: The SwiftStack Controller is an out-of-band management system that manages one or more Swift clusters and automates the deployment, integration, and ongoing operations of SwiftStack Nodes. As such, the SwiftStack Controller decouples the control and management of the storage nodes from the physical hardware. The actual storage services run on the servers where Swift is installed, while the deployment, management, and monitoring are conducted out-of-band by the SwiftStack Controller.

The SwiftStack product offers several benefits to operators:

Automated storage provisioning
: Devices are automatically identified by agents running on the SwiftStack Node, and an operator places those nodes in a region or zone. The SwiftStack Controller keeps track of all the devices and provides a consistent interface for operators to add and remove capacity.

Automated failure management
: Agents running on the SwiftStack Node detect drive failures and can alert an operator. Although Swift will automatically route around a failure, this feature lets operators deal with failures in a consistent way. Extensive dashboards on cluster statistics also let operators see how the cluster is operating.

Lifecycle management
: A SwiftStack Controller can be upgraded separately from Swift. A Controller can perform a rolling, no-downtime upgrade of Swift as new versions are released. It can be configured with a warm standby if desired. A Controller can also fold in old and new hardware in the same cluster. Agents identify the available capacity and will gradually rebalance data automatically.

User and capacity management
: Several authentication modules are supported by SwiftStack, including on-cluster accounts. You can create storage groups (which can be provisioned with an API), and integrate with the Lightweight Directory Acccess Protocol (LDAP) and OpenStack Keystone. Additionally, these show capacity and trending. A per-account utilization API provides the ability to do chargeback.

Additional access methods
: SwiftStack includes a web UI for users that can be custom-tailored with additional CSS to suit your organization. SwiftStack also includes the ability to provide filesystem access via the Common Internet File System (CIFS)/Network File System (NFS).

Other SwiftStack features include:

- Built-in load balancer
- SSL termination for HTTPS services
- Disk management tools
- Swift ring building and ring deployment
- Automated gradual capacity adjustments
- Health-check and alerting agents
- Node/drive replacement tools
- System monitoring and stats collection
- Capacity monitoring and trending
- Web client / user portal

Additional information on SwiftStack is available at the SwiftStack site (*http://swiftstack.com/product/*).

Now that you have some background, in Chapter 3 we'll start digging more deeply into Swift's architecture and how it works.

CHAPTER 3

Swift's Data Model and Architecture

Joe Arnold
Amanda Plimpton

This chapter aims to familiarize you with the different parts of Swift and how they work together to provide a storage system that is—among other things—durable, scalable, and highly concurrent.

We'll start with a conceptual overview of Swift's data model and then walk you through the different layers of Swift's architecture (clusters, regions, zones, nodes). After that you will learn about the types of Swift server processes (proxy, account, container, object), as well as consistency processes.

After discussing how data is housed and organized, we'll examine Swift's consistent hashing rings and how they determine the locations where data will be placed in the cluster. Finally, we'll wrap up the chapter by showing how you can simplify the management of Swift with the SwiftStack Controller and SwiftStack Node software.

Swift Data Model

OpenStack Swift allows users to store unstructured data objects with a canonical name containing three parts: *account*, *container*, and *object*. Using one or more of these parts allows the system to form a unique *storage location* for data.

`/account`
: The *account storage location* is a uniquely named storage area that will contain the metadata (descriptive information) about the account itself, as well as the list of containers in the account. Note that in Swift, an account is not a user identity. When you hear *account*, think *storage area*.

`/account/container`
: The *container storage location* is the user-defined storage area within an account where metadata about the container itself and the list of objects in the container will be stored.

`/account/container/object`
: The *object storage location* is where the data object and its metadata will be stored.

Because the parts are joined together to make up the locations, the container and object names do not need to be unique within the cluster. If three objects with the name `ObjectBlue` are uploaded to different containers or accounts, each one has a unique storage location, as shown in Figure 3-1. The storage locations for the three objects are:

```
/AccountA/Container1/ObjectBlue
/AccountA/Container2/ObjectBlue
/AccountB/Container1/ObjectBlue
```

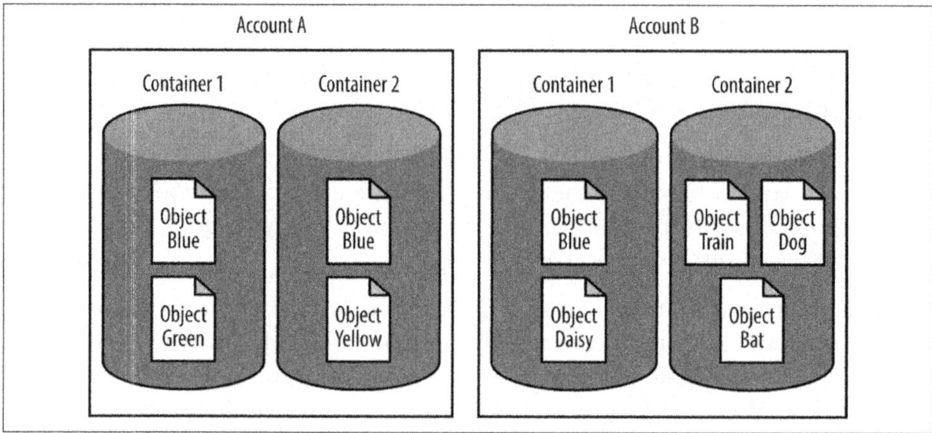

Figure 3-1. Objects can have the same name as long as they are in different accounts or containers

Now that we have discussed storage locations and their construction, let's look a little more closely at the three types of resources that they represent:

Accounts
: Accounts are the root storage location for data. Sometimes compared to a filesystem volume, accounts are uniquely named spaces in the system. Each account has a database that stores both the metadata for the account and a listing of all the containers within the account. Account metadata headers are stored as key–value pairs (name and value) with the same durability guarantees of all Swift data.

It is worth noting that the account databases do not contain objects or object metadata. The account databases are accessed when a user (authorized person or service) requests metadata about an account or a list of all the containers in an account.

Accounts can be designated for single-user access or for multiuser access depending on the permissions that are set. It is common to see single-user access for individual users or service accounts such as "backups," and multiuser access for projects where many team members will require access to the account. Swift users with the correct permissions can create, modify, and remove containers and objects within an account.

Remember that in Swift, an account is a storage account and not a user identity. When you see account, think storage location. We'll make this point repeatedly throughout the book because we've found that many people who are new to Swift struggle at first to distinguish between a Swift account (storage) and a Swift user (identity).

Containers

Containers are user-defined segments of the account namespace that provide the storage location where objects are found. Although containers cannot be nested, they are conceptually similar to directories or folders in a filesystem. Because they are one level down in storage location (*/account/container*), containers do not have globally unique naming constraints. Having two containers with the same name in different accounts (`/AccountA/Container1` and `/AccountB/Container1`) is perfectly valid. There is no limit to the number of containers a user may create within a Swift account.

Just as each account has a database, so does each container. Each container database has the metadata for the container and a record for each object that it contains. Container metadata headers are also stored as key–value pairs (name and value) with the same durability guarantees of all Swift data. One example of metadata for containers is the `X-Container-Read` header, which provides the authorization list for who can read objects in the container.

We should point out that, like account databases, the container databases do not contain the actual objects or object metadata. The container databases are accessed when a user requests a list of all the objects in a container or metadata about the container.

Within an account, you may create and use containers to group your data in logical ways. You can also attach metadata to containers, and use several Swift features to give containers different properties, such as turning them into websites.

Objects

Objects are the data stored in OpenStack Swift. They could be photos, videos, documents, log files, database backups, filesystem snapshots, or any other data. Each object typically includes the data itself and its metadata.

Metadata headers are stored as key–value pairs (name and value) with all the durability guarantees of the object data, and require no extra latency to retrieve. Metadata can provide important information about the object. For example, a video production house could store the video format and duration along with the content; a document could contain authorship information; or a genome sequence could contain information about the process by which it was generated.

Every object must belong to a container. When an object is stored in the cluster, users will always reference it by the object storage location (*/account/container/object*). There is no limit to the number of objects that a user may store within a container.

From the user's perspective, the object storage location is where to find an object. As we have mentioned in previous chapters, Swift is actually storing multiple copies of each object on drives across the cluster to ensure the reliability and availability of the data. Swift does this by placing the object in a logical grouping called a *partition*. A partition maps to multiple drives, each of which will have the object written to it. It should be noted that the partition we are talking about here is not related to the partitioning of hard drives. We'll discuss these internal mechanisms in greater detail later in this chapter. The key concept here is that users access an object by its storage location. The user does not know, and has no need to know, where in the cluster the object is physically located.

Swift Architecture

Swift data (the accounts, containers, and objects) are resources that eventually get stored on physical hardware. We refer to a machine running Swift processes as a *node*. A Swift *cluster* is a group of nodes that collectively run the full set of processes and services needed to act as a distributed storage system.

To ensure durability and isolate failures, you can organize the nodes in a cluster into *regions* and *zones* (Figure 3-2).

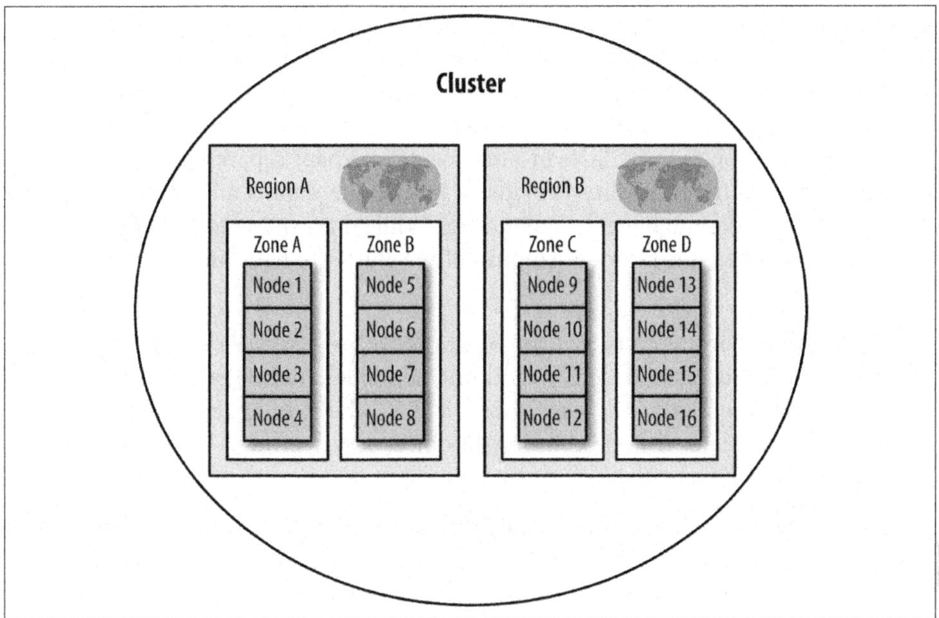

Figure 3-2. How nodes, zones, and regions are organized into a cluster

Regions

Swift allows the parts of the cluster that are physically separate to be defined as *regions*. Regions are often defined by geographical boundaries. For example, a new region might be defined for several racks of servers (nodes) that are placed in a higher-latency, off-site location away from the other nodes in the cluster. A cluster must have a minimum of one region; as a result, there are many single-region clusters where all the nodes belong to the same region. Once a cluster is using two or more regions, it is a multi-region cluster (MRC).

Multi-region clusters have certain read and write behaviors. In particular, when an MRC receives a read request, Swift will favor copies of the data that are closer, as measured by latency. This is called *read affinity*.

Swift also offers *write affinity*, but not by default. By default, Swift attempts to simultaneously write data to multiple locations in an MRC, regardless of the region. This is well suited for low-latency connections where the write requests, data transfer, and responses can be fast.

In the case of a high-latency connection, it might help to turn on *write affinity*. With write affinity, each write request creates the necessary number of copies of the data locally. Then the copies are transferred asynchronously to other regions. This allows faster write operations, at the cost of increased inconsistency between regions until the asynchronous transfers complete.

Zones
Within regions, Swift allows availability *zones* to be configured to isolate failures. An availability zone should be defined by a distinct set of physical hardware whose failure is isolated from other zones. In a large deployment, availability zones might be defined as separate facilities in a data center, perhaps separated by firewalls and powered by different utility providers. In a single data center deployment, the availability zones might be different racks. While there does need to be at least one zone in a cluster, it is far more common for a cluster to have many zones.

Nodes
Nodes are physical servers that run one or more Swift server processes. The main Swift server processes are proxy, account, container, and object. A node running an account or container server process will also be storing account or container data and metadata. A node running an object server process will also be storing objects and their metadata.

A collection of nodes that run all the processes needed for Swift to act a distributed storage system is referred to as a cluster. As discussed in this section, there are many ways to logically group the nodes in a cluster, mostly based on physical criteria. An additional way to group nodes is with storage policies.

Storage policies
Storage policies are a way for Swift operators to define space within a cluster that can be customized in numerous ways, including by location, replication, hardware, and partitions to meet specific data storage needs. A powerful and flexible tool, storage policies are set at the object level and implemented at the container level. This increased versatility of a Swift object storage cluster means that operators can create storage policies that target hardware tiering, increased data durability, geographic constraints, and more.

For example, one storage policy could distribute data across multiple regions, another could distribute replicas across a single region, and a third could be deployed only on fast storage media such as SSDs (Figure 3-3).

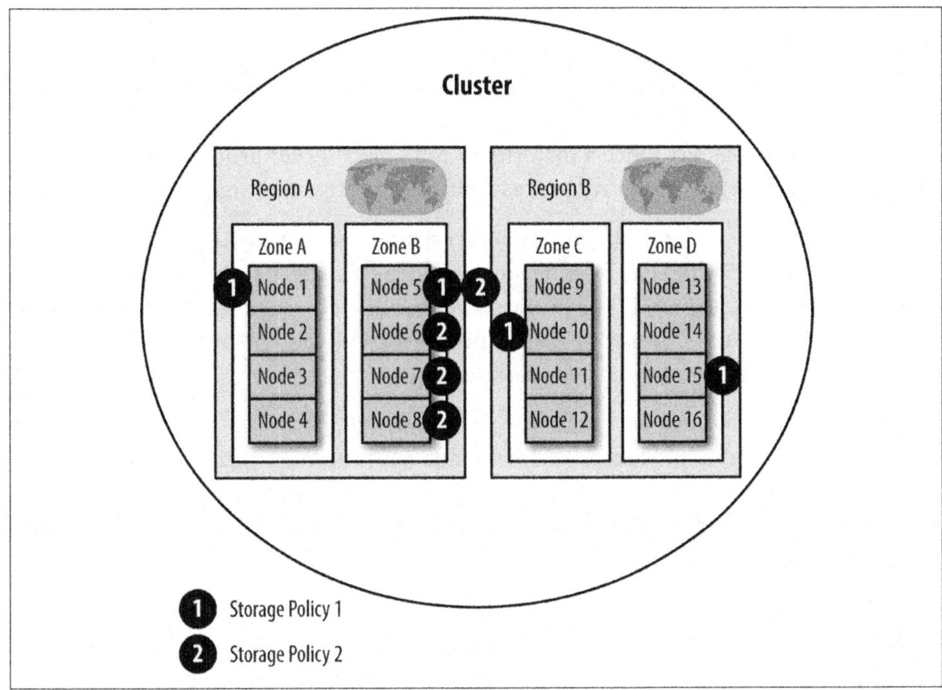

Figure 3-3. Some possible storage policies

Server Processes

Swift runs many processes to manage its data, and each node might run some or all of them. For redundancy and durability, it is usually desirable to have multiple nodes running each of the services. The main Swift server processes are proxy, account, container, and object. When the proxy server process is run by itself on a node, it is called a proxy node. When nodes run account, container, or object server processes, they also store the related type of data, so they are often referred to as storage nodes. Storage nodes will also have a number of other services running on them to maintain data consistency.

When we refer to the collective server processes running on nodes in a cluster, we refer to them as a server process layer; in other words, a proxy layer, an account layer, a container layer, or an object layer.

Let's take a closer look at the server processes.

Proxy layer
: The proxy server process is the only part of the Swift cluster that communicates with external clients. It coordinates the read and write requests from clients, and implements the read and write guarantees of the system.

For example, when a client sends a write request for an object to Swift, the proxy server process determines which nodes would store the object and sends the data to the object server processes on those nodes concurrently. If one of the primary nodes is unavailable, the proxy server process will choose an appropriate hand-off node to write data to. Once a majority of the object server processes respond with success, then the proxy server process returns a success response code to the client.

All messages to and from the proxy server process use standard HTTP verbs (such as `GET`, `PUT`, `POST`, `DELETE`) and response codes. We cover this communication in more detail in Chapter 4. The proxy server process also handles failures and coordinates timestamps. It uses a shared-nothing architecture, so it can be scaled as needed depending on projected workloads.

Account layer

The account server process provides metadata for the individual accounts and a list of the containers within an account. It stores its information in SQLite databases on disk. As with all Swift data, copies of the account data are made and distributed across the cluster.

Container layer

The container server process manages container metadata and a list of objects within each container. The server doesn't know where those objects are, only which objects are in a specific container. The listings are stored as SQLite databases. As with all Swift data, copies of the container data are made and distributed across the cluster. The container server process also tracks statistics such as the total number of objects and total storage usage for that container.

Object layer

The object server process provides a blob storage service that can store, retrieve, and delete objects on the node's drives. Objects are stored as binary files on the drive using a path containing its *partition*, discussed later in this section, and the operation's timestamp. This allows the object server process to store multiple versions of an object while serving up the latest version.

The metadata of an object is stored in the file's extended attributes (`xattrs`), which are supported by most modern filesystems. This design allows the object's data and metadata to be stored together and copied as a single unit.

Each object is stored as a single file on disk unless its size exceeds the maximum file size configured for the Swift cluster. This maximum file size defaults to a rather small value, 5 GB, in order to prevent a single object from filling up a disk while most of the cluster is empty. If an object to be stored is very large, it is divided into several segments and stored with a manifest to allow reassembly later.

Consistency Processes

Storing data on disk and providing an API to the data is not hard. The hard part is handling failures. Consistency processes are responsible for finding and correcting errors caused by data corruption or hardware failures. They are one of the main reasons we say Swift is durable.

Many consistency processes run under the hood to ensure data integrity and availability. Consistency processes run in the background on nodes where the account, container, or object server processes are running. The proxy server process has no associated consistency processes because it does not store account, container, or object data. The specific consistency processes that run depend on the server process:

- Account server processes are supported by the account auditor, account replicator, and account reaper consistency processes.
- Container server processes are supported by the container auditor, container replicator, container, updaters, and container sync consistency processes.
- Object server processes are supported by the object auditor, object replicator, object updaters, and object expirer consistency processes.

As you might have noticed, the auditors and replicators are the two main consistency processes used for all three of the storage-related (account, container, and object) server processes. The updaters are also present for container or object server processes. The rest of the consistency processes are specific to one server process. Let's take a closer look at these consistency processes.

Auditor
: Auditor consistency processes run in the background on all nodes that store data, so if the account, container, or object server process is running on a node, so will the corresponding auditor. These account, container, and object auditors continuously scan the disks on their node to ensure that the stored data has not suffered filesystem corruption. If an error is found, the auditor moves the corrupted data to a quarantine area.

Replicator
: Replicator consistency processes ensure that enough copies of the most recent version of the data are stored where they should be in the cluster. This allows the cluster to stay in a consistent state in the face of temporary error conditions, such as network outages or drive failures. The account, container, and object replicator processes run in the background on all nodes that are running the corresponding services. The replicator continuously examines its local node and compares the accounts, containers, or objects against the copies on remote nodes in the cluster. If one of the remote nodes has an old or missing resource, then the replicator will push its local copy out to that node to update or replace the data. This is called a

replication update. It should be noted that the replicators are only pushing their local data out to remote nodes; they do not pull remote copies in if their local data is missing or out of date.

The replicator also handles object and container deletions. Object deletion starts by creating a tombstone file (a zero-byte file with a name that ends with *.ts*) as the latest version of the object. The replicator pushes the tombstone file as the newest version to other replicas, and the object is removed from the entire system.

Container deletion requires that there be no objects in the container. The container database is then marked as deleted and the replicators push this version out, thus removing the container from the cluster.

Account reaper

An account deletion request sets the status of an account to "deleted" so that it will no longer be used. This also marks it for the *account reaper*. When the account reaper locates an account marked as deleted, it begins stripping out all objects and containers associated with the account, ultimately removing the account record itself. To provide a buffer against error, the reaper can be configured with a delay so that it will wait for a specified period of time before it starts deleting data.

Container and object updaters

The container updater consistency process is responsible for keeping the container listings in the accounts up-to-date. Additionally, it updates the object count, container count, and bytes used in the account metadata.

The object updater has a similar responsibility for ensuring the object listings in the containers are correct. However, the object updater is running as a redundancy. The object server is primarily responsible for updating the object listing in the container. Should it fail to do so, the updater takes over the attempt and will update the container listing as well as the object count and bytes used in the container metadata.

Object expirer

Object expiration allows designated objects to be automatically deleted at a certain time. These processes are the ones that purge the designated data. For more on expiring objects, see Chapter 7.

Locating the Data

With data for accounts, containers, and objects distributed across multiple nodes in the cluster, you might wonder how on earth these system components and services find any one piece of data in the cluster!

The short answer is that when a process on a node needs to find a piece of account, container, or object data, it goes to the local copy of the *rings* and looks up all the locations for that data on the account ring, the container ring, or one of the object rings. Swift stores multiple copies of each piece of data, so looking up where data is stored results in finding multiple locations. The process can then query the locations for the data.

The longer, more technical answer requires discussing what the rings are. Rings are a set of lookup tables distributed to every node in the cluster. Swift uses a modified version of consistent hashing for its rings. To understand the rings and how they are used for data placement, we will first look at hash functions and consistent hashing rings. After that, we will look at Swift's modified consistent hashing ring and how Swift rings are created.

To get started, let's talk about hashing. A real-world example of hashing occurs when you use a printed encyclopedia set. When you look up information in an encyclopedia, you shorten the information you need to just the first few letters (a basic form of hashing) and select that volume from the set based on the letter range that is visible on the spine. For example, if you are looking up greyhounds, you would select the *GOL - JYO* volume. Looking only at the first few letters of a word is a very simple hash function. Although it is effective for encyclopedias, we will need more sophisticated hash functions when storing data on multiple drives.

Ring Basics: Hash Functions

Before we take a closer look at consistent hashing in Swift, let's cover basic hashing by looking at how we can use a hash function to determine where to store objects. Hashing can be thought of as a method that takes a long string of data and generates a shorter fixed-length reference for it. A key point about this method is that it always returns the same results. With our encyclopedia example, no matter how many times you check the encyclopedia set for information about greyhounds, you will always be checking the *GOL - JYO* volume.

A relatively simple method of determining where to store an object would be to use the MD5 algorithm to get the hash of the object's storage location and then divide the hash value by the number of drives available for storage to get the remainder. The value of the remainder would map to a drive ID.

We did say *relatively* simple.

To make this clearer, let's look at an example. Let's name the object storage location */account/container/object* and use four drives for storage, which we'll call Drive 0 through Drive 3. If we had only two drives to store data on, we could get away with just putting objects with even hashes on one drive and odd hashes on the other. However, things get more complicated with three or more drives. Here we take the remainder (a modulo function) so we always get a number that will be equal to or less than the number of drives and allows the object placement to be somewhat even.

We start by using the MD5 function to get the hash of the storage location:

```
md5 -s /account/container/object
MD5 ("/account/container/object") = f9db0f833f1545be2e40f387d6c271de
```

Then we divide the hash result (a hexadecimal numerical value) by the number of drives, and find the remainder (the whole number left over from division).

While we applaud all those who can do hexadecimal division in their heads, let's make this easier for everyone by converting the hexadecimal value to decimal (the result is 332115198597019796159838990710599741918). Now we divide the hash value by the number of drives and determine the remainder. This function, the modulo operation, is represented in most programming languages by the `%` operator:

```
332115198597019796159838990710599741918 % 4 = 2
```

Because the remainder was 2, the object would be stored on Drive 2.

The biggest drawback to this kind of hashing function is that the calculation depends on dividing by the number of drives. Any time a drive is added or removed (a *capacity change*), that object would likely have a different remainder, which would map to a different drive. To demonstrate this, the following table shows which drive the object would be stored on as more drives are added. The hash of the object's storage location remains the same throughout.

Table 3-1. Which drive the object will be stored on

Total drive count	Remainder	Maps to
6	(hash) % 6 = 4	Drive 4
7	(hash) % 7 = 6	Drive 6
8	(hash) % 8 = 6	Drive 6
9	(hash) % 9 = 1	Drive 1
10	(hash) % 10 = 8	Drive 8

Notice that the object would have to be moved to a different drive almost every time a new drive is added or removed. This recalculation would need to happen for all data in the cluster and would result in the majority of the data being moved to different drives after a capacity change. The cluster would then have to spend resources making those moves, generating heavy network traffic, and data unavailability.

Ring Basics: Consistent Hashing Ring

Consistent hashing helps minimize the number of objects that move when capacity is added to or removed from a cluster. Instead of mapping each value directly to one drive, a range of values is associated with one drive. This is done by mapping all the possible hash values around a circle. Each drive is then assigned to a point on the circle based on a hash value for the drive. Although different methods can be used (hash of the drive's

IP address, hash of part of the drive's name, etc.), the result is that all the drives are placed in a fairly random order around the ring, as shown in Figure 3-4.

When an object needs to be stored, the object's hash is determined and then located on the circle. The system will then do a search clockwise around the circle to locate the nearest drive marker. This will be the drive where the object is placed. In Figure 3-4 you can see that the object would be stored on Drive 4. To make it easier for us to see which drive an object will be placed on after the system does its search, we marked the range of hashes that "belong" to a drive.

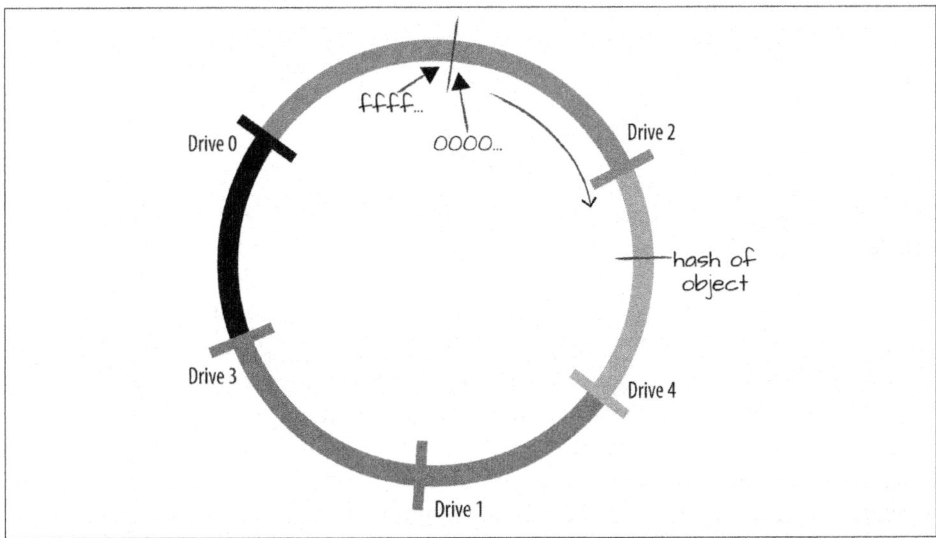

Figure 3-4. Drives and the hashing ring

With this hashing ring in place, you can add a drive or remove a drive and only a few objects will be moved. When a drive is added to the circle, the next drive clockwise from it will lose any objects whose hash is on the part of the hash range that now belongs to the new drive. Those objects will be copied over to the new drive. The rest of the objects, however, will not be disturbed. This is much more efficient than our original example, where nearly all the objects moved around.

To better visualize this, let's add a new drive, Drive 5, to our diagram. The nearest drive clockwise to it, in this case Drive 4, would give up all objects whose hash values match what is now part of the new drive's range. So the object that was on Drive 4 would now be moved to Drive 5 (Figure 3-5).

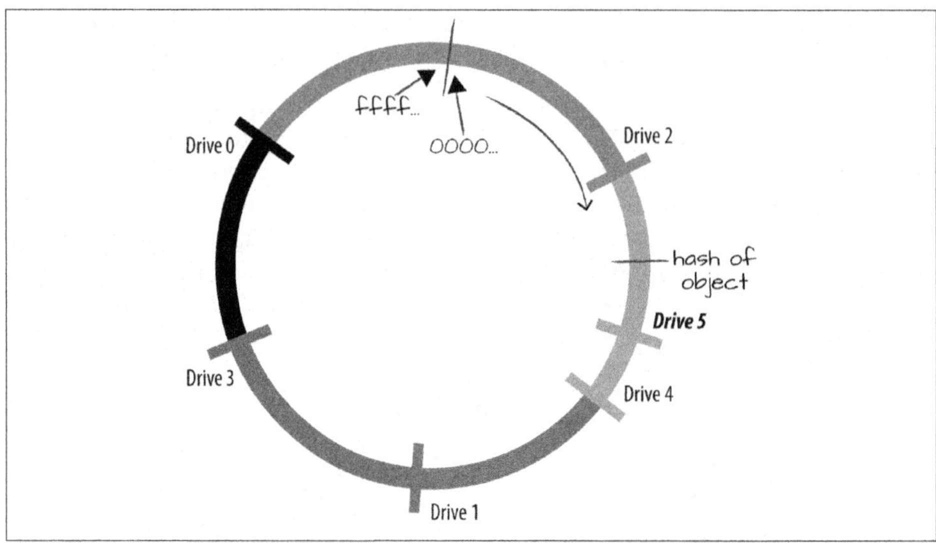

Figure 3-5. New drive added to a ring

Up to now we've been using a simplified version of a consistent hashing ring, with only one marker per drive in order to more clearly show what is happening. In practice, there are multiple markers placed around the circle for each drive. On most consistent hashing rings there would be significantly more markers, even hundreds, per drive placed on the ring. This would be difficult to show on a diagram, so we have added only a few extra markers to show the concept. These multiple markers mean that a drive maps to several small ranges of hash values instead of one big one (Figure 3-6). This scheme has two effects: a new drive will gain objects from more than one drive and the overall placement of objects will be fairly even.

When a new drive is added, it maps to several small hash ranges around the ring and each of the neighbor drives on the ring will give up the objects in those ranges. Moving a smaller number of objects from several different drives keeps data placement more even across all drives.

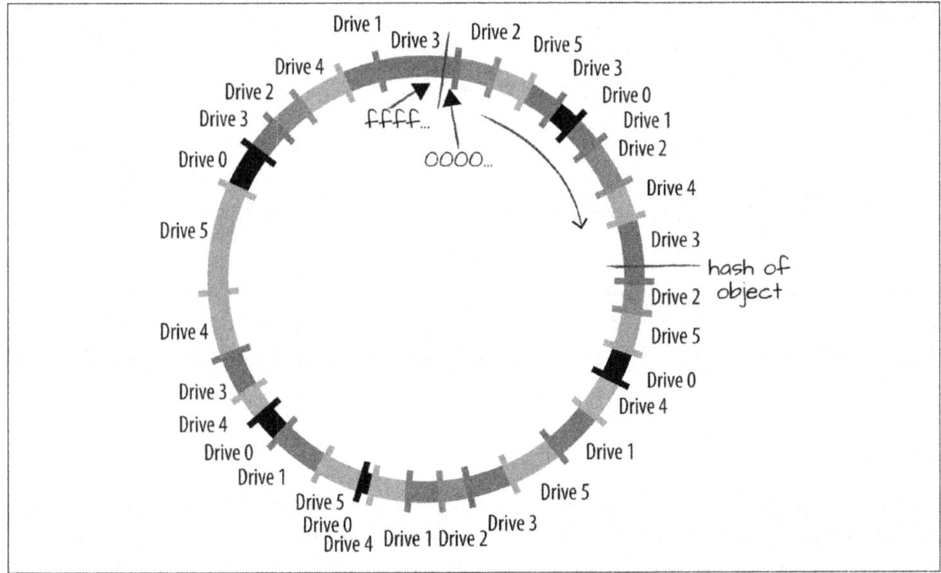

Figure 3-6. Many ranges for each drive

The Rings: Modified Consistent Hashing Ring

At the beginning of our discussion on locating data, we noted that Swift uses a modified consistent hashing ring. These modifications create a partitioned consistent hashing ring that uses replica count, replica lock, and data distribution mechanisms such as drive weight and unique-as-possible placement to build the individual Swift rings. One account ring will be generated for a cluster and be used to determine where the account data is located. One container ring will be generated for a cluster and used to determine where the container data is located. One object storage policy ring will be created for each storage policy in use and used to determine where object data is located.

Partitions

With an unmodified consistent hashing ring, there are numerous small hash ranges that become smaller or larger when drives are added or removed. This churn can result in objects not being available as they are moved during capacity changes.

To prevent this, Swift approaches the hashing ring differently. Although the ring is still divided up into numerous small hash ranges, these ranges are all the same size and will not change in number. These fixed-width *partitions* are then assigned to drives using a placement algorithm.

Let's take a closer look at how partitions are calculated and how drives are assigned to them.

Partition power

The total number of partitions that can exist in your cluster is calculated using the *partition power*, an integer randomly picked during cluster creation.

The formula to calculate the total number of partitions in a cluster is:

$$\text{total partitions in cluster} = 2^{\text{partition power}}$$

For example, if a partition power of 15 is chosen, the number of partitions your cluster will have is $2^{15} = 32{,}768$. Those 32,768 partitions are then mapped to the available drives. Although the number of drives might change in a cluster, the number of partitions will not.

Replica count

When a Swift ring is built, the *replica count* value is how many copies of each partition will be placed across the cluster. For example, if you have a replica count of three, then each partition will be replicated for a total of three copies. Each of the three replicas will be stored on a different device in the cluster for redundancy. When an object is put into the cluster, its hash will match a partition and be copied to all three locations of that partition.

The more replicas you have, the better protected you are against losing data when there is a failure (particularly if you distribute replicas across data centers and geographic regions). The replica count is set to a real number, most often to an integer such as 3.0. In the less common instance where a non-integer replica count is used, a percentage of the partitions will have one additional replica; for instance, a 3.15 replica count means that 15% of the drives will have one extra replica for a total of four. The main reason you might use a fractional replica count would be to make a gradual shift from one integer replica count to another, allowing Swift time to copy the extra data without saturating the network.

Partition replication includes designating handoff drives. This means that when a drive fails, the replication/auditing processes will notice and push the data to handoff locations. This dramatically reduces the MTTR (mean time to repair) compared to standard three-way mirroring or RAID. The probability that all replicated partitions across the system will become corrupt (or otherwise fail) before the cluster notices and is able to push the data to handoff locations is very small, which is another reason we say that Swift is durable. Depending on the durability guarantees you require and the failure analysis of your storage devices, you can set the replica count appropriately to meet your needs.

Replica locks

While a partition is being moved, Swift will lock that partition's replicas so that they are not eligible to be moved in order to ensure data availability. Locks are used both when the rings are being updated as well as operationally when data is moved. The exact length of time to lock the partition is set by the `min_part_hours` configuration option.

Distribution of Data

In addition to using the modified ring structure, Swift has two other mechanisms to distribute data evenly:

Weight
: Swift uses a value called *weight* for each drive in the cluster. This user-defined value, set when the drive is added, is the drive's relative weight compared to the other drives in the ring. The weight helps the cluster calculate how many partitions should be assigned to the drive. The higher the weight, the greater number of partitions Swift should assign to the drive.

Unique-as-possible
: To ensure the cluster is storing data evenly across its defined spaces (regions, zones, nodes, and disks), Swift places partitions using an algorithm called *unique-as-possible*. The algorithm identifies the least-used region, then zone, then server (IP:port), and then, if necessary, the least-used disk, and then places the partition there. The "least-used" formula also attempts to place the partition replicas as far from each other as possible.

  This calculated placement gives deployers the flexibility to organize their infrastructure as they choose and configure Swift to take advantage of what has been deployed, rather than forcing the deployer to change the hardware to conform to the application.

Creating and Updating the Rings

We have covered what the Swift ring structure is like and the key factors used in determining partition placement. Now let's look at the creation of the account ring, container ring, and object rings, and discuss what the internal structures of all the rings are like.

Rings are created and updated by the *ring-builder* utility. There are two steps in ring creation: updating the builder files and rebalancing the rings.

Creating or Updating Builder Files

During cluster creation, Swift uses the ring-builder utility to create *builder files*, which are a blueprint of sorts for creating the rings. A separate builder file is created for accounts, containers, and each object storage policy that contains information such as partition power, replica count, replica lock time, and the location of drives in the cluster. During capacity change in a cluster, Swift uses the ring-builder utility to update the builder file with the updated drive information.

It is important to note that the information in each builder file is separate from the others. So, for example, it is possible to add some drives to the account and container builder files but not the object files.

Rebalancing the Rings

Once the builder files are created or updated with all the necessary information, a ring can be built. The ring-builder utility is run using the `rebalance` command with the builder file as input. This is done for each of the rings: account, container, and object.

Once these new rings are created, they will have to be copied to all the nodes, where they replace the old rings.

Inside the Rings

Each time Swift builds a ring, two important internal data structures are created and populated based on the builder file information.

Devices list
: The ring-builder populates this list with all the devices that were added to the ring-builder file. Each entry for a drive includes its ID number, zone, weight, IP address, port, and device name (Figure 3-7).

Devices lookup table
: This table contains one row per replica and one column per partition in the cluster. Typically it is three rows by thousands of columns (Figure 3-8). The ring-builder calculates the optimal drive to place each partition replica on using the drive weights and the unique-as-possible placement algorithm. It then records the drive in the table.

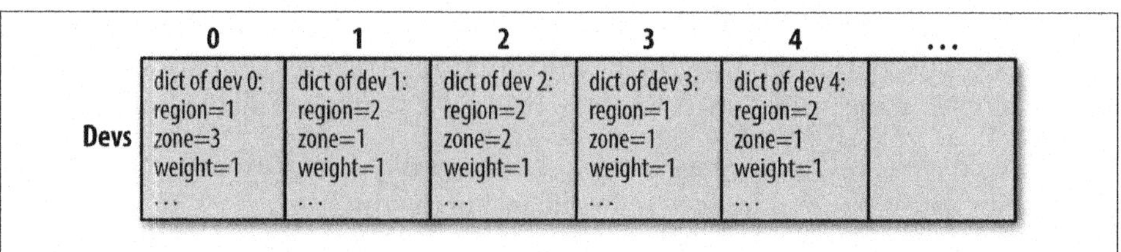

Figure 3-7. Content of Devices list

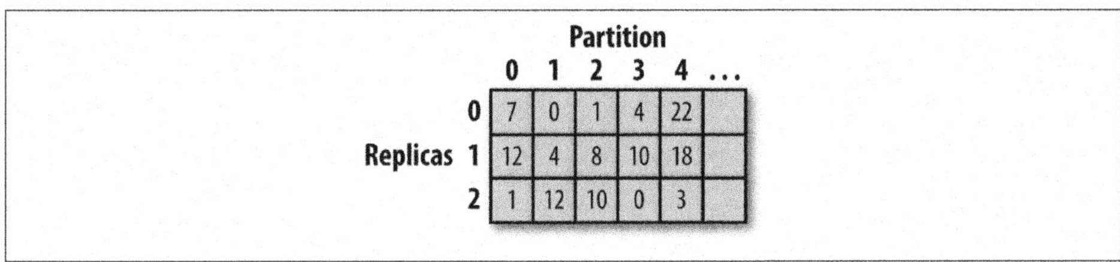

Figure 3-8. Layout of devices lookup table

These internal structures are what get called upon by any Swift process seeking to learn where its data is located. The Swift process will calculate the hash of the data that it is seeking. This hash value will then get mapped to a partition, which can be looked up in the partition column on the devices lookup table. The calling process will check each replica row at that specific column to see what drives the data is on. It then makes a second set of searches to the devices list to get the information it needs about those drives. From there, the process can call on all the data locations.

As you can tell, there is a great deal to say about how Swift is put together and about all the moving parts running behind the scenes. We encourage those who are interested in learning more to read the OpenStack Swift documentation.

Conclusion

In this chapter you've become acquainted with the key concepts Swift uses to organize, distribute, and serve data:

- Accounts and containers to create unique namespaces for objects
- Clusters, regions, zones, storage policies, and nodes—the basic units of Swift architecture
- Main server and consistency processes that handle and maintain the data
- The rings, which map partitions to physical locations

The next chapters cover how all these elements work together so that you can move from a conceptual understanding to becoming comfortable with installing, operating, and maintaining Swift.

CHAPTER 4
Swift Basics

Amanda Plimpton

In Chapter 3 you learned about the architecture of Swift and how it stores data. In this final chapter of Part I, we'll introduce you to the basics of accessing data in Swift. We'll show you how to use cURL, a command-line tool, to perform simple operations on your Swift cluster. In Part II of this book we will go more deeply into the API, introduce a few client libraries, explore some of Swift's advanced features, and learn how to build middleware with Swift.

Talking to the Cluster: The Swift API

Swift, like its animal totem, spends much of its time in motion. There are incoming requests to put data into the cluster, which result in multiple copies of the data being written to different nodes. There are also requests to get data out of the cluster, perhaps to restore a backup or to serve up content to websites or online games. For each request, Swift has to check who is making the request and whether it is allowed, before handling the request itself and responding. In addition to all that, there are the different server and consistency processes swarming behind the scenes, looking after the data. All this activity requires communication and coordination.

As mentioned in the previous chapter, the proxy server process is the only part of the Swift cluster that communicates with external clients. This is because only the proxy server process implements the Swift API. At this point, we can simply say that the Swift API is an HTTP-based set of rules and vocabulary that the proxy server process uses when communicating with external clients. We will cover the Swift API in greater detail in Chapter 5; for our purposes in this chapter, the salient point is that the proxy server process is the only process that can communicate outside the cluster, and that when it does, it listens for and speaks HTTP.

Using HTTP means that communication is done in a request-response format. Each request has a desired action (for example, uploading an object) that is expressed with an HTTP verb. Each response has a response code (for example, "200 OK") that indicates what happened to the request. Because the proxy server process communicates in HTTP, so should users that want to communicate with it. Let's look at (1) sending requests, (2) authorization and action, and (3) responses.

Sending a Request

If you send a request to a Swift cluster, it should contain the following components:

- Storage URL
- Authentication information
- HTTP verb
- Optional: any data or metadata to be written

Storage URL

The storage URL has two roles to play: it is how the request gets to the cluster, and it indicates where in the cluster the request is supposed to take place.

The format of the storage URL should seem familiar to anyone who has visited a website. For example, a storage URL for an object in a Swift cluster might look like this:

```
https://swift.example.com/v1/account/container/object
```

Storage URLs have two basic parts:

Cluster location (`swift.example.com/v1/`)
: The first part of the storage URL is an endpoint into the cluster. It is used by the network to route your request to a node with a proxy server process running so your request can be handled.

Storage location (`/account/container/object`)
: The storage location is composed of one or more identifiers that make up the unique location of the data. The storage location might be one of three formats, depending on which resource you are trying to reach with your request:

    - Account: `/account`
    - Container: `/account/container`
    - Object: `/account/container/object`

Object names might contain a slash character ("/"), so pseudo-nested directories are possible.

Authentication

The first thing Swift does with a request is verify who sent it. Authentication is done by comparing the information you provide to the information on the authentication server Swift uses.

Tools using Swift offer one of two ways to handle authentication:

- Passing the authentication credentials in with the request each time
- Passing in an authentication token that you obtain by making a special authentication request before making any storage requests

This is similar to visiting a company and having the option to present your ID at the check-in desk each time you enter the building, or get a daily visitor's badge that identifies you as someone who can come and go for the day without showing your ID again.

As Swift confirms that you are who you say you are, it also notes what data you are allowed to have access to. Swift uses this information once it knows what the request is for.

There is much more to say about both authentication and authorization, which is why we go into greater detail about them in Chapter 13. For now, the important thing to understand is that each storage request must include authentication information (either credentials or a token) because Swift will verify authentication each time.

HTTP Verbs

Let's look at the different actions that can be requested when communicating in HTTP. Swift uses the standard HTTP verbs as follows:

`GET`
: Downloads objects (with metadata), or lists the contents of containers or accounts.

`PUT`
: Uploads objects, creates containers, or overwrites metadata headers.

`POST`
: Updates metadata (accounts or containers), overwrites metadata (objects), or creates containers if they don't exist.

`DELETE`
: Deletes objects or empty containers.

`HEAD`
: Retrieves header information, including the metadata, for the account, container, or object.

Learn more about HTTP in Chapter 5 and more about custom metadata in "Custom Metadata" on page 83.

After successful authentication, Swift will examine a request to determine the storage location and action that is being requested, so it can check whether the request is authorized. Let's look a little closer at authorization.

Authorization and Taking Action

Although a user might have valid credentials to access a Swift cluster, he might not be authorized to be taking the action (HTTP verb) that he sent in the request. The proxy server will need to confirm authorization before allowing the request to fulfilled.

For example, if you send in a request with your valid authentication information, but try to add an object to someone else's account, you will be authenticated by the system but the request will be rejected because you are not authorized to write to someone else's account.

If the action is authorized, the proxy server process will call on the correct nodes to fulfill the request. The nodes will return the results of the request, which the proxy server process then sends back to you as an HTTP response.

Getting a Response

A response from the Swift cluster will contain at least two, and often three, components:

- Response code and description
- Headers
- Data (optional, depending on request type)

The response code and description lets you know if your request was completed. Broadly, there are five response code categories:

1xx (Informational)
: - Example: 100 Continue

2xx (Success)
: - Example: 200 OK

- Example: 201 Created

3xx (Redirection)
- Example: 300 Multiple Choices
- Example: 301 Moved Permanently

4xx (Client error)
- Example: 400 Bad Request
- Example: 401 Unauthorized

5xx (Server error)
- Example: 500 Internal Server Error

From this list you can tell that the 2xx codes are a good sign that your request was fulfilled. The headers that accompany the response might provide further information. If the request was to `GET` data, the data should be returned as well.

As you can see, although the request-response format is fairly simple (`GET`, `200 OK` or `PUT`, `401 Unauthorized`) there are a lot of moving parts that surround it to ensure that you can communicate with the cluster.

Now that we have gotten an overview of requests and responses, let's look at some of the tools you can use to make and receive them.

Communication Tools

Users and administrators often carry out the HTTP request-response communication using a client application. Swift client applications can take many forms, from tools such as command-line interfaces (CLIs) to sophisticated graphical user interfaces (GUIs) and web-based software.

A CLI is all you need to perform simple operations on a Swift cluster. Because the native language of the Swift system is HTTP, a command-line tool such as cURL (shipped with most Unix-like operating systems) is the best way to communicate with Swift at a low level.

However, sending HTTP requests one at a time, and extracting all the relevant information from the results, can be a bit tedious. For this reason, most people prefer to use Swift at a higher level. For example, developers use Swift client libraries (discussed in Chapter 6) instead of making the underlying HTTP calls themselves.

We take an in-depth look at those higher level communications in the next part of this book; first, however, let's look at basic communication with Swift.

Command-Line Interfaces

We will show commands from two CLIs, *cURL* and *Swift*. Both of these allow a user to send requests, one line at a time, to a Swift cluster. We'll discuss cURL first to show what the HTTP communication between a client and a Swift cluster looks like. Then we'll show you the Swift_CLI, which trades away some of the functionality that cURL provides, in order to offer a smaller but more human-readable set of commands.

Using cURL

Client for URLs (cURL) is a popular command-line tool for transferring data to and from a server using the URL syntax. It is often preinstalled on systems or is easily installed on the command line. cURL provides detailed control over HTTP requests, so it can handle all possible Swift requests. Because cURL takes the HTTP verbs explicitly, it is often used to provide examples for Swift.

cURL requests include the following:

1. `curl` command
2. `-X` *`<method>`* option to provide the HTTP verb (e.g., `GET`, `PUT`)
3. Authentication information (for now, we'll just represent that with [...], but see Chapter 5 for the basics of authentication with cURL)
4. Storage URL
5. Data and metadata (optional)

```
curl -X <HTTP-verb> [...] <Storage-URL> <object.ext>
```

Let's look at some sample HTTP `GET` requests for a user named Bob to see how cURL would be used for objects, containers, or accounts. One common way to use Swift is where every user has exactly one account. We will use that model here, so the storage URL for Bob's Swift account might be *http://swift.example.com/v1/AUTH_bob*. So, for this example, here are the ways Bob would perform some common tasks in Swift:

Create a new container

Make a `PUT` request to the new container's location:

```
curl -X PUT [...] http://swift.example.com/v1/AUTH_bob/container2
```

List all containers in an account

Make a `GET` request to the account's location:

```
curl -X GET [...] http://swift.example.com/v1/AUTH_bob
```

Upload an object

Make a `PUT` request to the object's location:

```
curl -X PUT [...] http://swift.example.com/v1/AUTH_bob/container1 -T object.jpg
```

List all the objects in a container
: Make a GET request to a container's location:

```
curl -X GET [...] http://swift.example.com/v1/AUTH_bob/container1
```

Download an object
: Make a GET request to the object's location:

```
curl -X GET [...] http://swift.example.com/v1/AUTH_bob/container1/object.jpg
```

We'll go into much greater detail about how to use the cURL command with Swift in Chapter 5.

Using Swift

The Swift CLI is part of the `python-swiftclient` package and can be installed on any computer running Python 2.6 or 2.7. Detailed installation instructions can be found on the OpenStack website (*http://bit.ly/openstack_clients*).

Just as the cURL CLI uses the `curl` command, the Swift CLI uses the `swift` command. The `swift` command simplifies things for users, by saving some typing and making several common types of requests easy. However, this simplification comes at a cost: the Swift CLI (the command-line tool) is not able to do everything that Swift (the storage system) can. There are some types of HTTP requests that the Swift CLI does not yet know how to send.

One reason the `swift` command is popular is because it provides users with human-friendly verbs (`upload` instead of `PUT`) to use when communicating with a cluster. It then translates the commands into the appropriate HTTP verbs.

One drawback with the Swift CLI is that is requires you to pass in your authentication information with each command.

Swift CLI subcommands

The commands you type in to the Swift CLI and the corresponding HTTP requests it issues are:

`delete` *(HTTP* `DELETE`*)*
: Delete a container or objects within a container

`download` *(HTTP* `GET`*)*
: Download objects from containers

`list` *(HTTP* `GET`*)*
: List containers in an account or objects in a container.

`post` *(HTTP* `POST`*)*
: Update metadata for account, container, or object (may also be used to create a container)

`stat` *(HTTP* `HEAD`*)*
: Display header information for account, container, or object

`upload` *(HTTP* `PUT`*)*
: Upload files or directories to a container

Let's look again at the HTTP `GET` requests from the cURL section, this time using the `swift` command.

Because the `swift` command requires the username, password, and authentication URL to be passed in with each request, it would look like this:

```
swift download -U myusername -K mysecretpassword  \
      -A https://swift.example.com/auth/v1.0 \
      http://swift.example.com/v1/AUTH_bob/container1/object.jpg \
```

We will represent that authentication information with [...] to make the commands easier to read.

List all containers in an account
: The `list` subcommand sends a `GET` request to the account's storage location:

```
swift list [...] http://swift.example.com/v1/AUTH_bob
```

List all the objects in a container
: The `list` subcommand sends a `GET` request to the container's storage location:

```
swift list [...] http://swift.example.com/v1/AUTH_bob/container1
```

Download an object
: The `download` subcommand sends a `GET` request to the object's storage location:

```
swift download [...] http://swift.example.com/v1/AUTH_bob/container1 object.jpg
```

Custom Client Applications

Although the command-line interfaces are fine for simple operations, many users will need more sophisticated client applications, with customization and integration.

Application developers can construct HTTP requests and parse HTTP responses using their programming language's HTTP library, or they may choose to use open source Swift libraries to abstract away the details of the HTTP interface.

Open source client libraries for Swift are available for most modern programming languages, including:

- Python
- Ruby
- PHP
- C#/.NET
- Java

More information about developing for the Swift API can be found in Chapter 6 and Chapter 7.

Example Scenarios

To describe how these pieces all come together, let's walk through two basic scenarios: uploading and downloading. These will help you understand more practically how Swift works.

Uploading (`PUT`)
: A client uses the Swift API to make an HTTP request to `PUT` an object into an existing container. After receiving the `PUT` request, the proxy server process determines where the data is going to go. The account name, container name, and object name are all used to determine the partition where this object will live. A lookup in the appropriate ring is used to map the storage location (`/account/container/object`) to a partition, and to the set of storage nodes where each replica of the partition is assigned.

  The data is then sent to each storage node, where it is placed in the appropriate partition. Once the majority of the writes have succeeded, the proxy server process can then notify the client that the upload request succeeded. For example, if you are using three replicas, at least two of the three writes must be successful. Afterward, the container database is updated asynchronously to reflect the new object in the container.

Downloading (`GET`)
: A request comes in to the proxy server process for `/account/container/object`. Using a lookup in the appropriate ring, the partition for the request is determined, along with the set of storage nodes that contains that partition. A request is sent to the storage nodes to fetch the requested resource. Once the request returns the object, the proxy server process can return it to the client.

Conclusion

In this chapter, we covered how to access a Swift cluster via the Swift API using command-line client tools (cURL and Swift). We also mentioned that custom client applications can be developed for the API with client libraries for popular programming languages. This introduction will serve you well as we explore using Swift in more depth in the following chapters.

PART II
Application Design with Swift

This section of the book is aimed at developers, ranging from those new to Swift and rusty on HTTP, all the way up to Swift veterans who want to develop their own middleware. We show you the principles of interacting with Swift through RESTful HTTP requests, which are the underlying basis for Swift libraries in many programming languages. Although most chapters show interaction using command-line tools in order to stay at a general level, we will also introduce you to libraries for several languages and will provide some full Python examples. The last chapter in this section discusses the development of middleware, which allows you to extend Swift.

CHAPTER 5

Overview of the Swift API

Jon Solera

This chapter will be most useful to developers and architects considering building a system that includes Swift, or those writing code against an existing Swift installation. In the first section, we'll offer a conceptual overview of Swift's architecture as background for understanding what uses Swift is best suited for. In the second section, we'll see how these theoretical concepts and practical realities influence Swift's implementation, and thus which applications do best on a Swift platform. In the third and final section, we offer an applied overview of how to work with the Swift API, covering basics such as authentication, data retrieval and storage, and how to update and best use metadata.

What Is an API, Anyway?

API stands for "application programming interface," which isn't much more illuminating if you're not clear on the term. An API is the set of rules for interacting with a software system. An API promises, "If you pass in this type of data in this manner, and if it meets these criteria, then you'll get back this result; otherwise, you'll get this type of error." More loosely, an API is the set of instructions for how to use a software system.

The Swift API is a set of rules that specify what types of HTTP requests you are allowed to send to a Swift cluster, what types of success and failure responses you'll get back under what circumstances, and what data those responses will contain. We'll discuss the details of Swift's API in this chapter.

But before we discuss how to use Swift, we'll provide a little theory and background that will help explain how Swift works, the design decisions that shaped its implementation, and how those design decisions affect how you use Swift.

The CAP Theorem

"No One-Size-Fits-All Storage System" on page 5 briefly introduced the CAP theorem, which we'll explore here in more detail since it can help us better understand Swift's architecture.

The CAP theorem, proposed in 2000 by Eric Brewer of UC Berkeley and formally proven in 2002 by Seth Gilbert and Nancy Lynch of MIT, states that it is impossible for a distributed service to simultaneously guarantee consistency (all servers and clients see operations occur in the same order), availability (all client requests receive a response at all times), and partition tolerance (the system is usable even when arbitrary network links are unavailable).

Partition tolerance, or the P in CAP—formally, "the network will be allowed to lose arbitrarily many messages sent from one node to another"—defines our concept of a distributed system. Systems that aren't partition tolerant are either single-node systems or not useful. The availability guarantee might seem easy—surely a server can simply try to communicate with its peers to update, and return an error code if it doesn't get a response from them?—but a subtlety makes it more complicated: we don't know whether the message was lost going from the server to the peer (in which case the peer has the old value), or from the peer back to the server (in which case the peer successfully updated). So when there is no acknowledgment, our original server doesn't know whether to respond with success or failure!

More recently, other researchers have refined the concepts behind the CAP theorem. At Yale, Daniel Abadi points out that unlike consistency and availability, partition tolerance is not something that a design can choose to trade off: either the system is partition tolerant (i.e., it is a correctly functioning distributed system of some kind), or it is not. What is more precisely of interest is how the system behaves under a network partition, and how it behaves when the network isn't partitioned. Abadi calls it "PACELC": during a partition (P), does the system prioritize availability (A) or consistency (C); else (E), if there is no partition, does it prioritize latency (L) or consistency (C)?

Others warn about the use of the term "consistency," which means something different in the CAP sense—a valid total ordering of operations—than it does in the ACID (atomicity, consistency, isolation, and durability) sense in databases, where it refers to database constraints not being violated.

A discussion of the proof of the CAP theorem (and its interesting edge cases) is beyond the scope of this book, but the theorem provides a simple rationale for why many distributed systems are designed to be either consistent (i.e., transactional, like a distributed database) or available (like Swift) but not both. It should be noted that this is an oversimplification of the result proven by the CAP theorem, and Brewer and others have written about how systems (including Swift) choose to be either consistent or available in some circumstances when they could have both properties. Nevertheless, it is certainly true that maintaining consistency and availability in the face of network partitions is difficult at best, introducing complexity and potential brittleness into the system, and at worst it's been proven impossible.

Swift is a classic AP system in the CAP theorem's sense: it provides high availability in the face of partition tolerance, but different clients might see operations in a different order and thus see inconsistent data. In fact, in certain unusual circumstances, it is possible for a single client to write a new value, see the write complete successfully, issue a read for that value, and retrieve the old data. You can successfully create an object, then immediately list the container and not see your object. Given time and sufficiently low system load, Swift is guaranteed to converge to a consistent state. However, applications must be designed to accommodate Swift being in an inconsistent state at times until consistency is restored. This might be a surprise for developers accustomed to ACID database guarantees.

Swift belongs to a class of systems described by the term BASE (basically available, soft state, eventual consistency), an *ever so slightly* contrived acronym intended to distinguish them from ACID systems. Of those descriptors, eventual consistency is the one that seems to be most challenging to developers accustomed to ACID.

Swift's Sweet Spot: High Availability, Redundancy, and Throughput

What kinds of applications are good candidates for a Swift-based architecture? What applications won't work well with Swift?

Due to Swift's eventual consistency, any application that has a transactional nature or needs ACID guarantees—such as a travel booking system that must ensure that two people never buy the same ticket, or a banking system that must ensure that two transactions don't withdraw the same money—generally will not be a good fit for Swift. Similarly, if your application requires that clients nearly always see the same data (and if that fails due to timing delays, that clients always agree afterward on the ordering of mixed read and write operations), you should not choose an AP system for your data storage. Although Swift can help guard against conflicts with headers like `Etag` and `If-Unmodified-Since`, locking or transactional operations are not the core strength of Swift or any AP system.

On the other hand, Swift excels at high availability, redundancy, throughput—and, of course, capacity. To focus on availability over consistency, Swift has no transaction or locking delays. Large numbers of simultaneous reads are fast. Even large numbers of simultaneous writes complete quickly: each write notes its timestamp, and eventual consistency ensures that even under extreme load, conflicts are resolved after some delay.

Swift is excellent for high availability: if the network is unreliable, a strongly consistent distributed system must grind to a halt, but Swift can continue to store and retrieve data. Having a configurable number of redundant copies of your data means that you can arbitrarily increase Swift's throughput for heavy loads, or increase Swift's durability in the face of multiple simultaneous drive failures.

Swift also supports *multi-region clusters*, where redundant servers are located not on different racks in the same data center, but rather anywhere in the world. Because this requires traffic over high-latency routes, the situation resembles a partitioned network, and the performance of any consistent system necessarily becomes horrible. Swift, on the other hand, not only continues to function, but provides distributed points of presence for low-latency Internet access. Although this is likely to have a negative impact on the resolution time required to regain consistency after each write, many systems are willing to accept that trade-off, which would render a strongly consistent system largely unusable.

In short, if your system is willing to accept the limits of Swift's eventual consistency guarantees in exchange for the benefits of high availability, redundancy, and throughput (and huge capacity), Swift is likely to be a good choice for your architecture. Examples of excellent uses for Swift include:

- Storing user data from web applications
- Parallel non-locking operations on massive Big Data datasets
- Serving heavy loads such as high-traffic websites
- Systems whose service level agreements (SLAs) include high availability or guaranteed durability
- Storing large independent files such as photos or videos
- Enterprise solutions such as storing shared project data or intranet service data
- Storing disk-image files such as backup snapshot images or data center machine-provisioning images

Swift API: Background

Fundamentally, Swift is accessed via a RESTful HTTP API. Many developers are already familiar with HTTP and some are familiar with the tricks and traps associated with it. REST is a term that has deviated in common usage from its original and more useful definition. It is often informally used simply to refer to a stateless communication protocol, while the original definition of REST is a much more expansive and powerful term that includes service discoverability and network optimization for servicing requests. Before discussing the Swift API, let's quickly review the basics of HTTP and REST to ensure consistent terminology.

Review of the Hypertext Transfer Protocol (HTTP)

Because Swift relies on HTTP verbs and headers for both user metadata and system parameters, it is useful to review HTTP methods. Although many software systems send data over HTTP, they often do so in ad hoc ways. Swift uses the semantics of HTTP (mostly) as the protocol's authors intended.

When you access a simple static web page in your browser, the browser performs a series of actions on your behalf:

1. It makes a TCP connection to port 80 of the server.
2. It issues the basic request for your web page to the server.
3. It provides a list of client headers to the server.
4. It receives the status code of the request from the server (e.g., `200 OK` or `404 File Not Found`).
5. It receives a list of server headers back from the server.
6. It receives the data—perhaps some HTML—from the server.
7. It might process the data based on the headers (e.g., if the headers specify gzip compression, the browser will uncompress the data returned by the server).
8. Finally, the browser renders the result (e.g., displaying HTML content as indicated by the markup).

Here is a representative HTTP request and response:

```
GET /path/to/page.html HTTP/1.1
Host: www.example.com
User-Agent: Mozilla/5.0 (X11; Ubuntu; Linux x86_64; rv:26.0) Gecko/20100101
Firefox/26.0
Accept: text/html,application/xhtml+xml,application/xml;q=0.9,*/*;q=0.8
Accept-Language: en-US,en;q=0.5
Accept-Encoding: gzip, deflate
Cookie: cookie1=aaa; cookie2=bbb
Connection: keep-alive
X-User-Full-Name: Alice Adams

HTTP/1.1 200 OK
Content-Encoding: gzip
Content-Type: text/html; charset=UTF-8
Date: Fri, 27 Dec 2013 23:24:03 GMT
Server: Apache/2.2.22 (Ubuntu)
Last-Modified: Thu, 23 Apr 2009 21:43:46 GMT
ETag: "b221a-13d-4683fc64ce880"
Accept-Ranges: bytes
Set-Cookie: cookie1=yyy; cookie2=zzz
Content-Length: 8317
X-Frame-Options: SAMEORIGIN
```

```
X-XSS-Protection: 1; mode=block

[content of the web page goes here]
```

In both the request and response, arguably the most important content is the first line. The first line of the request, `GET /path/to/page.html HTTP/1.1`, tells the server that the client is issuing a `GET` request against the URL */path/to/page.html* using the HTTP 1.1 protocol. The first line of the response informs the client that the server replied in the HTTP 1.1 protocol and indicated that the request was successful.

After the first line of the request, the client uses request headers to communicate additional information that affects the request, such as what formats, languages, and encodings it is willing to accept, what browser is being used, and some custom information in a header starting with `X-`. Take note of this convention of reserving the `X-` header namespace for application-specific purposes—Swift makes heavy use of that feature of HTTP.

The first line of the server response gives its status code and a standard text description, in this case "200" and "OK," respectively. There are many other status codes for the various success and error conditions, summarized in "Getting a Response" on page 44. Statuses in the 200-299 range are various types of success, while the 300-399 range is used for redirections, the 400-499 range for client errors, and the 500-599 range for server errors. (The informational 100-199 range is less commonly seen by developers and users, though it is actively used.)

After the first line of the response, the server provides some metadata in its headers, such as the length of the content, the date it was last modified, and the fact that the content is compressed with gzip. It also uses headers starting with `X-` for its own application-specific purposes.

This example showed a `GET` request, the most common type of request on the Web. `GET` requests are used to retrieve data. Servers should not interpret a `GET` request in a way that modifies data, but keep in mind that not all servers are good citizens in all circumstances. (For example, a website might offer users the ability to delete data and, in a poorly implemented system, that might be transmitted to the server as a `GET` request. While most modern sites would not do this, it has definitely happened in the past and it illustrates that you shouldn't depend on external systems to follow best practices.)

HTTP supports several other methods (also called *verbs*) besides `GET`. The `HEAD` method retrieves only the headers, not the actual data; it functions like a `GET` request that omits the data, which can be useful if the data is very large and if we might want to take action based on just the headers. The `PUT` method is used to store data on servers that support it, under appropriate circumstances, such as when the user is authorized to do so. The `DELETE` method requests that the server delete the information at the given URL, again depending on authorization. The `OPTIONS` method asks the server what methods are allowed for the given URL. Web browsers such as Firefox, Internet Explorer, and Chrome generally don't expose HTTP methods other than `GET` and `POST` to users, but the other HTTP methods can be invoked with command-line tools such as cURL or with client-side Javascript (AJAX). Modern web applications make extensive use of these HTTP methods.

Although the `GET`, `HEAD`, `PUT`, `DELETE`, and `OPTIONS` methods perform very different actions, they have one important common feature: all of them are *idempotent*. This means that repeated identical requests yield the same result as a single request. For example, if you `PUT` the same data to the server several times in a row, the result is the same as if you had `PUT` the data once. If you `DELETE` a URL several times in a row, again the result is the same as if you had performed a single `DELETE`. Issuing a `GET` or `HEAD` or `OPTIONS` request doesn't change the data on the server, so of course issuing several of them doesn't change the data, either.

The `POST` method, however, is different. `POST` is the HTTP method reserved for requests that might *not* be idempotent. For example, a `POST` might be used to create a new object, such as a new credit card transaction. If you issue the `POST` twice, you've created two transactions, not one—a very different result indeed!

This carefully structured use of the HTTP verbs was laid out in the original specification of HTTP 1.1 in the early 1990s. However, due to incomplete and revised specifications, early browsers based their protocols on HTTP 1.0 and only implemented `GET` and `POST`, leading to websites that only used `GET` and `POST`. But starting early in the new millennium, the usefulness of the other verbs has become obvious, and newer web development frameworks such as Rails depend on them.

In today's web development, nearly all frameworks use HTTP methods beyond `GET` and `POST`. Rails and Sinatra are the leading examples in the Ruby world; in Python, Tastypie and Piston are two representative examples among many ways to modernize Django in that regard. (Django itself, unfortunately, predates the common use of extended HTTP methods.) It will come as no surprise that Swift also uses these extended HTTP methods.

Representational State Transfer (REST)

Roy Fielding, one of the authors of the HTTP specification, wrote a PhD dissertation in 2000 introducing his concept of REST. Fielding's formulation included many interrelated concepts, including service discoverability, an idea of URIs referencing resources, a noun-based protocol in contrast with RPC-style verb-based protocols, caching and proxy behavior, a model of a network optimized for servicing requests, and other insightful observations. Sadly, the term "REST" is frequently misused to refer merely to stateless communication over HTTP, often with a create-read-update-delete (CRUD) API.

Although HTTP is a fine protocol for a service-oriented architecture, and stateless communication between entities provides many benefits (such as better isolation and testability of architectural components), Fielding's use of the term "REST" encompasses a much wider vision. In particular, the concept of service discoverability is a valuable idea that makes a RESTful service easy to develop against and easy to support across multiple versions with differing capabilities. The interested reader is urged to read Fielding's very accessible dissertation (*http://bit.ly/fielding_paper*).

Swift, HTTP, and REST

With that background, explaining the Swift API becomes quite simple. Swift uses a RESTful HTTP API. Data is retrieved with an HTTP `GET`, stored with a `PUT`, and deleted with (you guessed it!) a `DELETE` request. Metadata is stored in headers, so a `HEAD` request is often useful.

Swift does a better-than-average job of using HTTP status codes correctly, so that a 404 actually means "File Not Found" rather than "something isn't right somewhere." Clients may issue any of several extra HTTP client headers, specifying more advanced Swift features to apply to their requests.

Swift uses HTTP server headers to provide clients with many different types of metadata related to the request. As a developer, if you have a way to issue HTTP requests and receive responses (including headers), whether in the form of a Swift client library or a command-line tool such as cURL, you have all you need to start developing against Swift. Unlike many other systems, no special SDK (software development kit) is necessary—plain HTTP is all you need to access all of Swift's features.

Of course, not every client is authorized for every operation; Alice shouldn't be allowed to delete Bob's data, for example. The general problem is that of *authentication* (verifying who a user is) and *authorization* (determining what a user is allowed to do), collectively referred to as "auth." Swift allows system administrators to configure any of several auth systems, depending on their needs. The auth API is versioned, with auth versions 1 through 3 in active use; we will mostly discuss version 1 auth in this book because it is the simplest and suitable for many needs. In version 1 auth, a request is made to the auth system, with the `X-Auth-User` and `X-Auth-Key` headers set; if the user gives the correct key (password), then Swift issues a response containing an `X-Auth-Token` header. That token is used on subsequent requests to prove that the client has successfully authenticated. The response to a successful authentication request also contains an `X-Storage-Url` header, specifying the root URI of the user's primary account. Auth requests will be discussed in more detail later in this chapter in "Using the Swift API" on page 61.

Swift's RESTful HTTP API produces a system that is easy for developers to understand and characterize. Each API call is a single HTTP round trip. With the exception that a valid auth token must be retrieved for use in later operations, each HTTP round trip requires no other knowledge about the system. This ability to control and observe its state makes Swift easier to test and qualify as part of your architecture than other platforms. You can replicate HTTP content with command-line tools such as cURL in order to confirm system behavior, but when building applications, most developers will want to use a Swift library for their preferred language. In the next chapter, we will provide examples from the `python-swiftclient` library, with some discussion of other language bindings.

Using the Swift API

Although we'll discuss the Swift API in more detail in later chapters, here we present an overview to help readers understand what the RESTful HTTP API looks like, and to help you see how integrating Swift into an existing architecture can be relatively simple. This section assumes a working Swift installation, a valid username and password, and a storage account for that username available in the cluster.

About Your Swift Cluster

Before you even try to access any data, you might want to get some information about your Swift cluster. What version of Swift is it running? What values are configured for its parameters, such as maximum object size? What features are enabled by middleware in its pipeline? This information is all available via the Swift cluster info API, which can be accessed with a simple `GET` request to the path */info* under the Swift cluster's base URL. For example, if your Swift cluster's base URL is *http://swift.example.com*, you can get the cluster info with a `GET` request to the URL *http://swift.example.com/info*. The cluster info API is public; no authentication is required.

The response to an info request will be a JSON dictionary such as the following:


```
{
  "tempauth": {
    "account_acls": true
  },
  "slo": {
    "max_manifest_segments": 1000,
    "min_segment_size": 1048576,
    "max_manifest_size": 2097152
  },
  "swift": {
    "max_file_size": 5368709122,
    "account_listing_limit": 10000,
    "max_meta_count": 90,
    "max_meta_value_length": 256,
    "container_listing_limit": 10000,
    "version": "1.12.0.37.g45feab5",
    "max_meta_name_length": 128,
```

```
        "max_object_name_length": 1024,
        "max_account_name_length": 256,
        "max_container_name_length": 256
    }
}
```

A Swift client application can retrieve and parse the cluster info, and use the results to determine how to proceed based on the cluster's advertised capabilities. This is one way in which Swift implements the RESTful principle of discoverability.

Authentication

With a few exceptions (such as the info request described in the previous section), an authentication token ("auth token") is a prerequisite for nearly all Swift operations. From a cold start, the first step in a Swift operation is to authenticate and receive an auth token. Because Swift allows administrators to plug in their auth system of choice, the *auth URL* (that is, the URL to which requests for authentication are sent) is separate from the *storage URL* (which specifies where data is stored) of the user's primary account. In order to authenticate to Swift, you need to have the cluster's auth URL—and, of course, your username and password.

Your authentication request then looks like this:

```
curl -i -X GET -H 'X-Auth-User: myusername' -H 'X-Auth-Key: mysecretpassword' \
    https://swift.example.com/auth/v1.0
```

In this example, *https://swift.example.com/auth/v1.0* is the auth URL. Generally, Swift traffic should happen over the encrypted HTTPS connection, in order to protect all data on the wire (credentials and tokens for an auth request, or the stored content itself).

The auth system then produces a response. If there is no problem with the Swift installation, and your username and password are correct, then the authentication response code is `200 OK` and the response headers will return with the auth token and the storage URL of your username's primary account, which will look like this:

```
X-Auth-Token: AUTH_tkdc764d39fd1c40c9a293cbea142b90d7
X-Storage-Url: https://swift.example.com/v1/AUTH_myusername
[other HTTP headers]
```

Auth tokens have a configurable expiration time, with a default of 24 hours. During that period, this auth token will prove your identity to the auth system, which can then check to see whether you are authorized to perform the operation you are requesting. If you present an auth token that was previously working but you receive an `HTTP 401` response, then your auth token has likely expired and you should re-authenticate to receive a new token.

The *storage URL* returned by the auth response is the root of the storage area of the user's primary Swift account. *Account* is a bit of a confusing term. In the context of Swift, think of an account as an area where data is stored. Like a bank account, a Swift account may be owned by one person or co-owned by multiple people. A given *user*, such as Alice or Bob, might have access to multiple Swift *accounts*, because the cluster might be set up with one account (storage area) per project team, or per service, or any of several other strategies. So the storage URL returned by the auth request is not necessarily the only storage URL that the user may access.

It is even more important to think of Swift accounts as storage areas when considering Swift's data hierarchy. At Swift's basic level, an account has containers and a container has objects. Unlike a traditional filesystem, however, containers can't be placed in other containers, and objects can't be placed directly in an account without a container. The URL of every object in a Swift cluster looks like *https://swift.example.com/v1/myaccount/mycontainer/myobject*, with exactly one account (storage area) name, one container name, and one object name. So it makes sense to emphasize this:

Swift *users* are *identities*. Swift *accounts* are *storage areas*.

Keep that in mind as we discuss storing and retrieving data, because we will be discussing accounts constantly!

Retrieving Data

Now that you have an auth token, you can issue requests to the storage system. You might have a storage URL from an external source (such as a configuration file, your colleague, or the Swift cluster administrator), but for now let's assume that you're interested in the data in your primary account—the storage URL returned by the auth system's response. If you've successfully authenticated as described in the previous section, you might store your token and storage URL in environment variables, which can be used to simplify requests to the storage system. For example, suppose you store your token in the environment variable `TOKEN` and the storage URL in the environment variable `STORAGE_URL`. If you've already created two containers named *my_photos* and *my_videos* in this account, then this might be a request and response:

```
curl -i -X GET -H "X-Auth-Token: $TOKEN" "$STORAGE_URL"

HTTP/1.1 200 OK
X-Account-Bytes-Used: 458
X-Account-Container-Count: 2
X-Account-Object-Count: 2
[...other headers...]

my_photos
my_videos
```

The 200 response indicates a successful request. If you had tried to access an account for which you did not have authorization, you would receive a `403 Forbidden` response. (`401 Unauthorized` indicates an authentication failure; `403 Forbidden` indicates an authorization failure.) Swift provides metadata about the resource in the headers of its response: in this case, you learn that this account has two containers in it, with only one object in those containers, using a total of 458 bytes. After the metadata, the content of the response appears. This request was a `GET` on an account (storage area) resource; the response is a list of containers in that account.

Swift Header Names Are Case-Insensitive

Swift makes the choice to be case-insensitive with header names, though not with header values. You can pass in `x-auth-user: alice` or `X-Auth-User: alice` (or `x-aUtH-uSER: alice`), and they will all work equivalently. Note that these are all different from `X-Auth-User: ALICE`, however! The header name is case-insensitive, but the header value must use upper- and lowercase letters properly.

Similarly, if you do a `GET` on a container (such as *$STORAGE_URL/my_photos*) rather than on an account as in the previous example, the content of the response would be a list of objects in that container, and the headers of the response would contain metadata about the container such as the number of objects in it. And if you do a `GET` on an object... well, you retrieve the object, of course! (And yes, you also get metadata in the headers.)

If you are interested only in the metadata, you can use a `HEAD` request instead of a `GET`. This avoids the network load of retrieving and sending potentially large objects (or even the potentially large container listing or account listing), and just gives you the information you want.

When you retrieve the listings of an account or a container, you might want them in a format that is easy to parse. You can append `?format=json` to your resource's URL (such as an account's storage URL) to have Swift return your response in JSON, or `?format=xml` for an XML response:

```
% curl -X GET -H "X-Auth-Token: $TOKEN" "$STORAGE_URL?format=json"

[
  {"count": 1, "bytes": 458, "name": "my_photos"},
  {"count": 0, "bytes": 0, "name": "my_videos"}
]

% curl -X GET -H "x-auth-token: $TOKEN" "$STORAGE_URL/my_photos?format=json"

[
  {
```

```
        "hash": "0450d6d21f1aa2aa1fe4a354c8e62c8f",
        "last_modified": "2014-01-16T20:01:04.329970",
        "bytes": 458,
        "name": "happy.png",
        "content_type": "image/png"
    }
]

% curl -X GET -H "x-auth-token: $TOKEN" "$STORAGE_URL/my_photos?format=xml"

<?xml version="1.0" encoding="UTF-8"?>
<container name="my_photos">
 <object>
  <name>happy.png</name>
  <hash>0450d6d21f1aa2aa1fe4a354c8e62c8f</hash>
  <bytes>458</bytes>
  <content_type>image/png</content_type>
  <last_modified>2014-01-16T20:01:04.329970</last_modified>
 </object>
</container>
```

In these examples, observe that with the `?format=...` query parameter, a `GET` request on an account still returns a list of containers, but with some useful metadata included in the data structure. Similarly, a `GET` request on a container still returns a list of objects in the container, but with useful metadata included in the data structure. In both the JSON and the XML example, the returned data and the implementation of lists and attributes are structured in a manner appropriate to the format. Given a JSON parser or XML parser, it would be easy to parse this data and make use of it.

Storing Data

You save data to a Swift cluster with an HTTP `PUT` method. This applies not only to the process of adding an object to a container, but also when adding a container to an account. If a Swift cluster administrator wants to add a new account to the Swift cluster, that is also done as a `PUT`.

In all cases, you execute a `PUT` to the URL of the resource you want to create, as opposed to the URL of the parent resource or any other scheme. If you want to create a new container called *my_music* to go along with *my_photos* and *my_videos*, issue this command:

```
curl -i -X PUT -H "X-Auth-Token: $TOKEN" $STORAGE_URL/my_music
```

A successful `PUT` creates the container, which didn't exist before. The `-i` option lets you see the headers returned by Swift, which look like this:

```
HTTP/1.1 201 Created
Last-Modified: Thu, 16 Jan 2014 19:53:21 GMT
Content-Length: 0
```

```
Date: Thu, 16 Jan 2014 19:53:20 GMT
[...]
```

The 201 response code indicates a successful PUT. You will now see your new container along with the other two, if you issue a GET to the account.

When you PUT an object, you also need to provide the data that will be stored in the object. When developing an application, you will use the methods provided by your Swift library. But we can also do this on the command line with cURL, by uploading a local file as shown in Example 5-1:

Example 5-1. Storing a new object

```
curl -i -X PUT -H "X-Auth-Token: $TOKEN" $STORAGE_URL/my_music/my_song.mp3 \
  -T /tmp/song.mp3
```

cURL uses the `-T` *`filename`* flag to provide the object data. This use of cURL is suitable for testing, or small scripts. In a more complex software development effort, Swift libraries such as `python-swiftclient` would provide equivalent functionality with more efficiency by allowing streaming data rather than requiring a file on the filesystem, and not spawning a subshell to run cURL.

Deleting Data

Deleting an object is as easy as you would expect:

```
curl -i -X DELETE -H "x-auth-token: $TOKEN" \
  $STORAGE_URL/junk_container/junk_object
```

Swift prevents accidental mass deletion of data by requiring that a container be empty before you can delete it. If you try to delete a non-empty container, you will get an HTTP response of `409 Conflict` as shown here:

```
% curl -i -X DELETE -H "x-auth-token: $TOKEN" $STORAGE_URL/junk_container

HTTP/1.1 409 Conflict
Content-Length: 95
Content-Type: text/html; charset=UTF-8
X-Trans-Id: txe0fa9bced54448ecb3753-0052d84131
Date: Thu, 16 Jan 2014 20:29:37 GMT

<html>
  <h1>Conflict</h1>
  <p>There was a conflict when trying to complete your request.</p>
</html>
```

However, once you delete all the objects in the container, the previous request will succeed. (See "Bulk Operations Middleware" on page 88 for an efficient way to delete multiple objects, such as to empty a container.)

Updating Metadata

The HTTP POST method is used to update the metadata of an existing object, container, or account. (For historical reasons, a PUT to a container also updates metadata rather than overwriting it, but this use isn't recommended.) A POST to an object updates its metadata without the overhead of resending the object's content. For instance, in Example 5-1, we stored an MP3 file. When someone retrieves it, we might want its Content-Type header to be set correctly. We could have done this in the original PUT, but we can easily update it now:

```
curl -i -X POST -H "X-Auth-Token: $TOKEN" -H "Content-Type: audio/mpeg" \
  $STORAGE_URL/my_music/my_song.mp3
```

This request results in a few hundred bytes rather than several megabytes of traffic through the system.

In addition to Internet-standard metadata such as Content-Type, Swift also allows and encourages you to set custom metadata on your objects, containers, and accounts. When developing a Swift-based system, consider what metadata might improve your system's performance, help your users understand what they're retrieving, or indicate which of several resources is most appropriate. There are so many possible uses for metadata that we can't begin to discuss them all, but here are a few:

- Information about authors of a work
- Image dimensions or audio duration
- Financial references, such as account number, invoice number, or sales transaction ID
- Origin of the data in the file
- Language of the content

Swift enforces some limits on the size of metadata. (These limits are given in the Swift cluster info available at the */info* URL.) Metadata is usually much smaller in size than the content of the object, so don't expect to store megabytes of information in the metadata. However, storing some carefully chosen metadata can provide your system with surprising flexibility to optimize for performance, minimize traffic, or provide a better user experience.

Conclusion

We hope this chapter has given you both some conceptual background on Swift's architecture and a useful overview of the Swift API. Our goal was to help you understand more fully how Swift is designed and whether it's a good fit for your needs. If it is a good fit, we hope you've been able to get started issuing basic commands. The next chapter focuses on building applications using Swift client libraries, which are more efficient at carrying out extended operations with Swift than the basic commands you've learned so far.

CHAPTER 6

Swift Client Libraries

Jon Solera

The previous chapter introduced the Swift HTTP API, and demonstrated how it can be used with low-level HTTP tools such as cURL. Introducing the API with examples in cURL highlighted the key pieces of information that are exchanged (such as auth credentials and tokens), and how they map to the underlying wire protocol, particularly with the use of HTTP headers. But pragmatically, using cURL for extended Swift sessions can get tedious and repetitive. Although cURL is commonly used to run quick experiments against a Swift cluster, for more extended uses we tend to turn to client libraries in our language of choice. Fortunately, Swift works with a wide array of open source libraries and languages.

This chapter offers an overview of some of the open source client libraries that have been developed for Swift. Although we'll draw most of our examples from Python—the language in which Swift is written—there are strong similarities across Swift client libraries. This means you'll also gain insights into how to use client libraries beyond Python.

Client Libraries

Open source client libraries have been developed for Swift in many languages, including Python, Ruby, PHP, C#/.NET, Java, and others. By looking at the HTTP communication in the previous chapter, we've seen what information these libraries need to:

- Send auth credentials for an auth request
- Receive an auth token (and the storage URL for the primary account) for an auth response
- Send the auth token and other information in HTTP request headers for a storage request

- Receive metadata in the HTTP response headers and content in the response body for a storage response

All client libraries attempt to streamline the send-and-receive process and make it more idiomatic to their language. Most client libraries provide some assistance in parsing responses as well.

A list of Swift client libraries can be found at *http://swift.openstack.org/associated_projects.html*. Some of the most popular libraries according to language are here:

- Python (*http://bit.ly/python-lib*)
- Ruby (*http://bit.ly/fog-lib*)
- PHP (Rackspace library) (*http://bit.ly/rackspace-lib*)
- PHP (Zend library) (*http://bit.ly/zend-lib*)
- C#/.NET (*http://bit.ly/stacknet-lib*)
- Java (*http://bit.ly/java-sdk*)
- Others (SDKs) (*http://bit.ly/other-sdk*)

We'll cover the `python-swiftclient` Python bindings in depth here, with some additional examples from other client libraries. These examples will show the similarities between different client libraries, even across language boundaries, and give you insight into other libraries. But most of our focus will indeed be on Python, Swift's native language, because the `python-swiftclient` library is well developed, easy to use, and supported by the OpenStack project itself.

The Authentication Exchange

Let's start by taking a look at the authentication exchange. To review, a client needs three pieces of information to authenticate to a Swift cluster: a username, a password, and an auth URL. For this example, we assume that the Swift cluster's auth URL is *http://swift.example.com/auth/v1.0*, and we're authenticating as user `alice` with password `passw0rd`.

Recall that in the previous section, we authenticated with cURL in the following way:

```
curl -D- -X GET -H 'X-Auth-User: alice' -H 'X-Auth-Key: passw0rd' \
  https://swift.example.com/auth/v1.0
```

If the username/password combination had been invalid, we would have received an HTTP response code of `401 Unauthorized`. However, we sent a valid username and password, so we received the response code `200 OK`, and the HTTP response included the following headers:

```
X-Storage-Url: https://swift.example.com/v1/AUTH_alice
X-Auth-Token: AUTH_tkdc764d39fd1c40c9a293cbea142b90d7
```

Because that is how Swift's HTTP API handles authentication, we expect that in any client library, we authenticate by invoking some function and passing in an auth URL, username, and password, and the function returns an auth token and probably also a storage URL for the primary account associated with that user. Let's see how this plays out in `python-swiftclient`, which actually gives you two interface choices. You can use a procedural `get_auth()` function, which returns a storage URL and auth token:

```
>>> import swiftclient
>>> authurl, username, password = (
...    'http://swift.example.com/auth/v1.0', 'alice', 'passw0rd')
>>> storageurl, token = swiftclient.get_auth(authurl, username, password)
```

Or you can use an object-oriented method centered around the `Connection` class, as shown here:

```
>>> import swiftclient
>>> authurl, username, password = (
...    'http://swift.example.com/auth/v1.0', 'alice', 'passw0rd')
>>> conn = swiftclient.Connection(authurl=authurl, user=username, key=password)
```

We recommend the second choice, which automatically retries requests that fail due to network connection issues, but Swift supports both APIs. However, users should note that credentials returned by the first API cannot be used to generate a `Connection` object for the second API. `Connection` objects do support access to their underlying storage URL and token, but mixing the two APIs isn't recommended.

Storage Requests: Basic Usage

If you authenticate using the procedural `get_auth()` function and get back a storage URL and token, then you can issue basic `GET` requests to accounts, containers, and objects, as shown here. In this example, we have a container named *my_photos* in our account, and an object named *happy.png* in that container:

```
>>> acct_headers, containers = swiftclient.get_account(storageurl, token)
>>> cont_headers, objs = swiftclient.get_container(
...    storageurl, token, 'my_photos')
>>> obj_headers, obj = swiftclient.get_object(
...    storageurl, token, 'my_photos', 'happy.png')
```

The `python-swiftclient` library's function-based API that we just demonstrated is used in a manner very similar to how we used cURL in the previous chapter. As a preferable alternative with cleaner method interfaces, consider the object-oriented `Connection` API, as follows:

```
>>> conn = Connection(authurl=authurl, user=username, key=password)
>>> acct_headers, containers = conn.get_account()
```

```
>>> cont_headers, objs = conn.get_container('my_photos')
>>> obj_headers, obj = conn.get_object('my_photos', 'happy.png')
```

In both cases, your return values will look like this:

```
>>> acct_headers
{
  'content-length': '96',
  'accept-ranges': 'bytes',
  'x-timestamp': '1389900015.90491',
  'x-trans-id': 'txad3196fe1c5f43db81ae8-0052d9926f',
  'date': 'Fri, 17 Jan 2014 20:28:31 GMT',
  'x-account-bytes-used': '458',
  'x-account-container-count': '2',
  'content-type': 'application/json; charset=utf-8',
  'x-account-object-count': '1'
}
>>> containers
[
  {'count': 1, 'bytes': 458, 'name': 'my_photos'},
  {'count': 0, 'bytes': 0, 'name': 'my_videos'}
]
>>>
>>> cont_headers
{
  'content-length': '157',
  'x-container-object-count': '1',
  'x-container-meta-my-other-metadata': 'Bar',
  'x-container-meta-my-metadata': 'Foo',
  'x-container-bytes-used': '458',
  'x-timestamp': '1389900015.93242',
  'x-trans-id': 'txb138978a46154a6e96460-0052dd804b',
  'date': 'Mon, 20 Jan 2014 20:00:11 GMT',
  'content-type': 'application/json; charset=utf-8',
  'accept-ranges': 'bytes'
}
>>> objs
[
  {
    'bytes': 458,
    'last_modified': '2014-01-16T23:49:42.936030',
    'hash': '0450d6d21f1aa2aa1fe4a354c8e62c8f',
    'name': 'happy.png',
    'content_type': 'image/png'
  }
]
>>>
>>> obj_headers
{
  'content-length': '458',
  'accept-ranges': 'bytes',
  'x-object-meta-my-other-metadata': 'Bar',
  'last-modified': 'Thu, 16 Jan 2014 23:49:43 GMT',
```

```
    'etag': '0450d6d21f1aa2aa1fe4a354c8e62c8f',
    'x-timestamp': '1389916182.93603',
    'x-trans-id': 'tx15ad1a1c9c9f462b8b261-0052dd811c',
    'date': 'Mon, 20 Jan 2014 20:03:40 GMT',
    'content-type': 'image/png'
}
>>> obj
'\x89PNG\r\n\...'
```

Note that `python-swiftclient` has parsed the headers that we saw via cURL and turned them into a dictionary object for us—a native and idiomatic Pythonic data type that is easy to access in ways you're likely to find useful. These advantages, along with more intuitive naming, motivate most developers to prefer client libraries over raw HTTP when they have the choice.

The `swiftclient` library removes much of the repetitiveness of typing everything out on a cURL command line, while clearly mapping between library calls and the underlying HTTP. The previous example demonstrated `GET` operations; there are corresponding library calls for `HEAD`, `PUT`, `POST`, and `DELETE`. (There are no methods to `PUT` or `DELETE` accounts, because those operations are done only by a cluster administrator.)

Note that, in addition to managing the auth token, the `swiftclient` module's `Connection` methods also automatically retry operations that experience network failures. This is another reason you might prefer the Connection API over the lower-level functions.

The remaining methods work exactly as you'd expect, analogously to the previous examples. For example, to retrieve account metadata you would make an HTTP `HEAD` request to the account resource, which translates into invoking the `head_account` method:

```
>>> conn.head_account()
{
    'content-length': '0',
    'x-account-container-count': '2',
    'x-account-object-count': '2',
    'x-account-bytes-used': '2048'
}
```

The `put_object` function and method each take an additional parameter: a representation of the data to be stored. If your data is small, you can simply pass a Python string containing the data:

```
>>> some_data = "Hi Mom!  Look, I'm on Swift!"
>>> conn.put_object(container_name, object_name, some_data)
'546e8a12a999e4f63a1e669fd6967355'
```

The `put_object` method returns the object's MD5 hash, which you can use to validate that the object stored in the cluster exactly matches the object on the local disk.

If you are uploading very large files, you can pass a file-like Python object containing the data to PUT. So, for example, you can invoke put_object like this:

```
>>> with open('/path/to/local/file') as localfile:
...     conn.put_object(container_name, object_name, localfile)
'f6036bba6d1ad119aca7b78a5b641432'
```

By accepting a file-like object rather than in-memory data, the swiftclient API is able to stream data to Swift, rather than attempt to read all the data into memory.

Client Libraries in Other Languages

Once you understand Swift's underlying HTTP requests from last chapter's examples, a client library API such as swiftclient now should make intuitive sense. Here are some Swift client libraries in other languages, which we hope make similar sense, as they rely on the same basic methods to send and receive data, including metadata, auth credentials, and auth tokens. In each case, we'll demonstrate basic usage, in order to show the patterns across multiple languages.

Ruby

The ruby-openstack library (*http://bit.ly/ruby-os-lib*) provides Ruby language bindings for OpenStack Compute (Nova) and Object Storage (Swift), and supports v1 and v2 authentication schemes. The bindings are similar to python-swiftclient's Connection class. For example, here's how you would list objects in a container:

```
>> os = OpenStack::Connection.create(
    :auth_url => API_URL,
    :username => USERNAME,
    :api_key => API_KEY,
    :service_type => "object-store")
>> container = os.container('my_photos')
>> container.objects
=> ["happy.png"]
```

PHP

Rackspace officially supports Swift in its new library, php-opencloud (*http://bit.ly/rackspace-lib*), which is currently undergoing active development. It has an object-oriented interface not unlike the ruby-openstack library discussed in the previous section. This client library works best with a version 2 auth system, such as Keystone. Here's how you list objects in a container:

```
$ostore = $conn->ObjectStore();
$container = $ostore->Container('animals');
$objects = $container->ObjectList();
while($object = $objects->Next()) {
    printf("Object %s size=%u\n",
```

```
            $object->name, $object->bytes);
    }
```

Java

Several Java language bindings are available, but the `jclouds` library (*http://bit.ly/jclouds-lib*) seems to be the favorite. It supports OpenStack Swift, Nova, and Amazon S3 object storage. Being Java, it tends to be more verbose than the libraries previously described. Here's how to list objects in a container:

```
import org.jclouds.ContextBuilder;
import org.jclouds.blobstore.BlobStoreContext;
import org.jclouds.blobstore.domain.PageSet;
import org.jclouds.openstack.swift.CommonSwiftAsyncClient;
import org.jclouds.openstack.swift.CommonSwiftClient;
import org.jclouds.openstack.swift.domain.ObjectInfo;
import org.jclouds.rest.RestContext;

[...]

BlobStoreContext context = ContextBuilder.newBuilder('swift')
  .endpoint("https://swift/auth/v1.0")
  .credentials('username', 'password')
  .buildView(BlobStoreContext.class);

RestContext<CommonSwiftClient, CommonSwiftAsyncClient> swift =
context.unwrap();

PageSet<ObjectInfo> objects = swift.getApi().listObjects('my_photos');

for (ObjectInfo object : objects) {
    System.out.println(object.getName() + ": " +
        object.getBytes() + " bytes");
}
```

This quick tour through the Swift client libraries of various languages is intended to show the commonalities across them. By understanding Swift and seeing an example in one language, we hope you'll be able to understand the usage in other languages and other libraries without detailed examples.

Storage Requests: Advanced Usage

Because client libraries have much in common, this section on advanced usage should be helpful not only to Python developers, but also to developers using other bindings.

All the `swiftclient` API methods take many optional parameters. For instance, you can explicitly define a chunk size for both `PUT` and `GET` operations, which divides data up for more efficient transfers (explained further in "Chunk Size" on page 221):

```
>>> obj_headers, obj_generator = conn.get_object(
...     container_name, huge_object_name, resp_chunk_size=1<<20)
>>> for chunk in obj_generator:
...     myfile.write(chunk)

>>> myfile = open('/path/to/large/file')
>>> conn.put_object(container_name, another_huge_object_name, my_file,
...     chunk_size=65536)
'0450d6d21f1aa2aa1fe4a354c8e62c8f'
```

If a file-like object is provided but no `chunk_size` is given, `chunk_size` defaults to 64K.

Arbitrary HTTP headers, such as custom metadata, can be passed with the `swift client` library. The various request methods also accept an optional parameter named `headers`:

```
>>> conn.put_object(container_name, object_name, my_data,
...     headers={'X-Object-Meta-Color': 'mauve'})
```

Normally, failed requests are indicated by raising exceptions, and developers don't distinguish between the various success response codes. (In many situations, you don't care whether your `PUT` returned a `201` or a `202`.) However, easy programmatic access to the HTTP response is available, via the parameter named `response_dict`:

```
>>> rd = {}
>>> conn.put_object(container_name, object_name, my_data, response_dict=rd)
>>> rd
{
  'status': 200,
  'reason': 'OK',
  'headers': {'content-length': '458', ...},
  'response_dicts': [
    {similar dict for each sub-request}
  ]
}
```

Additional Considerations When Using Python

`python-swiftclient` can also help with encoding non-ASCII characters and with difficulties that can arise from unreliable network connections.

If you use any non-ASCII characters in your request URL, headers, or body, they will need to be encoded. `python-swiftclient` has provisions in place to encode Unicode data consistently as UTF-8.

In many environments, network connections are unreliable and suffer from intermittent errors. Retrying failed requests is often desirable. `python-swiftclient`'s `Connection` constructor allows you to specify a retry count for any failed requests, allowing all requests made with that `Connection` to transparently retry failed requests, saving the developer a bit of effort and code. You can even control the initial backoff delay for the retry, and the maximum backoff that will be allowed. (Currently, no access is given to the backoff multiplier, which is fixed at 2.)

If a client is interrupted during a long `PUT`, it might be able to try again if it has the ability to reset its input. Some inputs, such as a string, can trivially be reread as often as necessary. Others, such as files, can be reread with appropriate method calls (such as `seek()` and `tell()`, in this case). Still others, such as sockets, can't be reset: once bytes are read from a socket, the socket has no way to rewind and make those bytes readable again. If the data source that you pass to a `python-swiftclient put_object()` method can be reset, `python-swiftclient` retries your `PUT` after resetting your data source—again, transparently to you.

These more advanced considerations are more likely to vary from one client library to another, and therefore might not be as useful to developers using libraries other than `python-swiftclient`. However, they give you a feeling for what sorts of features a client library can provide in order to make the developer's task easier.

Conclusion

We've demonstrated some of the most common and useful features of the `python-swiftclient` library. Other libraries have similar features, which should be fairly easy to understand when compared to these examples. Of course, by allowing the passing of arbitrary HTTP headers, the `swiftclient` library provides access to all the underlying Swift features, even when no syntactic sugar makes them more accessible. For more information about development using `swiftclient`, consult the API documentation (*http://bit.ly/swiftclient-web*).

CHAPTER 7
Advanced API Features

Jon Solera

While CRUD (create, read, update, delete) operations, covered in Chapter 6, are the foundation of any storage system, Swift also provides a rich API that offers developers many useful, more advanced features. Along with its included middleware, Swift makes it possible to minimize the amount of custom development required to configure a powerful and flexible system. This chapter will provide synopses and use cases, and refer you to more detailed documentation for many of Swift's most interesting features. If one of these features solves a problem for you, use it! If not, feel free to ignore or disable it. Although they are part of a default installation, none of these are necessary for the basic use of Swift. But they are really helpful when you need them.

In order to make this functionality as easy to use as possible, we also provide code samples using simple command-line HTTP requests (with cURL) at the end of the chapter. You could also use the `swift` command-line utility (installed via the `python-swiftclient` package), which usually results in simpler commands, or use an API library in the language of your choice. We use cURL in our code samples so that the HTTP verbs and headers are visible, which makes it easier to convert to other interfaces, because they might use other terminology (e.g., an HTTP `PUT` is called an `upload` by the `swift` CLI).

A number of features in this chapter call for you to pass `X-` headers in requests, a mechanism discussed in "Storage Requests: Advanced Usage" on page 75.

Large Objects

Swift sets a maximum object size (default 5 GB) in order to make sure that objects are spread out fairly evenly across disks. If you plan to store objects larger than the maximum size, you can use the static large object (SLO) or dynamic large object (DLO) middleware. Because, at its lowest level, Swift doesn't store objects larger than the maximum size, both static and dynamic large objects are broken into multiple *segments* that the middleware can later retrieve and concatenate. See the Swift documentation for an overview of large objects (*http://bit.ly/largeobjects*).

Static large objects rely on a user-defined *manifest* that explicitly lists the segments that make up the object. This allows Swift complete flexibility in storing segments in distributed locations and retrieving them again in parallel to be reassembled. Using SLOs has the additional advantage of being self-documenting with respect to the segments that make up a given large object. We recommend SLOs over DLOs unless there is a specific need for DLOs. Details about manifest syntax and the API for SLOs can be found in the SLO documentation (*http://bit.ly/slo-docs*).

Dynamic large objects allow the set of segments to be defined by a container name and an object prefix, thus determining the names of segments dynamically instead of from a manifest. For example, you can upload several files named *bigfile-part-0001*, *bigfile-part-0002*, and *bigfile-part-0003* into a container named *large_file_segments*, and create a manifest indicating that all files with the prefix *large_file_segments/bigfile-part-* should be interpreted as segments of a large object called *bigfile* (not *bigfile-part-* or anything like that) in a container called *large_files* (not *large_file_segments*—the concatenated object may reside in a different container, or not, as you choose). In contrast with SLO manifests, which contain a full list of segments, DLO manifests simply specify the container and object name prefix for the segments. The manifest is uploaded at the URL from which the resulting concatenated DLO should be retrieved.

If a new segment *bigfile-part-0004* is uploaded later, future retrievals of *large_files/bigfile* will automatically include the new segment. However, bear in mind that container listings are subject to Swift's eventual consistency. It's possible to upload a new segment, be informed that the operation completed successfully, and then retrieve the large object only to find that the large object doesn't include the new segment.

Because DLOs are dynamic, they have no way to realize that there might be a new segment that hasn't yet populated across the cluster. (In contrast, SLOs have a manifest that lists the segments explicitly, so if a segment doesn't exist, they can definitively indicate an error.)

You can read details about the API for DLOs in its documentation online (*http://bit.ly/dlo-docs*).

Although we suggest favoring SLOs over DLOs to avoid potential consistency issues (i.e., potentially not retrieving a recently uploaded segment), DLOs might be the best solution for some applications. One use might be uploading log file segments once per hour, while always being able to retrieve the concatenation of all (or most) of the segments. Another might be archiving a live video stream while allowing real-time access to the partial stream. In general, applications that benefit from non-atomic streamed data tend to be good applications for DLOs. However, in addition to avoiding consistency issues, SLOs allow segments to be located in any container in the account, and allow segments to have arbitrary names.

When using large objects (either SLOs or DLOs), upload the segments first, before creating the manifest, in order to avoid errors retrieving nonexistent segments.

Object Versioning

If you want to guard against accidental overwriting of an object, or if you want to automatically keep a history of different versions of an object, Swift's object versioning is the answer. To enable versioning in your target container, first create a separate auxiliary container to hold old versions of the target container's objects, then activate object versioning in the target container by setting its `X-Versions-Location` metadata header to the name of the auxiliary container holding the old versions.

For example, you can create a container named *fragile_data* and a container named *old_versions*, and then set the `X-Versions-Location` header of *fragile_data* to the value *old_versions*. After that, *fragile_data* will be the location of the latest version of its objects, and all previous versions will be found in the *old_versions* container. If an object in the *fragile_data* container is deleted, the next most recent version is moved from the *old_versions* container to the *fragile_data* container. (The *old_versions* container can still be accessed directly, if desired.)

Object versioning requires configuring the container servers, by adding the line `allow_versions = True` to your container server configuration file (e.g., `/etc/swift/container-server.conf`).

For more details on versioning, read the Swift documentation online (*http://bit.ly/versioning-docs*).

Object Expiration

Object expiration allows designated objects to be automatically deleted at a certain time; for example, to save disk space by purging temporary data, or for legal or policy compliance. Use this feature by setting an object's `X-Delete-At` header metadata to a particular timestamp. Eventually, the object auditor and replicator (see "Server Processes" on page 27) will examine that object, and if the current time is later than the `X-Delete-At` timestamp, they will delete the object.

`X-Delete-At` should be set to a time represented by an integer number of seconds since the Unix Epoch (1970-01-01, at midnight UTC). For convenience, you may alternatively use a header named `X-Delete-After`, which will be mapped to an `X-Delete-At` header value by the middleware. If the current time is 1,400,000,000 seconds since the Epoch, and you set `X-Delete-After` to 86,400 for an object, then that object will expire and be subject to deletion starting at the time 1,400,086,400.

More details about expiring objects can be found at the Expiring Object Support web page (*http://bit.ly/ex-os*).

Temporary URL Middleware (TempURL)

Some applications create data that needs to be temporarily public. For example, a file-sharing application might allow you to upload files and briefly grant access to another user via a time-limited URL, often referred to as a Temporary URL (TempURL). Because the URL expires after a fixed time, the system doesn't need to track and remove outstanding access.

Because TempURLs contain their expiration time in a tamper-proof manner, an excellent implementation from a security standpoint. No action needs to occur in order to revoke access. There is no process that might fail and thereby open a security hole. If the current time is later than the timestamp in the TempURL, then the TempURL has expired and will not be honored.

TempURLs have many applications. Another example would be if an organization wants to accept a payment from a customer and provide a link to proprietary content while discouraging the customer from emailing the link to others who didn't pay.

TempURL middleware allows not only temporary `GET` permission, but temporary permission to perform any HTTP verb that its creator chooses. For example, you could create a container into which files could be uploaded only if a user had a valid `PUT` TempURL. (This is often done in conjunction with form post operations for accepting uploads directly from web forms rather than using the Swift API.)

TempURLs are based on cryptographic signatures of the raw object URL, the HTTP method, and a timestamp. When generating a temporary URL, those values are concatenated together and signed with the *TempURL key*, which is stored as privileged account metadata. (Privileged metadata is readable and writeable only by people with admin access to the account, usually the account owners.)

If the signature is verified, and the timestamp has not yet expired, the client may access the URL with the given method. See the documentation (*http://bit.ly/openstack-config*) and the sample code at the end of this chapter for more information.

Form Post Middleware

One common Swift use case is allowing users to use an HTML form to upload files. Form Post middleware saves you the trouble of writing server-side code to verify authorization, parse the HTML response, and map it to a Swift API call. With this middleware, Swift itself can accept the form post of the uploaded file for storage. Form Post middleware also lets you:

- Upload multiple files designated on the same form, prepending a static prefix to each given filename.
- Redirect to another URL (such as a "thank you" page) after the upload completes.
- Set a maximum allowed file size, to prevent system abuse as well as attacks by careless or malicious users.

Because Form Post middleware is often used to allow web-based uploads to users who are not authenticated in Swift (perhaps because the system is available only to trusted users), it is often used in conjunction with a TempURL that you have generated to allow `POST` operations.

More information about Form Post middleware is available in the Swift documentation. (*http://bit.ly/form-post-docs*)

Custom Metadata

We've seen several instances of metadata in request headers that will be stored by the Swift system. Examples from this chapter include the TempURL secret key, the manifests of large objects, the expiration timestamp of an object, and containers for use in object versioning.

Note that metadata may be associated with an account (e.g., the TempURL secret key), with a container (e.g., the corresponding object versioning container for objects in this container), or with an object (e.g., the expiration timestamp).

Metadata is very useful for many purposes. Swift makes it easy to add your own metadata: simply add your own header to a `PUT` or `POST` request. You may add metadata to an account, a container, or an object. Your custom metadata header must start with `X-Account-Meta-` for account metadata, with `X-Container-Meta-` for container metadata, or with `X-Object-Meta-` for object metadata. Swift will store the metadata and include it as a header when a `HEAD` or `GET` operation is performed on the account, container, or object.

Use Swift metadata to save applications the trouble of maintaining a separate database about Swift resources. Metadata is stored with all the durability guarantees of data, and requires no extra latency to retrieve. For example, a video production house could store the video format and duration along with the content; a document could contain authorship information; and a genome sequence could contain information about the process by which it was generated. In all these cases, the metadata can be retrieved with a fast `HEAD` request, rather than a slow-running `GET`, which downloads the data (which might be very large).

PUTting and POSTing Metadata

Both accounts and containers support two different ways of changing metadata. If you PUT to an account or a container and include metadata in your request, you remove whatever metadata was there before and replace it with the metadata you provide. However, if you POST to an account or container and include metadata in your request, you alter only the metadata fields you include. In other words, let's say that the previous metadata contained the following:

```
X-Container-Meta-A: 1
X-Container-Meta-B: 2
X-Container-Meta-C: 3
```

If you PUT to this container with `X-Container-Meta-B: 100`, you update the "B" value, but you also delete the "A" and "C" values. However, if you POST to the container with that metadata, you update the "B" value and retain the previous "A" and "C" values.

PUT and POST grant the user the option of replacing or updating account and container metadata. However, for historical reasons, *the rules for object metadata are different.* In the case of object metadata, a POST behaves like a PUT. Let's say your object's metadata previously contained the following:

```
X-Object-Meta-A: 1
X-Object-Meta-B: 2
X-Object-Meta-C: 3
```

You might think that if you POST to this object with the header `X-Object-Meta-B: 100`, it would follow the pattern of account or container metadata, and you would update the "B" value while retaining the previous "A" and "C" values. *This is not the case!* For objects, POST and PUT both overwrite all previous metadata! (PUT also overwrites the actual object data, of course.) There is no way to update object metadata and leave values untouched, short of issuing a HEAD request to read it, modifying it in memory locally, and then issuing a POST request to write the modified data. (And that is subject to race conditions, if anyone else is modifying that data.)

Metadata: PUT vs. POST

There are *two* surprises about the differences between PUT and POST in storing metadata. The first is the "update vs. overwrite" issue. The second is the different behavior of object metadata, as compared with account or container metadata.

Cross-Origin Resource Sharing (CORS)

Swift supports cross-origin resource sharing (CORS), which lets application developers upload data to Swift or host web content directly from Swift without having to build and maintain a separate proxying layer to get around the Web's same-origin security model. In web applications, the *same-origin* policy has become a browser standard to prevent several types of security issues. For example, in general it is dangerous to allow a script originating from *http://host1.foo.com* to access the Document Object Model (DOM) of a page from *http://host2.foo.com*, and browsers prohibit attempts to do so. However, if two pages coordinate with each other, each can explicitly allow the other to access it. It's considered safe for a page to explicitly grant access to another host.

If you are using your Swift cluster to host resources (such as JavaScript) that will be displayed on websites, you likely want to use CORS to tell browsers to grant an exemption to the same-origin policy in this particular case. For example, you might want to allow a web application hosted at *http://app.example.com* to upload images directly to *http://images.example.com*—which might be backed by a Swift cluster.

Swift allows users to set CORS headers on data stored in Swift. CORS headers in Swift are implemented on a per-container basis. To use CORS headers on data in your Swift cluster, set the appropriate metadata headers on your containers. Setting this container metadata causes all requests for objects in that container to return with the CORS headers and respond appropriately to `OPTIONS` requests. The headers you can set on your containers are:

```
X-Container-Meta-Access-Control-Allow-Origin
X-Container-Meta-Access-Control-Max-Age
X-Container-Meta-Access-Control-Allow-Headers
X-Container-Meta-Access-Control-Expose-Headers
```

These are standard container metadata headers (as described earlier in "Custom Metadata" on page 83), but when a CORS request is made to the container or to an object in the container, these metadata entries cause Swift to set corresponding CORS headers on the response.

"Cross-Origin Resource Sharing" on page 94 shows how to put together such a request. Also see the Swift documentation (*http://bit.ly/swift-cors*), and a useful blog post (*http://bit.ly/using-cors*).

Swift Cluster Info

We mentioned Swift's cluster info discoverability in "About Your Swift Cluster" on page 61 in Chapter 5. We'll now discuss how developers might take advantage of this capability.

Because Swift is under active development, with new powerful functionality added to every release, developers might wish to test the capabilities of a given Swift cluster to determine whether it has a particular feature. In addition to presence/absence tests, Swift cluster info provides key–value lookups for some parameters. Developers may use parameter values to guide decisions about how to use the cluster.

Current cluster information includes the presence or absence of certain key features (such as account ACLs) and many configuration values (such as maximum file size and maximum name lengths). Because cluster info is a relatively new feature, it is regularly being updated with additional information. See the end of this chapter for an example of how you might use the cluster info functionality. Try it out against your own Swift cluster—you might find the information useful.

Swift cluster info is critical for applications intended to run against multiple Swift clusters with a variety of configurations, or against a Swift cluster with configuration options that might change (such as when developing against a test cluster but planning to move to a differently configured production cluster).

For example, your application might automatically create SLOs by segmenting large data files uploaded by the user. Your application will need to know the maximum allowed file size in order to choose a good segment size. Or if you allow file uploads, your application can determine whether the Swift cluster has Form Post middleware enabled (and use it if it's there).

Range Requests

Although Swift is excellent at storing large volumes of data (including big files), sometimes network issues, software bugs, or human error will cause a lengthy download to fail when it was nearly complete. If your application has been streaming data to disk, it might need only the last small portion of the object from Swift.

For this reason, Swift supports range requests to retrieve only the portion of the object desired by the client, reducing latency and load on the cluster. Range requests can also be used to stream reasonably sized chunks to the user, in situations where the whole object might not be wanted. For example, many video websites have found that users often casually browse only the first few seconds of a video.

The Swift proxy process itself also takes advantage of this API feature. When the proxy node communicates with its object nodes, an interruption might occur partway through reading an object. In that case, the proxy server process will contact a different replica for that object, issuing a range request starting after the last byte it successfully received from the first object node. This all happens behind the scenes, so the client doesn't even notice—it's just one of the many redundancy features that Swift provides.

More information is available in the Get Object documentation (*http://bit.ly/get-object*).

Domain Remap Middleware

Domain Remap middleware provides an easy way to refer to an account or container by a DNS hostname instead of a path component. Swift usually refers to an object by a URL such as *http://swift.example.com/v1/account/container/object*. If instead you'd prefer to reference *http://account.swift.example.com/container/object* or *http://container.account.swift.example.com/object*, Domain Remap middleware comes to your aid.

This feature is useful in certain types of content distribution applications. If your Swift cluster hosts different types or tiers of content, it might be convenient for your content to appear to users as originating from different domains. For example, your Swift cluster might hold photos and video from sports events, and you might want to make it available to users at URLs such as *http://football.video.swift.example.com/filename.jpg*. If you use Domain Remap middleware, and if you have an account called *video* with a container called *football*, you can implement this without any custom code. Create a CNAME record in your DNS configuration pointing from *football.example.com* to *football.video.swift.example.com* to enable a simpler URL.

Another middleware package, cname_lookup, can be used in conjunction with Domain Remap to provide friendly domain names that map directly to a specific account or container. This feature enables more concise hostname mappings. With cname_lookup enabled, Swift will use DNS to resolve the canonical name for any hostname that does not already end in the configured storage domain. That allows administrators to configure arbitrary domains such as *football.example.com* that point to other accounts or containers.

Note that if your account name is *AUTH_acct*, the domain name becomes *auth-acct.swift.example.com*, because underscores are not allowed in domain names and domain names are case-insensitive. This also applies to container names with underscores.

This setup generally requires wildcard DNS, which is beyond the scope of this book.

Static Web Hosting

StaticWeb middleware lets you serve HTML content directly from containers in your Swift cluster, bypassing the need for a custom application. StaticWeb does this by allowing you to set metadata on a container specifying the named object to display in response to a `GET` on the container. *index.html* is the traditional value, but you can use any name you want.

If you want the content to be public, you will need some mechanism to grant access. A common solution is container access control lists (ACLs), which can be used either to make a container completely publicly readable, or to make a container publicly readable from a given HTTP referrer. Alternatively, if you use SwiftStack Auth as your authentication system, it can set a cookie upon a successful authentication. This cookie contains the auth token, and the SwiftStack Auth middleware verifies the cookie's auth token to grant access.

StaticWeb middleware handles the container `GET` request (i.e., the *index.html* page), sets `Content-Type` to `text/html`, and allows for several other useful features:

- Container listings, which can be styled with a CSS file
- "Pseudo-directories," which may be listed (and styled) just as container listings are
- Custom error pages, which may be specified in addition to default error pages

Depending on your requirements, StaticWeb middleware might be an easy way to implement high-availability web hosting, because redundancy, throughput, and capacity issues can all be handled directly by Swift. The entire website can be easily hosted simply by placing files in the Swift cluster. Furthermore, if you place geo-aware DNS services in front of the nodes of a multi-region Swift cluster, you can implement a simple kind of content delivery network (CDN), minimizing latency to nearby web clients.

The SwiftStack Web Console product, for example, uses this feature to enable a drag-and-drop web interface for object management.

More details about StaticWeb middleware configuration can be found in the Swift documentation (*http://bit.ly/staticweb*).

Content-Type Header

The `Content-Type` header can be used to serve web content directly from Swift. If a client sets `Content-Type` on a `PUT` request, the same `Content-Type` will be returned on a future `GET`. Browsers recognize many `Content-Type` headers and can either display or present the content natively (e.g., audio or video), or call other appropriate applications to display the data (e.g., Microsoft Word documents).

This feature is so easy to use that it doesn't require much additional explanation. But it's worth highlighting the enormous benefits of serving content directly from Swift—including not only redundancy and throughput, but also the potential for geo-aware points of presence within multi-region clusters. For these reasons, we want to bring this feature to the attention of developers, so they can simplify their architecture.

Bulk Operations Middleware

Bulk Operations middleware lets you upload or delete multiple Swift objects with a single HTTP request. Bulk uploading consists of uploading an archive file that will be uncompressed on the server side. Bulk deletion is performed via a `POST` request that lists the containers and objects to be deleted; the Swift proxy then issues the multiple internal `DELETE` requests. In both cases, the developer (and the custom code) avoid the network overhead of multiple HTTP requests and round-trip times, and the effort of aggregating the multiple responses into a useful summary return value.

Bulk upload is an efficient way of importing moderately large amounts of data. Although not quite up to the task of Big Data petabyte-order uploads, bulk upload can easily manage thousands of files and many gigabytes of data.

Bulk delete is the preferred way to purge large numbers of files; for example, when deleting a container with thousands of objects. Bulk delete can also be used to delete the contents of a Swift account, but in that case there is an alternative worth considering: If a cluster administrator executes a `DELETE` on the account itself, then a background process will eventually delete all the contents of the account.

Code Samples

In the following examples, we will demonstrate basic use of the Swift features described in this chapter. All examples depend on your storage URL, and require you to be authenticated, so we assume you have set the environment variables `TOKEN` and `STORAGE_URL`, perhaps with the following shell commands:

```
USERNAME=your_Swift_account_name
KEY=your_Swift_account_key_or_password
AUTH_URL=your_Swift_cluster's_authentication_URL
TOKEN=$(curl -s -i -H "x-auth-user: $USERNAME" -H "x-auth-key: $KEY" \
  "$AUTH_URL" | perl -ane '/X-Auth-Token:/ and print $F[1];')
STORAGE_URL=$(curl -s -i -H "x-auth-user: $USERNAME" -H "x-auth-key: $KEY" \
  "$AUTH_URL" | perl -ane '/X-Storage-Url:/ and print $F[1];')
```

If you are using a non-TempAuth-style auth system (one that does not take its input via the `X-Auth-User` and `X-Auth-Key` headers), adjust the token generation command accordingly.

The following examples use cURL from the command-line shell.

Static Large Objects

Create a container to hold the segments called `large_file_segments`, and a different container called `large_files` from which large objects will be downloaded:

```
curl -i -X PUT -H "x-auth-token: $TOKEN" "$STORAGE_URL/large_file_segments"
curl -i -X PUT -H "x-auth-token: $TOKEN" "$STORAGE_URL/large_files"
```

Next, upload the segments:

```
curl -i -X PUT -H "X-Auth-Token: $TOKEN" \
  "$STORAGE_URL/large_file_segments/obj1-part1" --data-binary "segment1..."
curl -i -X PUT -H "X-Auth-Token: $TOKEN" \
  "$STORAGE_URL/large_file_segments/obj1-part2" --data-binary "segment2..."
curl -i -X PUT -H "X-Auth-Token: $TOKEN" \
  "$STORAGE_URL/large_file_segments/obj1-part3" --data-binary "segment3..."
```

Now create the JSON manifest, using the Etag and Content-Length values from the headers of the segments:

```
MANIFEST="["
for seg_path in /large_file_segments/obj1-part1 \
                /large_file_segments/obj1-part2 \
                /large_file_segments/obj1-part3; do
  ETAG=$(curl -I -s -H "X-Auth-Token: $TOKEN" "$STORAGE_URL$seg_path" \
      | perl -ane '/Etag:/ and print $F[1];')
  SIZE=$(curl -I -s -H "X-Auth-Token: $TOKEN" "$STORAGE_URL$seg_path" \
      | perl -ane '/Content-Length:/ and print $F[1];')
  SEGMENT="{\"path\":\"$seg_path\",\"Etag\":\"$ETAG\",\"size_bytes\":$SIZE}"
  [ "$MANIFEST" != "[" ] && MANIFEST="$MANIFEST,"
  MANIFEST="$MANIFEST$SEGMENT"
done
MANIFEST="${MANIFEST}]"   # append closing bracket
```

Upload the manifest, creating the SLO:

```
curl -i -X PUT -H "X-Auth-Token: $TOKEN" \
    "$STORAGE_URL/large_files/obj1?multipart-manifest=put" \
    --data-binary "$MANIFEST"
```

Finally, retrieve the large object:

```
curl -i -X PUT -H "X-Auth-Token: $TOKEN" "$STORAGE_URL/large_files/obj1"
```

Dynamic Large Objects

As in the SLO example, we will first create a container to hold the segments, and a different container from which large objects will be downloaded:

```
curl -i -X PUT -H "x-auth-token: $TOKEN" "$STORAGE_URL/large_file_segments"
curl -i -X PUT -H "x-auth-token: $TOKEN" "$STORAGE_URL/large_files"
```

Next, we upload the individual segments:

```
curl -i -X PUT -H "X-Auth-Token: $TOKEN" \
  "$STORAGE_URL/large_file_segments/obj1-part1" --data-binary "segment1..."
curl -i -X PUT -H "X-Auth-Token: $TOKEN" \
  "$STORAGE_URL/large_file_segments/obj1-part2" --data-binary "segment2..."
curl -i -X PUT -H "X-Auth-Token: $TOKEN" \
  "$STORAGE_URL/large_file_segments/obj1-part3" --data-binary "segment3..."
```

Creating the empty manifest object is easier than in the SLO case, because we only need to specify the container and object name prefix. (However, we don't get the robustness that the SLO middleware's more substantial manifest can provide.)

```
curl -i -X PUT -H "X-Auth-Token: $TOKEN" \
  -H 'X-Object-Manifest: large_file_segments/obj1-part' \
  "$STORAGE_URL/large_files/obj1" --data-binary ''
```

And now we're ready to download the large object:

```
curl -i -X GET -H "X-Auth-Token: $TOKEN" "$STORAGE_URL/large_files/obj1"
```

Object Versioning

Object versioning stores old versions of an object in a separate container. If you overwrite the object with a new version, the old version will be copied to the "versions location" container. If you delete the object, Object Versioning middleware will prevent actual deletion, and instead revert the current version of the object to the object's previous version, discarding the current version of the object. Only when you delete the earliest version of the object will that object be completely deleted.

To start this example, create a container to hold the current objects, and a different container that will contain the old versions:

```
curl -i -X PUT -H "X-Auth-Token: $TOKEN" $STORAGEURL/fragile_data
curl -i -X PUT -H "X-Auth-Token: $TOKEN" $STORAGEURL/old_versions
```

Activate object versioning on the *fragile_data* container, with *old_versions* as the backup container:

```
curl -i -X PUT -H "X-Auth-Token: $TOKEN" -H "X-Versions-Location: old_versions" \
    $STORAGEURL/fragile_data
```

Now we can upload and overwrite data, and old data will be copied to the *old_versions* container:

```
curl -i -X PUT -H "X-Auth-Token: $TOKEN" "$STORAGE_URL/fragile_data/obj1" \
  --data-binary '111'
curl -i -X PUT -H "X-Auth-Token: $TOKEN" "$STORAGE_URL/fragile_data/obj1" \
  --data-binary '222'
curl -i -X PUT -H "X-Auth-Token: $TOKEN" "$STORAGE_URL/fragile_data/obj1" \
  --data-binary '333'
```

At this point in the example, the directories' contents are as follows:

- *fragile_data* contains only *obj1*, with the contents *333*.
- *old_versions* contains objects *obj1.0* and *obj1.1*, with contents *111* and *222*.

This can be verified by inspecting the container contents with the following commands:

```
curl -i -X GET -H "X-Auth-Token: $TOKEN" "$STORAGE_URL/fragile_data"
curl -i -X GET -H "X-Auth-Token: $TOKEN" "$STORAGE_URL/old_versions"
```

If we delete the current version, the previous version is restored:

```
curl -i -X DELETE -H "X-Auth-Token: $TOKEN" "$STORAGE_URL/fragile_data/obj1"
```

TempURL (Time-Limited URLs)

TempURL middleware lets you create tamper-proof temporary URLs that contain a timestamp and a cryptographic signature. If anyone tries to access the URL after the timestamp, the attempt is unsuccessful. The timestamp in the URL can't be changed without invalidating the cryptographic signature, and of course TempURL middleware rejects all access attempts that contain invalid signatures.

To create a valid temporary URL, the TempURL middleware package must be enabled for the cluster, and you must have administrative access to the account in question. (Usually this means that you are the account owner.) Admin access to the account allows you to view or set the *TempURL key*.

The cryptographic signature requires a secret key, which is stored as account metadata. Unlike most account metadata, this key is *privileged metadata*, and only the account owner (or someone with administrative access to the account) may see it when retrieving account metadata.

Say you want to generate a temporary URL to allow `GET` requests to the object at *https://swift.example.com/v1/AUTH_acct/cont/obj*. For convenience, assume we set the environment variable `$STORAGEURL` to this value. Now, in order to generate the temporary URL, we'll need to split `$STORAGEURL` into the server component (*https://swift.example.com*) and the path component (*/v1/AUTH_acct/cont/obj*). We also need to extract the account URL from `$STORAGEURL` (which is an object in this case, but in general might be an account or a container). Here's one way to do that:

```
STORAGE_SERVER="${STORAGEURL/\/v1*/}"
STORAGE_PATH="${STORAGEURL/*\/v1/\/v1}"
STORAGE_ACCT=$(echo $STORAGEURL | sed -e 's!/v1/\([^/]*\)/.*!/v1/\1!')
```

We'll also need to set the account's secret key for signing temporary URLs, if it isn't already set:

```
TEMPURL_KEY="secret123"
curl -X POST -H "X-Auth-Token: $TOKEN" \
  -H "X-Account-Meta-Temp-URL-Key: $TEMPURL_KEY" "$STORAGE_ACCT"
```

Now we can use the `swift-temp-url` tool, distributed with Swift, to generate the temporary URL. Recall that we will need to specify the following:

- Which HTTP verb to allow, e.g., `GET`
- How long, in seconds, before the access should expire
- The path component of the URL to which we are granting access
- The cryptographic secret key with which we are signing the temporary URL

```
TEMPURL_PATH="$(swift-temp-url GET 60 "$STORAGE_PATH" "$TEMPURL_KEY")"
```

$TEMPURL_PATH now contains the path component (but not the server name or protocol) of the temporary URL. To generate the complete URL, prepend the value in $STORAGE_SERVER that we extracted earlier.

This temporary URL can be used to download the object even without presenting credentials such as an auth token:

```
curl "$STORAGE_SERVER$TEMPURL_PATH"
```

Form Post

Form Post middleware, which allows users to upload data to Swift by using a web form, presents a small challenge. Unlike the other examples in this chapter, the use of Form Post can't be demonstrated from the command line. Instead, we show how to programmatically generate a form that can be used with Form Post middleware:

```
#!/usr/bin/env python

import hmac
from hashlib import sha1
from time import time

# Parameters determined by developer
swift_base_url = 'http://swift.example.com'
path = '/v1/account/container/object_prefix'
filenames_to_upload = 'file1 file2 file3'.split()
redirect = 'https://myserver.com/some-page'
max_file_size = 104857600
max_file_count = 10
timeout = 600
key = 'mykey'

expires = int(time() + timeout)
# We cryptographically sign the following five parameters to ensure that the
# end user can't tamper with them:
hmac_body = '%s\n%s\n%s\n%s\n%s' % (path, redirect,
    max_file_size, max_file_count, expires)
signature = hmac.new(key, hmac_body, sha1).hexdigest()

form_header = """
  <form action="%{swift_url}s" method="POST" enctype="multipart/form-data">
     <input type="hidden" name="redirect" value="%(redirect)s" />
     <input type="hidden" name="max_file_size" value="%(max_file_size)s" />
     <input type="hidden" name="max_file_count" value="%(max_file_count)s" />
     <input type="hidden" name="expires" value="%(expires)s" />
     <input type="hidden" name="signature" value="%(signature)s" />
""" % {
  'swift_url': "%s/%s" % (swift_base_url, path),
  'redirect': redirect,
  'max_file_size': max_file_size,
  'max_file_count': max_file_count,
```

```
        'expires': expires,
        'signature': signature,
    }

    form_footer = """
          <input type="submit" />
        </form>
    """

    form_files = ''.join(['  <input type="file" name="%s" /><br />\n' % filename
                          for filename in filenames_to_upload])

    print "%s\n%s\n%s\n" % (form_header, form_files, form_footer)
```

Cross-Origin Resource Sharing

CORS allows your Swift objects to indicate that a given website has permission to access them, in spite of web browsers' default rules regarding the same-origin policy.

CORS is specialized and somewhat complex, and a tutorial on CORS is beyond the scope of this book. If you believe CORS will help your application, please refer to resources such as the following:

- Wikipedia entry on the same-origin policy (*http://bit.ly/so-policy*)
- Wikipedia entry on CORS (*http://bit.ly/cors-wiki*)
- Swift documentation on CORS middleware (*http://bit.ly/swift-cors*)
- A SwiftStack blog post on using CORS middleware (*http://bit.ly/using-cors*)

With that understanding, here is an example of using Swift's CORS middleware to set CORS headers appropriately. First, we create a container for use with the website *http://webapp.example.com* and set the metadata appropriately. (Note that CORS is enabled at the container level.)

```
curl -i -X PUT -H "X-Auth-Token: $TOKEN" \
  -H "X-Container-Meta-Access-Control-Allow-Origin: http://webapp.example.com" \
  $STORAGE_URL/webstuff
```

We create an object in that container:

```
curl -i -X PUT --data-binary 1234 -H "X-Auth-Token: $TOKEN" \
  -H "X-Container-Meta-Access-Control-Allow-Origin: http://webapp.example.com" \
  $STORAGE_URL/webstuff/obj
```

Now we can make CORS requests and see what happens.

The first request is the CORS pre-flight request. The draft spec defines a successful response as having a 200 status code and anything else as a CORS pre-flight request failure.

```
curl -i -X OPTIONS -H "X-Auth-Token: $TOKEN" \
  -H "Origin: http://webapp.example.com" \
  -H "Access-Control-Request-Method: POST" $STORAGE_URL/webstuff/obj
```

The response to the previous request will contain headers that look like this:

```
Access-Control-Allow-Origin: http://webapp.example.com
Access-Control-Allow-Methods: HEAD, GET, PUT, POST, COPY, OPTIONS, DELETE
Access-Control-Allow-Headers: x-auth-token
Allow: HEAD, GET, PUT, POST, COPY, OPTIONS, DELETE
```

This is the CORS way of indicating that the *http://webapp.example.com* website has permission to do any of those HTTP verbs on this resource, and the browser should not consider this a security threat (e.g., a malicious script from *http://webapp.example.com* trying to gain unauthorized access to resources in the Swift cluster) because the Swift cluster is explicitly stating that *http://webapp.example.com* is expected to access this resource and has permission to do so.

The CORS pre-flight request indicated that we are allowed to use the `POST` method (as well as several other methods), because we got a `200 OK` response. We can make the actual request:

```
curl -i -X POST -H "X-Auth-Token: $TOKEN" -H "Content-Type: text/plain" \
  -H "Origin: http://webapp.example.com" $STORAGE_URL/webstuff/obj
```

In this case, Swift responds with a 202—success!

Custom Metadata

Custom metadata is passed in headers that begin with `X-Account-Meta`, `X-Container-Meta`, or `X-Object-Meta`, as appropriate for the resource that the metadata references. For example, here is an example of setting account metadata:

```
curl -i -X POST -H "X-Auth-Token: $TOKEN" \
  -H "X-Account-Meta-Favorite-Even-Prime: 2" "$STORAGE_URL"
```

Your custom metadata header will be visible on the next `GET` or `HEAD` of the resource.

Note that if you were setting metadata on a container or object instead of an account, you would adjust the metadata header name appropriately:

```
curl -i -X POST -H "X-Auth-Token: $TOKEN" \
  -H "X-Container-Meta-Used-For-Web: No" "$STORAGE_URL/privatecontainer"
```

Swift Cluster Info

Swift's Cluster Info API is a little unusual in two regards. First, it does not require a token or other form of authentication. Second, it is not accessed via the auth URL or any storage URL. The URL for a Swift cluster's info can be constructed by appending */info* to the cluster's root URL, e.g., *https://swift.example.com*. Since `$STORAGE_URL` is the storage URL for an account (rather than a container or object), the Swift root URL can be generated like this:

```
SWIFT_ROOT_URL=$(echo $STORAGE_URL | perl -pe 's!/[^/]+/[^/]+$!!')
curl -i -X GET "$SWIFT_ROOT_URL/info" ; echo
```

The output of the previous cURL command might look like this:


```
{
  "swift": {
    "max_file_size": 5368709122,
    "account_listing_limit": 10000,
    "max_meta_count": 90,
    "max_meta_value_length": 256,
    "container_listing_limit": 10000,
    "version": "1.11.0.55.gdb63240",
    "max_meta_name_length": 128,
    "max_object_name_length": 1024,
    "max_account_name_length": 256,
    "max_container_name_length": 256
  },
  "tempauth": {
    "account_acls": true
  }
}
```


Note that Swift's Cluster Info API returns its results as a JSON dictionary. Note also that the keys of the dictionary include "swift" (for info on core Swift parameters) as well as names of middleware packages (e.g., "tempauth"). In this way, middleware packages can indicate their own info without requiring a change in core Swift code.

Range Requests

Range requests allow users to retrieve only a portion of an object; for example, to continue an interrupted download. The following example retrieves the second 10-kilobyte chunk of the object:

```
OBJ="$STORAGE_URL/mycontainer/myobject"
curl -X GET -H "X-Auth-Token: $TOKEN" -H "Range: bytes=10240-20480" "$OBJ"
```

The range-request API is as easy as adding this header. Note that the HTTP response code will be `206 Partial Content` rather than `200 OK`. You can also request multiple (even overlapping) ranges, and receive a multi-part response:

```
curl -X GET -H "X-Auth-Token: $TOKEN" -H "Range: bytes=10240-20480,30720-40960" \
  "$OBJ"
```

The range-request API is very flexible in its syntax for allowing you to specify ranges. See the Get Object Details web page (*http://bit.ly/get-object*) for more details.

Domain Remapping

Domain remapping requires correct configuration of your domain's DNS. Assuming you have the appropriate subdomains set up to point to your Swift cluster (which we will assume to be located at *swift.example.com*), you will set the following value in your *proxy-server.conf* file:

```
[domain-remap]
storage_domain = .swift.example.com
```

This configures the Domain Remap middleware package to look for requests ending with `.swift.example.com` (including the leading dot, indicating that the request is directed to a subdomain); extract account (and optionally container) information from the subdomain; and rewrite the request. You will be able to see the action of this middleware with the following example.

First, we set up some environment variables:

```
SERVER=${STORAGE_URL%/*/*}
DOMAINNAME=${SERVER##*/}
ACCT=${STORAGE_URL/*\//}
CONT=my_container
OBJ=my_object
```

With these parameters, a conventional request would look like this:

```
curl -X GET -H "X-Auth-Token: $TOKEN" "https://$SERVER/v1/$ACCT/$CONT/$OBJ"
```

However, the Domain Remap middleware package allows you to access the same object at any of several new URLs. In this next example, we move the account name from the URL path to the domain name, and access a path off the virtual server *https://auth_alice.swift.example.com*:

```
curl -X GET -H "X-Auth-Token: $TOKEN" "https://$ACCT.$SERVER/$CONT/$OBJ"
```

Similarly, this next example moves both the account name and the container name from the URL path to the domain, and contacts the virtual server *https://my_container.auth_alice.swift.example.com*:

```
curl -X GET -H "X-Auth-Token: $TOKEN" "https://$CONT.$ACCT.$SERVER/$OBJ"
```

Note that if you leave the leading dot off your configured value of the `storage_domain` parameter (e.g., `storage_domain = swift.example.com`), the Domain Remap middleware package will insert a leading dot for you.

Also note that the Swift API version, seen as the `/v1/` in the `STORAGE_URL`, vanishes under domain remapping.

Static Web Hosting

The Static Web middleware package makes it easy to host a website from a Swift container. First, make the container publicly readable, and optionally allow public listing of the container's contents. Then define an index web page. Optionally, you can define a CSS stylesheet for the file listings.

This example assumes that you have a container named `website` that you want to use as a website.

Note that the container access control syntax is different from the account access control syntax. The following command demonstrates how to make a container publicly readable, with no authentication required. (Alternatively, we could require Swift authentication and only display this site to authorized viewers.)

```
curl -X POST -H "X-Auth-Token: $TOKEN" -H 'X-Container-Read: .r:*' \
  "$STORAGE_URL/website"
```

Next, we create an index file, which users will see when they browse to the container. (Alternatively, we could have users see a directory listing when they browse to the container, by setting `X-Container-Meta-Web-Listings` to "true".)

```
curl -X POST -H "X-Auth-Token: $TOKEN" \
  -H 'X-Container-Meta-Web-Index: my-index.html' "$STORAGE_URL/website"
```

You can now also enable optional features, such as custom error pages.

At this point, requests sent to this container will behave like a static website.

It's important to understand what functionality is provided by core Swift, and what the Static Web middleware package adds. Core Swift stores the objects, and allows them to be retrieved via HTTP and served with the `Content-Type` that they are designated to have. This is a large amount of the task of setting up a website! The Static Web middleware package provides the following additional functionality:

- A `GET` on a container will return the designated index page, instead of a listing of objects, if `X-Container-Meta-Web-Index` is set.
- A `GET` on a container will return an HTML page styled with the given CSS (if any), instead of a listing of objects, if `X-Container-Meta-Web-Listings` is set. (The object containing the CSS is given by `X-Container-Meta-Web-Listings-css`, if it is set.)
- A custom error page may be specified for HTTP errors by setting `X-Container-Meta-Web-Error`.
- Artificial "directory" objects may be created, to simulate hierarchy in the container.

These functions make a Swift container look more like a website, but the basic functionality of serving data (such as HTML files, JavaScript files, or images) with appropriate Content-Type headers (text/html, image/png, etc.) is all the default behavior of core Swift.

Content-Type

It is easy to set the Content-Type header, like any other metadata header. We provide the following example only to show how simple it is, and to encourage designers of Swift-based systems to have their systems set the content type of the data they store, in order to make it more easily viewable (e.g., through web browsers).

Here's how easy it is to upload some data, and mark it as a PNG file:

```
curl -i -X PUT -H "X-Auth-Token: $TOKEN" "$STORAGE_URL/large_files/obj2" \
  --data-binary @/tmp/myimage.png -H "Content-Type: image/png"
```

Thanks to that single extra header at the end, retrieving the object's URL from a browser should now display an image, rather than bytes.

Bulk Upload

Bulk uploads are performed by uploading a tar file and appending the query parameter to the request. The tar file may optionally be compressed with either *.gz* or *.bz2* compression:

```
curl -X PUT -H "X-Auth-Token: $TOKEN" \
  "$STORAGE_URL/cont123?extract-archive=.tar" --data-binary @/tmp/files.tar
```

This will send the file */tmp/files.tar* to Swift, which will extract the archive and place each normal file from the extracted archive into the container *$STORAGE_URL/cont123*. Instead of specifying a container in your upload URL, you may also omit the container and ensure that your tar file contains exactly two levels of path structure. Entities other than normal files (such as symlinks, directories, or devices) will not be processed by Swift.

Valid values for the extract-archive parameter are .tar, .tar.gz, and .tar.bz2. (Bulk uploads must use the tar utility for concatenation, and may optionally use either gzip, bzip2, or nothing for compression.)

Bulk upload has many options, and also includes mechanisms for checking for partial failures. See the Swift documentation for more details, or SwiftStack's documentation on bulk operations (*http://bit.ly/bulk-opers*).

Bulk Delete

Bulk delete is the best way to remove large numbers of objects in a few requests. It's the only mass-delete mechanism in Swift—you cannot DELETE a non-empty account or container! (Well, cluster administrators can delete accounts, but normal users can't.

Normal users can't even delete their own accounts.) If you want to remove large numbers of files, issue a bulk delete and then do a simple HTTP `DELETE` on the container.

Bulk delete requires a `POST` to the account. It accepts input in the form of a newline-separated list of resources to delete. Containers may be included in this list, but they must be empty at the time of their deletion. Resources are addressed by their relative paths within the account, as in the following:

```
printf "/cont111/obj1\n/cont111/obj2\n/cont111\n" | \
  curl -X POST -H "X-Auth-Token: $TOKEN" \
  "$STORAGE_URL?bulk-delete" --data-binary @-
```

cURL reads the `POST` data from standard input, which it gets from the `printf` command: the names of two objects followed by a container. The bulk delete operation processes these deletions in order, first deleting the two objects, then deleting the presumably now empty container.

See the Swift documentation, or SwiftStack's documentation on bulk operations (*http://bit.ly/bulk-opers*), for more information.

Conclusion

Although most developers and administrators are initially attracted to Swift for its durability, throughput, and low cost, Swift is hardly a bare-bones storage system. The API features described in this chapter can be used to assemble several types of complex systems, with very little custom development effort. It's unlikely that any particular application will need all these features at once, or even most of them. But as a developer, it's useful to know the capabilities of Swift as an architectural component. That knowledge can save a great deal of custom coding, testing, and integrating.

CHAPTER 8

Developing Swift Middleware

Jon Solera

Using nothing more than the default Swift installation, you can solve many of the challenges of distributed storage. In case that doesn't meet your needs, Swift ships with several helpful middleware packages to extend the functionality of your Swift installation. However, sometimes developers must address specific, custom requirements. Swift's open design makes it easy to add your own significant new functionality through middleware, with comparatively little effort. Middleware is a great way to customize Swift to meet your particular needs.

Middleware does have its complications, however. This chapter aims to provide you with a conceptual overview of how Swift middleware works. Swift is built on Python's Web Services Gateway Interface (WSGI) model, and is configured using the Python Paste framework, both of which require some attention. Middleware can be somewhat counterintuitive, as it "wraps" core Swift (and other layers of middleware). So in a sense, you need to design your system inside out—requests will be passed through layers of middleware and possibly altered at each stage before reaching core Swift. After providing this background, this chapter will then acquaint you with how to write Swift middleware, and will work through a range of examples. Finally, we'll give you some ideas about how you might use middleware.

Introduction to WSGI

The WSGI framework is a fundamental component of Swift's architecture. Developers have good reasons to both praise and curse WSGI, sometimes in the same sentence. WSGI's greatest strength is its middleware model: middleware "wraps" other middleware and so on, down to the actual application in the center—in this case, Swift. This makes life easier for both developers and deployers, because each middleware layer doesn't need to know anything about the other layers, including the innermost application layer (in this case, core Swift). So middleware code can be very straightforward.

On the downside, WSGI's programming model can be confusing to wrap your head around. We'll try to help with that in this and following sections.

Here's how a system with several layers of middleware might work. A request comes in and possibly is modified by the outermost middleware before it moves one layer inward. Then the next middleware has the option to tweak the request before passing it inward again, and so forth (Figure 8-1). When it reaches the end of the middleware pipeline, the mutated request is processed by Swift, and a response is generated. This response then travels back out the pipeline in reverse. Each middleware package now has the opportunity to modify the response. Of course, any given middleware object might choose to let a request or response pass through unchanged, and this is often what happens. Once the outermost middleware has processed the response (or let it through unchanged), the final response is returned to the user.

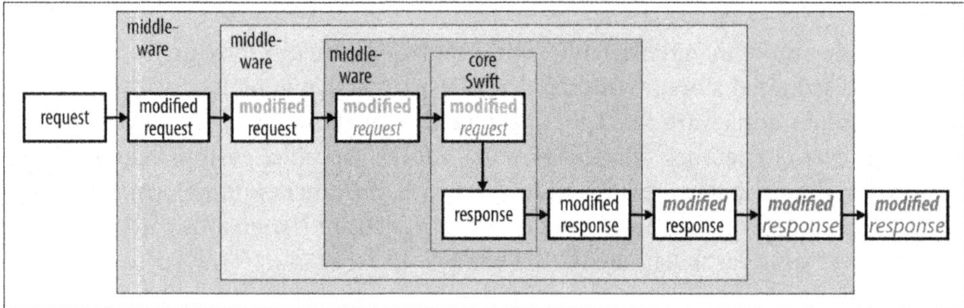

Figure 8-1. How layers of middleware work in WSGI

At each point in the inbound pipeline, middleware might choose to short-circuit the rest of the pipeline and return a response or an error. For example, auth middleware returns an error if an unauthenticated user tries to perform an operation requiring authentication. Health-checking middleware can choose to return a successful response to any health-check request directed to it, without passing that request "inward." In these short-circuit cases, the request is not passed to any downstream middleware or to core Swift (Figure 8-2).

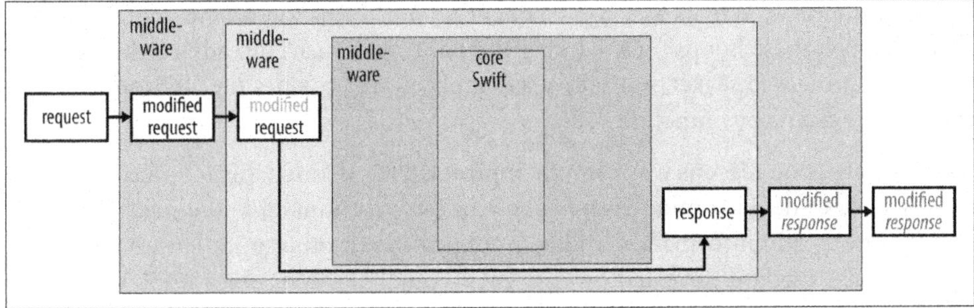

Figure 8-2. Short-circuiting the handling of a request

So, in summary, each middleware layer optionally inspects a request, modifies it, or both, and then either passes it along or provides a response that short-circuits the rest of the middleware pipeline. Similarly, each middleware layer can optionally inspect a request, modify it, or both on its return trip.

Programming WSGI

A WSGI application isn't a web server—it doesn't listen on port 80 for incoming requests, and so on. Instead, a separate WSGI-compliant web server fills that role, and hands off requests to your WSGI application. In order to hand off requests, the web server gives your application two things: the *request environment*, a dictionary-like object containing all the useful information from the request (including HTTP headers, HTTP request method, client IP address, path, query parameters, etc.), and a function that the web server will invoke when your application is ready to start responding to the request. Note that responding to the request—sending bytes out over port 80—is the web server's responsibility, not your application's. Your application just needs to give the web server some headers and some response content.

Therefore, a WSGI application is coded as a function that takes two parameters: a dictionary-like object containing the request environment information, and a function that can be invoked to start sending the response to the client. In other words, a WSGI application implements the interface shown here:

```
def app(environ, start_response):
  body = 'The WSGI request environment looks like this: %r' % environ
  response_headers = [
    ('Content-Type', 'text/plain'),
    ('Content-Length', str(len(response_body)))
  ]
  start_response('200 OK', response_headers)
  return [body]
```

Many online WSGI tutorials start right at that interface definition, without the introduction, which can make things a bit confusing. A reader might very well think, "What a strange interface! Why is `start_response()` defined this way? Why are we made to jump through these hoops?" (Assuming the poor reader isn't already confused about the fact that the web server, not the WSGI application, provides the environment and the `start_response()` function…)

But there are good reasons why the WSGI protocol has defined this interface, and they mostly have to do with middleware. The request environment is the mechanism for middleware to add information and communicate with other middleware. `start_response()` is a method provided by the WSGI-compliant web server itself. Once your application invokes `start_response()`, the headers are sent and can no longer be modified. Up until that point, middleware can add, change, or remove headers.

This would be a good time to show you what middleware looks like. The example that follows is a template or trivial example of WSGI middleware. The code does nothing except to play nice with WSGI and the rest of the middleware pipeline:

```
class TrivialMiddleware(object):
  def __init__(self, app):
    self.app = app

  def __call__(environ, start_response):
    return self.app(environ, start_response)
```

Let's consider how this works. Somewhere running on this machine is a WSGI-compliant web server that is configured to dispatch requests to WSGI applications. (Remember, a "WSGI application" isn't an independent process, but simply a function or other callable that implements an interface as described above.) The web server's functionality acts more or less like the following pseudocode:

```
def start_response(response_status, response_headers):
  # send HTTP status and headers to the connected client over port 80

class WsgiWebServer(object):
  def __init__(self, app):
    self.app = app

  def serve(self):
    while True:
      request = listen_for_web_request_on_port_80()
      environ = make_wsgi_environ_from_request(request)
      response_body = self.app(environ, start_response)
      send_response_body_to_client(response_body)
```

Now imagine that, rather than being configured to serve the application called `app`, this WSGI-compliant web server instead serves `TrivialMiddleware(app)`. The constructor for `TrivialMiddleware` takes an app as a parameter, so the initialization works fine. Then for each request, instead of invoking `app(environ, start_response)`, the server invokes the `TrivialMiddleware` instance's *`call`* method. That method just passes back the value of app(environ, start_response). So far we've accomplished nothing new, but we've demonstrated how to construct a middleware pipeline of the type described earlier.

Streaming and Making Modifications to Data

The TrivialMiddleware class simply passed the response back to the user unchanged, but it is easy to write middleware to modify the body of a response. Remember that the return value of the application function is an iterable. This allows very large responses to be streamed, rather than read into the web server's memory all at once. If you know your responses will always be small, you can instantiate the entire response in memory, but that is generally not advised. Here is an example of middleware that forces all response body text to uppercase, reading the entire response into memory:

```
class UppercaseMiddleware(object):
 def __init__(self, app):
  self.app = app

 def __call__(environ, start_response):
  body = self.app(environ, new_start_response)
  return [ chunk.upper() for chunk in body ]
```

And here is another implementation that returns a generator instead of a list, thus avoiding the need to read the entire response into memory:

```
class UppercaseMiddleware(object):
 def __init__(self, app):
  self.app = app

 def __call__(environ, start_response):
  body = self.app(environ, new_start_response)
  return ( chunk.upper() for chunk in body )
```

In this case, there is effectively no cost to make the middleware stream its data and play nicely with large responses. In more complex cases, it might be tempting to simplify the code by reading the entire response into memory. If you are certain about the size of responses you will be processing, this can work—but proceed with extreme caution, especially in code dealing with large-scale storage!

If the innermost application invokes start_response, how can the outermost middleware change the headers? When the outermost middleware needs to do this—say, by adding a new header—it passes a slightly different start_response method to the next middleware in the pipeline, as follows:

```
class HeaderAddingMiddleware(object):
  def __init__(self, app):
    self.app = app

  def __call__(environ, start_response):
```

```
    def new_start_response(status, headers):
      return start_response(status, headers + ('X-New-Header', 'Foo'))
    return self.app(environ, new_start_response)
```

Well, isn't that wacky! Changing the body was straightforward. But instead of changing a header, we pass in a function that, if it should be invoked, would do whatever `start_response` would do, but with one extra header. And naturally, all the middleware downstream in the pipeline will think this is the only `start_response` function in existence, so this is what will get invoked by the innermost application. Unless, of course, some other middleware wraps this `start_response` function in its own wrapper!

That's the downside of WSGI: the call chain, flow of control, and division of responsibilities can all be quite confusing. But the power to define a middleware pipeline makes WSGI a compelling interface.

More information, such as a WSGI tutorial (*http://bit.ly/wsgi-tutorial*), can be found online in several locations.

Configuring Middleware Through Paste

Swift is configured and deployed using the Python Paste framework, specifically its PasteDeploy module. In Paste terminology, middleware packages are "filters" on an application. Paste uses INI-style configuration files to define apps and filters, offering an easy way to set configuration variables for each component. We'll discuss some basic usage here, but refer to the Python Paste website's PasteDeploy section (*http://pythonpaste.org/deploy/*) for a more comprehensive reference.

Let's look at a simple configuration file for a Swift proxy server process, *proxy-server.conf*:

```
[DEFAULT]
bind_port = 80
expose_info = True

[pipeline:main]
# artificially simplified -- a real pipeline would have, e.g., auth middleware
pipeline = healthcheck proxy-logging proxy-server

[app:proxy-server]
use = egg:swift#proxy
account_autocreate = True
object_chunk_size = 8192
node_timeout = 10

[filter:healthcheck]
use = egg:swift#healthcheck
disable_path = /etc/swift/PROXY-HEALTHCHECK-DISABLED-503

[filter:proxy-logging]
```

```
use = egg:swift#proxy_logging
set access_log_facility = LOG_LOCAL2
```

This is, of course, a very simplified config file, with many necessary configuration settings missing (such as auth middleware), but it will be useful for discussing Paste deployment.

In this pipeline, the core proxy server code is wrapped by two middleware filters: `healthcheck` at the outermost layer, and `proxy-logging` in the middle layer. If a request is intercepted by the `healthcheck` middleware (which returns a response and short-circuits the rest of the pipeline), then `proxy-logging` never sees it, and neither does the core proxy server code itself.

This configuration file also defines several configuration variables that the various pipeline components will use. For example, the `disable_path` configuration variable is used by the `healthcheck` middleware. As the name suggests, if the specified file exists, health checking is disabled.

The pipeline shown above makes use of middleware that has been packaged as Python "eggs." What if you want to install middleware that hasn't been packaged as an egg? (This is common for testing custom middleware, or even installing custom middleware in a production system.) In that case, simply replace the `use` declaration of the config file with a `paste.filter_factory` declaration:

```
[filter:my-custom-middleware]
# the next line requires mymodule to be on sys.path
paste.filter_factory = mymodule.my_filter_factory
my_custom_config_param = 'my_param_value'
```

Paste provides the plumbing to get configuration variables through to the middleware that needs them. The first step is the somewhat magical `use` setting defined in each stanza, which points to the Python egg where the middleware is packaged. (Or the `paste.filter_factory` setting, which performs the same role when the middleware is not packaged in an egg.) This value tells Paste where to find the definition of the filter or app described. In a default Swift installation, all the non-custom middleware is defined in the Python *egg-info* directory, which was installed with Swift. This directory contains a file named *entry-points.txt*, which has contents like the following:

```
[paste.app_factory]
account = swift.account.server:app_factory
object = swift.obj.server:app_factory
container = swift.container.server:app_factory
proxy = swift.proxy.server:app_factory

[paste.filter_factory]
healthcheck = swift.common.middleware.healthcheck:filter_factory
proxy_logging = swift.common.middleware.proxy_logging:filter_factory
# etc.
```

As you might guess, the `paste.app_factory` and `paste.filter_factory` stanzas define useful application and filter names for the configuration file to refer to. (An *application* differs from a *filter* only in that an application lives at the end of the pipeline, and therefore can't pass a request inward to the next layer of middleware. An application is therefore intended to generate a response to all requests that it receives.) The `paste.filter_factory` stanza tells Paste that when it sees a reference to `healthcheck` (in the pipeline, for example), it can instantiate such a beast by invoking the `filter_factory` method in the `swift.common.middleware.healthcheck` module. If you look in that module for such a method, you'll find a simple wrapper function that looks like this:

```
def filter_factory(global_conf, **local_conf):
  conf = global_conf.copy()
  conf.update(local_conf)

  def healthcheck_filter(app):
    return HealthCheckMiddleware(app, conf)
  return healthcheck_filter
```

This wrapper function allows Paste to define how to make each element of the pipeline wrap (filter) the appropriate inner layers. Here, `filter_factory` is a function that takes a configuration dictionary and keyword parameters, and returns a function (`healthcheck_filter`, in this example) suitable for wrapping a WSGI app (such as the core proxy server code, or proxy server code that has already been wrapped in some middleware) in `HealthCheckMiddleware` configured with these parameters.

In order to recognize the configuration values from the Paste deployment configuration file, the constructor of `HealthCheckMiddleware` needs to look a bit different from the basic WSGI example in "Programming WSGI" on page 103:

```
class HealthCheckMiddleware(object):
  def __init__(self, app, conf):
    self.app = app
    self.disable_path = conf.get('disable_path', '')
```

Note that instead of taking one parameter (in addition to `self`), this constructor takes two. Paste is responsible for parsing the configuration file and passing the relevant information in dictionary form as the middleware constructor's second parameter, via the `filter_factory` function referenced in the *entry-points.txt* file in the egg that is named in the `use` stanza of the *proxy-server.conf* file. Pretty confusing, right?

The good news is that you usually don't need to concern yourself with any of this. Just put your config variables in the *proxy-server.conf* file, and they magically make it into your middleware. However, if you're writing your own middleware from scratch, you will need to verify that the plumbing exists. In addition to the notation of `use = egg:swift#healthcheck` (where the function referenced by `healthcheck` is defined in the `swift` egg's *entry-points.txt* file), Paste supports other ways to refer to filter factory functions and app factory functions. In particular, as mentioned above, the `paste.fil` ter_factory declaration is likely to be useful to custom middleware developers. See the Paste Deploy documentation (*http://pythonpaste.org/deploy*) for more information.

Production Swift installations usually rely on an automated configuration manager such as the SwiftStack Controller software. Automated configuration management simplifies the process of deploying new configuration files, greatly reduces the opportunity for human error, and often provides a level of abstraction that makes Swift's low-level settings easier to comprehend and evaluate. For this reason, we strongly recommend an administrative tool such as SwiftStack Controller for managing production Swift clusters. Obviously, mixing manual config tweaks and automated config management is likely to lead to undesirable results. If you use configuration management software such as SwiftStack Controller, check the documentation to learn how to include your custom middleware in configuration deployments.

How to Write Swift Middleware

Let's look at a full implementation of HealthCheckMiddleware as an example. Its functionality is described in the class docstring:

```
import os
from swift.common.swob import Request, Response

class HealthCheckMiddleware(object):
  """
  Healthcheck middleware used for monitoring.

  If the path is /healthcheck, it will respond 200 with "OK" as the body.

  If the optional config parameter "disable_path" is set, and a file is
  present at that path, it will respond 503 with "DISABLED BY FILE" as the
  body.
  """

  def __init__(self, app, conf):
    self.app = app
    self.disable_path = conf.get('disable_path', '')

  def GET(self, req):
    """Returns a 200 response with "OK" in the body."""
    return Response(request=req, body="OK", content_type="text/plain")

  def DISABLED(self, req):
    """Returns a 503 response with "DISABLED BY FILE" in the body."""
    return Response(request=req, status=503, body="DISABLED BY FILE",
      content_type="text/plain")

  def __call__(self, env, start_response):
    req = Request(env)
    if req.path != '/healthcheck':
```

```
      return self.app(env, start_response)
    handler = self.GET
    if self.disable_path and os.path.exists(self.disable_path):
      handler = self.DISABLED
    return handler(req)(env, start_response)

def filter_factory(global_conf, **local_conf):
  conf = dict(global_conf, **local_conf)
  return lambda app: HealthCheckMiddleware(app, conf)
```

There is one new feature here: the use of `Request` and `Response` objects in `swift.common.swob`. In this module, a `Request` is a wrapper for the WSGI environment and headers. A `Response`, however, is a much more complicated animal. It wraps the response code, headers, and body, as you might expect. But in addition to its use as a wrapper or container, it can also serve as a WSGI application! In the same way that middleware might return `self.app(env, start_response)` (which invokes `start_response` somewhere to start sending an HTTP response), middleware might also create a variable `resp = Response(request=req, status=200, body="OK")`, and return `resp(env, start_response)` instead of passing control to the WSGI application that it wraps. This use of the `Response` class, effectively as a WSGI application rather than a wrapper/container for response data, can be a bit surprising to the uninitiated.

With that in mind, let's see what `HealthCheckMiddleware` does. When called, it instantiates a `Request` and checks whether the request's path is */healthcheck*. If not, it just passes the request down the pipeline by calling `self.app(env, start_response)` and returning its value unaltered. However, if the path is */healthcheck*, the middleware doesn't pass the request down the pipeline at all. Instead, it assigns a handler—either the normal `GET` handler by default, or the `DISABLED` handler if `disable_path` is set and such a file is present—and returns the return value of that handler. As it happens, in both cases the handler is a `swob.Response` object, which simply sets `Content-Type` and returns the status code and body given in its constructor.

Inside Out

WSGI middleware's modular, callback-based design can make the flow of control a bit confusing, but we've seen all the pieces already. If a WSGI application named `app` is wrapped by several layers of middleware, such as `InnerMW` and `OuterMW`, the WSGI-compliant web server will be invoking `OuterMW(InnerMW(app))(env, start_response)`. Middleware almost always needs to know what it wraps, so its constructor should store a copy of its parameter, `app`. Also, every element of the chain must have a *call* method that accepts those parameters. The middleware can choose to do nothing by simply passing the request through, returning `self.app(env, start_response)` as the `TrivialMiddleware` class above does. `HealthCheckMiddleware` is one notch more complex, taking a different action if the request path is */healthcheck*.

It all makes sense (more or less) if, like a WSGI-compliant web server, you look at it inside out.

Some Simple Examples

Let's go through a couple more examples that are fairly simple, to demonstrate the patterns. Here's a simple middleware component that prevents deletion from your Swift cluster (although overwriting is still allowed):

```
class DeletionPreventingMiddleware(object):
  def __init__(self, app):
    self.app = app

  def __call__(self, env, start_response):
    if env['REQUEST_METHOD'] != 'DELETE':
      return self.app(env, start_response)
    return Response(request=req, status=405, body="Deletion prohibited",
      content_type="text/plain")
```

You still need to import `swob.Response` and write the filter factory function, but the preceding code is the extent of the custom development required to create new middleware that performs a useful, if simple, function.

Here's another simple but useful middleware component that compresses all object `PUT` data:

```
from bz2 import BZ2Compressor
from itertools import chain, ifilter
from swift.common.swob import Request

class BzipCompressionMiddleware(object):
  def __init__(self, app):
    self.app = app

  def __call__(self, env, start_response):
    if env['REQUEST_METHOD'] != 'PUT':
      return self.app(env, start_response)
    req = Request(env)
    version, account, container, obj = req.split_path(1, 4, True)
    if not obj:
      # request path had no object component -- account or container PUT
      return self.app(env, start_response)

    # We're doing an object PUT -- wrap the input stream
    # Make sure to avoid reading everything into memory
    not_blank = lambda somestr: somestr != ''
    bz = BZ2Compressor()
    compressed = chain((bz.compress(i) for i in env['wsgi.input']),
                       (bz.flush() for i in (1,)))
    env['wsgi.input'] = ifilter(not_blank, compressed)
    return self.app(env, start_response)
```

Note the use of `itertools.ifilter` to provide a generator rather than reading the entire object into memory. If these are objects we want to compress, then they're probably very large. Due to the `bz2` module's API, we needed to sneak in a call to `flush()` within that generator, and then filter out its possibly blank return value.

For extra usefulness, this middleware should also be augmented to intercept object `GET` requests, uncompress the fetched result, and return the uncompressed content. To the end users, nothing would look different—but the data would magically be stored on disk in compressed format.

You could write very similar code to automatically encrypt all object `PUT`s, although key management would require some careful attention. If that were addressed, perhaps by allowing a `reseller_admin` user to `POST` an encryption key at startup, you could write a couple dozen lines of middleware that converts Swift to an at-rest encryption solution.

And that is the power of middleware! In very little custom code, sometimes only a few dozen lines, you can add powerful functionality and customizations to your Swift service.

Doing More in Middleware

We're starting to get a picture of what sorts of functionality might be implemented by middleware. But as a middleware author, you have even more powerful tools available than we've seen thus far—and as with all power tools, some advice and caution is useful so that you don't hurt yourself.

As part of the proxy server process, middleware has access to additional information from the storage server processes (account, container, and object). When needed, both the core proxy server and any middleware can query these storage server processes for information about the resources in the course of processing a request. To save middleware programmers (and core Swift authors) from the effort of caching these results, the functions `get_account_info()` and `get_container_info()` are provided. If your middleware needs metadata, use these methods rather than retrieving it independently, to take advantage of the caching and reduce the system load on Swift. We'll see these methods used in later examples.

As another word of caution, middleware authors should be mindful of the impact of their middleware on performance (especially the performance of queries irrelevant to their component), because middleware can and often does generate additional HTTP requests or service calls. We've already mentioned `get_account_info()` and `get_container_info()`, which get their information either from a Memcache server or directly from the account and container nodes. But it is also possible to generate additional requests that are external to Swift, especially when integrating Swift as a component in a larger system.

Suppose we wanted middleware to automatically submit an object to a keyword indexing process, so that objects could be searched on their metadata—a potentially useful feature for our system's end users. In our imagined example, we have an external indexer to which we can submit requests such as *http://indexer.example.com/index?page=<swift-object-url>&keywords=<indexing-keywords>*.

We just need to write middleware that submits a request to this external indexer every time an object is stored in Swift.

Consider one way we might write this middleware. In this example, we'll do our indexing work if the header `X-Object-Meta-Search-Keywords` is provided in a `PUT` or `POST` request:

```
import requests

class IndexingMiddleware(object):
  def __init__(self, app):
    self.app = app

  def __call__(self, env, start_response):
    if env['REQUEST_METHOD'] not in ('PUT', 'POST'):
      return self.app(env, start_response)
    req = Request(env)
    version, account, container, obj = req.split_path(1, 4, True)
    if not obj:
      # request path had no object component -- nothing to index
      return self.app(env, start_response)

    # We're doing an object PUT or POST -- any keywords?
    keyword_str = req.headers.get('X-Object-Meta-Search-Keywords')
    if not keyword_str:
      return self.app(env, start_response)

    keywords = keyword_str.split()
    url_template = \
          'http://indexer.example.com/index?page=%(page)s&%(params)s'
    index_request_url = url_template % {
      'page': req.path,
      'params': '&'.join(('keyword=%s' % i for i in keywords))
    }

    # This could have high latency, and should be wrapped in a timeout.
    # However, the proxy's WSGI-compliant web server (Eventlet) would
    # still be able to accept other requests and spawn other threads
    # to handle them.

    result = requests.post(index_request_url)

    # It would be smart to check result.status_code and perhaps set a
    # response header to indicate whether the indexing was successful...
```

```
        return self.app(env, start_response)
```

Although some of the error checking is omitted from this example, it demonstrates how middleware can easily integrate with external services. Bear in mind the additional latency and return early when possible.

A more robust and lower-latency way to interact with external services would be to enqueue a work job upon successful uploading of the original object:

```
import requests

class JobEnqueueingMiddleware(object):
  def __init__(self, app):
    self.app = app

  def __call__(self, env, start_response):
    if env['REQUEST_METHOD'] != 'PUT':
      return self.app(env, start_response)
    req = Request(env)
    version, account, container, obj = req.split_path(1, 4, True)
    if not obj:
      # request path had no object component -- no job to enqueue
      return self.app(env, start_response)

    # We're doing an object PUT -- should we enqueue a job?
    enqueue_job = req.headers.get('X-Object-Meta-Enqueue-My-Work-Job')
    if not enqueue_job:
      return self.app(env, start_response)

    enqueue_url = 'http://workjobs.example.com/newjob?swift_path=%(url)s'
    # in real code, you would url-encode the following!
    job_request_url = url_template % { 'url': req.path }
    result = requests.post(enqueue_url)
    # It would be smart to check result.status_code and perhaps set a
    # response header to indicate whether the job was successfully enqueued

    return self.app(env, start_response)
```

The official Swift documentation shows how you can create "web hook" middleware, which sends a `POST` request to a URL (the URL being configured on a per-container basis) on every successful object `PUT`. This is a more generalized version of the `JobEnqueueingMiddleware` above, suitable for any service that can be configured to accept a `POST` containing the object URL as its input. The following example introduces two other new concepts (the `@wsgify` decorator from `swift.common.swob`, and system metadata as exemplified by the `SYSMETA_WEBHOOK` constant), but the overall structure should be familiar:

```
from swift.common.http import is_success
from swift.common.swob import wsgify
from swift.common.utils import split_path, get_logger
```

```
from swift.common.request_helper import get_sys_meta_prefix
from swift.proxy.controllers.base import get_container_info

from eventlet import Timeout
from eventlet.green import urllib2

# "x-container-sysmeta-webhook"
SYSMETA_WEBHOOK = get_sys_meta_prefix('container') + 'webhook'


class WebhookMiddleware(object):

  def __init__(self, app, conf):
    self.app = app
    self.logger = get_logger(conf, log_route='webhook')

  @wsgify
  def __call__(self, req):
    obj = None
    try:
      (version, account, container, obj) = \
        split_path(req.path_info, 4, 4, True)
    except ValueError:
      # not an object request
      pass
    if 'x-webhook' in req.headers:
      # translate user's request header to sysmeta
      req.headers[SYSMETA_WEBHOOK] = \
        req.headers.pop('x-webhook', '')
    if 'x-remove-webhook' in req.headers:
      # empty value will remove the sysmeta data
      req.headers[SYSMETA_WEBHOOK] = ''
    # account and object storage will ignore x-container-sysmeta-*

    # Request pre-processing complete.  Pass the request down the pipeline.
    resp = req.get_response(self.app)
    # Now take action based on the response.

    if obj and is_success(resp.status_int) and req.method == 'PUT':
      # POST to the webhook, if any, only on successful object PUT requests
      container_info = get_container_info(req.environ, self.app)
      # container_info may have our new sysmeta key
      webhook = container_info['sysmeta'].get('webhook')
      if webhook:
        # create a POST request with obj name as body
        webhook_req = urllib2.Request(webhook, data=obj)
        with Timeout(20):
          try:
            urllib2.urlopen(webhook_req).read()
          except (Exception, Timeout):
            self.logger.exception(
              'failed POST to webhook %s' % webhook)
```

```
            else:
              self.logger.info(
                'successfully called webhook %s' % webhook)
      if 'x-container-sysmeta-webhook' in resp.headers:
        # translate sysmeta from the backend resp to
        # user-visible client resp header
        resp.headers['x-webhook'] = resp.headers.pop(SYSMETA_WEBHOOK, '')
      return resp


  def webhook_factory(global_conf, **local_conf):
    conf = dict(global_conf, **local_conf)
    return lambda app: WebhookMiddleware(app, conf)
```

In this example, `@wsgify` allows the developer to structure the middleware's *`call`* method to accept a `swift.common.swob.Request` as input and return a `swift.common.swob.Response` as output. It also catches any raised `HTTPExceptions` and translates them to responses. This interface can be much more intuitive than the classic WSGI alternative, in which the *`call`* method accepts the `env` and `start_response` parameters, but it's entirely optional.

We also used the `swift.common.swob.Request` object's `get_response()` method to pass the request down the pipeline and intercept its response on the way out. For this middleware functionality, we needed to take further action dependent on the response (`POST`ing to the webhook only if the response indicates a successful initial HTTP PUT operation). Examining the `Response` object returned by `get_response()` provides a reliable way to structure that control flow.

Another new concept here is the idea of system metadata. We looked at user metadata in the previous chapter, Chapter 7. User metadata is intended for use by Swift clients and end users. System metadata, on the other hand, is intended for use by the Swift system, including its middleware. By using system metadata instead of user metadata, the developer gets several benefits:

Namespacing
: There is no risk of name collisions with user metadata.

Protection
: System metadata is propagated by headers that are automatically stripped out of both incoming requests and outgoing responses.

Automatic persistence
: Headers with the `sysmeta` prefix (such as the header name in the variable `SYSMETA_WEBHOOK` in the previous example) are persisted to the appropriate resource database (account, container, or object) with no additional code, and automatically populated in the responses from the resource server processes to the proxy server processes. The middleware has access to the system metadata as the request is exiting Swift, but all system metadata will be stripped before the response is sent to

the user (unless middleware copies it into an externally visible header, as it does in the previous example with `X-Webhook`).

For these reasons, middleware that makes use of persistent data—such as the association between a container and its webhook URL in the previous example—should use the system metadata infrastructure.

A Look Back and a Look Forward

Middleware introduces a great deal of power to modify Swift's HTTP API. To summarize what we've seen so far, a middleware component can:

- Modify requests, by mutating the WSGI environment
- Short-circuit the pipeline and return an error response (or a successful response, e.g., `HealthCheckMiddleware`)
- Modify the content of a request or response. Generators should be used to stream large requests and responses (e.g., for compression and decompression)
- Alter response headers by passing a modified `start_response` function down the pipeline
- Define new URL endpoints, and handle those endpoints specifically (`HealthCheckMiddleware`, various auth middleware)
- Define and handle new HTTP verbs—generally not recommended, but possible
- Issue additional HTTP requests to Swift or to an external service, with caution regarding latency (e.g., `IndexingMiddleware`, `JobEnqueueingMiddleware`, `WebhookMiddleware`)

These features let developers extend their storage systems in incredible ways, centralizing complex operations on the server side and allowing client applications to become simpler. Many middleware developers create middleware components to meet a very specific need at their own company, which makes a middleware-friendly platform such as Swift extremely appealing. Other middleware functions are broadly useful, and several of these have been developed, tested, and distributed with the core Swift installation. We can't guess your specific needs, but we can give you several examples and hope to seed your imagination.

In that spirit, here are some middleware components that can probably be implemented in fewer than 100 lines of code:

- Image resizing, either locally in the proxy with Python Wand, or via a call to an external server—we recommend storing the raw input image, then enqueueing a work job to process it.

- Logging or gathering stats on certain types of requests
- Denial-of-service attack mitigation (e.g., to handle badly behaved internal clients —better practices exist for handling external DoS attacks)
- Transcoding uploaded data—store a raw format, have the system transcode to a different format behind the scenes

And, of course, the ideas we've already seen:

- Intercepting certain requests, such as preventing `DELETE`s
- In-flight compression/decompression
- At-rest encryption
- Sending uploaded data to an external work job queue for post-processing
- Dynamic "web hooks" on upload: setting an owner-specified URL as an endpoint for `POST`ing the names of uploaded objects, for handling by an external system

In addition, the previous chapter (Chapter 7) lists middleware distributed with Swift, which is no different from middleware you might write yourself. That should provide plenty of additional ideas about what middleware can do for you.

Conclusion

Swift is a powerful and flexible storage system on its own, but its ability to support middleware vastly expands the possibilities. If you are designing a system that processes data on its way to or from storage, triggers additional actions on storage events, or needs to maintain any type of invariant around the storage, you will find it easier and more robust to implement those features in server middleware rather than in your storage clients. Effectively, you gain the ability to delegate more functionality to your storage system—but you retain the ability to keep any unneeded functionality out of your pipeline, thus simplifying your overall system design, reducing the risk of bugs in unused features, and easing the tasks of system maintenance and debugging.

The complexity doesn't vanish, of course: the choice to add middleware in your pipeline must be made with an eye toward security and latency, and of course you must understand the middleware's functionality and behavior when deciding to add it. But once the desired functionality is part of your storage system, your architectural block diagram becomes simpler because any stored data goes through the middleware pipeline and meets your requirements when stored. Swift becomes a storage system customized precisely for your exact needs.

PART III
Installing Swift

This part explains how to install Swift, both by using its fundamental commands and by using the SwiftStack product.

CHAPTER 9

Installing OpenStack Swift from Source

Hugo Kuo
Amanda Plimpton

In this chapter, you'll learn how to get a Swift cluster up and running. We will cover the download and installation of OpenStack Swift direct from source and go into detail about the configuration options. This will provide a foundation for understanding any automation tools you might use during deployment. Chapter 10 covers installing Swift using SwiftStack.

The instructions in this chapter show a fairly generic installation for a small deployment. The exact values you use when you are installing will vary depending on your needs and the physical or virtual machine(s) you are using. There are many configuration options and installation decisions to make; we will note potential land mines, so you can learn from our (sometimes painful) experiences.

User Access Rights

You will need the correct permissions to run many of these commands. Depending on your environment, using an account with sudo access or using `sudo su` may be the best option.

Downloading OpenStack Swift

The official releases of OpenStack Swift are available on GitHub (*https://github.com/openstack/swift*). For each major release of OpenStack there is a version of Swift.

We recommend deploying and staying current with the latest released version of OpenStack Swift. Given Swift's frequent release schedule you should check which versions of Swift have been tagged for release on GitHub (*https://github.com/openstack/swift/tags*). Swift tags follow the typical major.minor.release style; for example, 1.13.0.

Dependencies

Depending on your distribution, there might be some dependencies that will need to be installed on your system before we install Swift.

On apt-based systems (Debian and derivatives):

```
apt-get install git curl gcc memcached rsync sqlite3 xfsprogs \
                           git-core libffi-dev python-setuptools

apt-get install python-coverage python-dev python-nose \
                       python-simplejson python-xattr python-eventlet \
                       python-greenlet python-pastedeploy python-netifaces\
                       python-pip python-dnspython python-mock
```

On yum-based systems (RHEL, Fedora, and CentOS):

CentOS 6 might require the installation of the EPEL repo before installing the dependencies:

```
#For Centos 6 systems
rpm -Uvh http://dl.fedoraproject.org/pub/epel/6/x86_64/epel-release-6-8.noarch.rpm
```

The following packages will most likely need to be installed:

```
yum update
yum install git curl gcc memcached rsync sqlite xfsprogs git-core \
                 libffi-devel xinetd python-setuptools python-coverage \
                 python-devel python-nose python-simplejson pyxattr \
                 python-eventlet python-greenlet python-paste-deploy \
                 python-netifaces python-pip python-dns python-mock
```

After you install the dependencies, you will install the Swift command-line interface and Swift. After installation, you will need to configure and initialize the Swift processes before your cluster and node(s) will be up and running.

Installing the Swift CLI (python-swiftclient)

Install the Swift command-line interface (CLI) from GitHub with the following commands:

```
cd /opt
git clone https://github.com/openstack/python-swiftclient.git
cd /opt/python-swiftclient; sudo pip install -r requirements.txt;
python setup.py install; cd ..
```

Installing Swift

Installing Swift from GitHub is similar to installing the CLI; use the following commands:

```
cd /opt
git clone https://github.com/openstack/swift.git
cd /opt/swift ; sudo python setup.py install; cd ..
```

Fedora 19+ users might need to run the following if the installation of Swift fails:

```
#For Fedora 19+
pip install -U xattr
pip install -r swift/requirements.txt
```

Copying in Swift Configuration Files

Create a directory for Swift and then copy in the sample configuration files so you can use them as a template during configuration:

```
mkdir -p /etc/swift
cd /opt/swift/etc
cp account-server.conf-sample /etc/swift/account-server.conf
cp container-server.conf-sample /etc/swift/container-server.conf
cp object-server.conf-sample /etc/swift/object-server.conf
cp proxy-server.conf-sample /etc/swift/proxy-server.conf
cp drive-audit.conf-sample /etc/swift/drive-audit.conf
cp swift.conf-sample /etc/swift/swift.conf
```

At this point, you should be able to run the `swift-init` command with the help flag and get the help message:

```
swift-init -h
```

This command is similar to `service` or `start|stop`; it allows you to start/stop/reload Swift processes. However, don't try to start Swift up just yet.

Configuring Swift

Before starting the processes, the newly installed Swift needs configuring. You will need to create the builder files, add the drives, and build the rings. After that we will discuss how to set up logging, start services, and check our work.

Adding Drives to Swift

Storing data on hard drives is the fundamental purpose of Swift, so adding and formatting the drives is an important first step.

Swift replicates data across disks, nodes, zones, and regions, so there is no need for the data redundancy provided by a RAID controller. Parity-based RAID, such as RAID5, RAID6, and RAID10, harms the performance of a cluster and does not provide any additional protection because Swift is already providing data redundancy.

Finding drives

First, you need to identify what drives are in your system and determine which should be formatted and which are system drives that shouldn't be formatted.

From the command line of the machine, run:

```
df
```

It will return something similar to:

```
Filesystem       1K-blocks        Used     Available        Use%     Mounted on
/dev/sda1        27689156         8068144  18214448         31%      /
none      1536448  672      1535776  1%       /dev
none      1543072  1552     1541520  1%       dev/shm

none      1543072  92       1542980  1%       /var/run
none      1543072  0        1543072  0%       /var/lock
```

This should list all mounted filesystems. Just note which drive is used for booting so you don't accidentally format it later; very often it is the sda device mounted on the root / directory. But you can can verify that by poking around in */proc/mounts* and finding which directory is the *rootfs*:

```
cat /proc/mounts
```

It will return something similar to:

```
rootfs / rootfs rw 0 0
none /sys sysfs rw,nosuid,nodev,noexec,relatime 0 0
none /proc proc rw,nosuid,nodev,noexec,relatime 0 0
none /dev devtmpfs
rw,relatime,size=1536448k,nr_inodes=211534,mode=755 0 0
none /dev/pts devpts
rw,nosuid,noexec,relatime,gid=5,mode=620,ptmxmode=000 0 0
fusectl /sys/fs/fuse/connections fusectl rw,relatime 0 0
/dev/disk/by-uuid/c9402f9d-30ed-41f2-8255-d32bdb7fb7c2 / ext4 rw,relatime 0 0
none /sys/kernel/debug debugfs rw,relatime 0 0
none /sys/kernel/security securityfs rw,relatime 0 0
none /dev/shm tmpfs rw,nosuid,nodev,relatime 0 0
none /var/run tmpfs rw,nosuid,relatime,mode=755 0 0
none /var/lock tmpfs rw,nosuid,nodev,noexec,relatime 0 0
binfmt_misc /proc/sys/fs/binfmt_misc binfmt_misc
rw,nosuid,nodev,noexec,relatime 0 0
gvfs-fuse-daemon /home/joe/.gvfs fuse.gvfs-fuse-daemon
rw,nosuid,nodev,relatime,user_id=1000,group_id=1000 0 0
```

The output tells you that the root filesystem is /, which you know from the `df` command is mounted on */dev/sda1*. That is where the system will boot.

To find out what other block devices the operating system knows about, look in the */sys/block* directory. This should list all the block devices known to the system:

```
ls /sys/block
```

The command will return something similar to:

```
loop0 loop3 loop6 ram1  ram12 ram15 ram3 ram6 sda sdd sdg sdj sdm
loop1 loop4 loop7 ram10 ram13 ram19 ram4 ram7 sdb sde sdh sdk
loop2 loop5 ram0 ram11 ram14 ram2 ram5 ram8 sdc sdf sdi sdl
```

The devices you're interested in are the ones starting with sd in this output, but other systems might have different prefixes. Also review which filesystems are formatted by running the following, which you might need to run as root:

```
blkid
```

It will return something similar to:

```
/dev/sda1: UUID="c9402f9d-30ed-41f2-8255-d32bdb7fb7c2" TYPE="ext4"
/dev/sda5: UUID="b2c9d42b-e7ae-4987-8e12-8743ced6bd5e" TYPE="swap"
```

The TYPE value will tell you which filesystem is on the device (e.g., xfs or ext4). Naturally, you should not use ones that have swap as their type.

Labeling drives

It's important to keep track of which devices need to be mounted to which system location. This can be done with mounting by labels in a separate upstart script created for Swift. Labeling the drive will ensure the drive gets that name every time the OS reboots. If you don't do this, the next time the OS boots, a device with your data might come up under a different device name. This would lead to all sorts of unexpected behaviors when the cluster reboots.

We suggest *not using the fstab file* for this purpose. */etc/fstab* is used to automatically mount filesystems at boot time. Make sure that the only items listed there are critical for the booting of the machine, because the machine might hang upon boot if it can't mount a device. This is likely when running a big box full of disks.

Unless you are experienced in and confident about the need for it, do not use "nobarrier." See The XFS FAQ (*http://bit.ly/xfs-faq*) for more details.

Start building up a list of devices that the system knows about that need to be formatted. Identify all the devices in */sys/bock* that are not formatted (or not formatted in the manner specified here).

You should label each device so you can keep an inventory of each device in the system and properly mount the device. To add a label, use the -L option to the mkfs.xfs command. For instance, the following assigns the label d1 to the device */dev/sdb* and the label d2 to the device */dev/sdc*:

```
mkfs.xfs -f -L d1 /dev/sdb
mkfs.xfs -f -L d2 /dev/sdc
```

Go in this manner through all your drives that will be formatted.

Swift uses extended attributes, and the XFS default inode size (currently 256) is recommended.

Notice that we didn't create device partitions. Partitioning is an unnecessary abstraction for Swift because you're going to use the entire device.

Mounting drives

The next step is to tell the operating system to attach (mount) the new XFS filesystems somewhere on the devices so that Swift can find them and start putting data on them.

Create a directory in */srv/node/* for each device as a place to mount the filesystem. We suggest a simple approach to naming the directories, such as using each device's label (d1, d2, etc):

```
mkdir -p /srv/node/d1
mkdir -p /srv/node/d2
```

For each device (dev) you wish to mount, you will use the `mount` command:

```
// _mount -t xfs -o noatime,nodiratime,logbufs=8 -L_ <dev label> <dev dir>
```

Run the command for each device:

```
mount -t xfs -o noatime,nodiratime,logbufs=8 -L d1 /srv/node/d1
mount -t xfs -o noatime,nodiratime,logbufs=8 -L d2 /srv/node/d2
...
```

Swift user

After the drives are mounted, a user needs to be created with read/write permissions to the directories where the devices have been mounted. The default user that Swift uses is named `swift`. Different operating systems have different commands to create users, looking something like this:

```
useradd swift
```

Next, give the `swift` user ownership to the directories:

```
chown -R swift:swift /srv/node
```

Creating scripts to mount the devices on boot

The `mount` commands we ran earlier take effect only during the current boot. Because we need them to run automatically on reboot, we'll put the commands in a script called *mount_devices* that contains the `mount` commands we just ran. This new script should be created in the */opt/swift/bin/* directory:

```
mount -t xfs -o noatime,nodiratime,logbufs=8 -L d1 /srv/node/d1
mount -t xfs -o noatime,nodiratime,logbufs=8 -L d2 /srv/node/d2
...
mount -t xfs -o noatime,nodiratime,logbufs=8 -L d36 /srv/node/d36
```

Next, create an Upstart script in the */etc/init* directory called *start_swift.conf* with the following commands:

```
description "mount swift drives"
start on runlevel [234]
stop on runlevel [0156]
exec /opt/swift/bin/mount_devices
```

There are many good resources online that can explain more about Upstart scripts and runlevels. (*http://bit.ly/runlevels*)

Be sure the script is executable:

```
chmod +x /opt/swift/bin/mount_devices
```

Test the scripts by rebooting the system:

```
reboot
```

When the system restarts, log on and make sure everything mounted properly with the configuration settings by running the `mount` command:

```
mount
```

You should see something similar to:

```
/dev/sda1 on / type ext4 (rw,errors=remount-ro, commit=0)
...
...
/dev/sdc on /srv/node/d1 type xfs
(rw,noatime,nodiratime,logbufs=8)
```

Storage Policies

Released with Swift 2.0, storage policies let Swift operators define space within a cluster that can be customized in numerous ways, including by location, replication, hardware, and partitions to meet specific data storage needs. More information on storage policies can be found on the Openstack website (*http://bit.ly/os-storage*).

To implement storage polices, you must create them in the cluster and then apply them to containers. Creating user-defined storage policies is a two-step process. The policies are first declared in the *swift.conf* file with name and index number. Then their index number is used to create the corresponding builder files and rings.

It's important to understand that in the absence of user-defined policies, Swift defaults to an internally referenced storage policy 0, which is applied to all containers. There will always be a minimum of one storage policy per cluster as a result. In addition to being the system default, this storage policy 0, named *Policy-0*, allows for backward compatibility with clusters created before the storage policies feature was added to Swift.

If you want to use a different name for storage policy 0, you can add it to the *swift.conf* file. It is considered a best practice to add all storage policies, including storage policy 0, to the *swift.conf* file and explicitly list which policy is the default.

Creating storage policies

Each user-defined storage policy is declared with a policy index number and name. If a policy is deprecated or the default, there are additional fields that can be used. The general format for a storage policy is:

```
[storage-policy:N]
name =
default =
(optional) deprecated=

//Here's an example
[storage-policy:1]
name =  level1
(optional) deprecated=yes
```

The storage policy index, `[storage-policy:N]`, is required. The `N` is the storage policy index whose value is either 0 or a positive integer. It can't be a number already in use, and once in use it can't be changed.

The policy name (`name =`) is required and can only be letters (case-insensitive), numbers, and dashes. It can't be a name already in use, but the name can be changed. Before such a change, however, consider how it will affect systems using the current name.

One storage policy must be designated as the default. When defining one or more storage policies, be sure to also declare a policy 0. This makes it easier to manage the policies and prevents errors. As mentioned earlier, if there are no user-defined polices, then the default will be an internally referenced storage policy 0. A different policy can be designated as the default at any time; however, consider the impact it will have on the system before making the change.

When storage policies are no longer needed, they can be marked as deprecated with `deprecated=yes` rather than being deleted. A policy can't be both the default and deprecated. When deprecated, a policy:

- Will not appear in */info*
- Enables `PUT`/`GET`/`DELETE`/`POST`/`HEAD` requests to succeed on preexisting containers
- Can't be applied to a new container (a `400 Bad Request` will be returned)

Although storage policies are not necessary for this installation, we have included some to provide examples of how they are added and used.

To declare a storage policy, edit the *swift.conf* file in the */etc/swift/* directory. The suggested placement in the file for storage polices is below the `[swift-hash]` section:

```
[swift-hash]
# random unique strings that can never change (DO NOT LOSE)
swift_hash_path_prefix = changeme
swift_hash_path_suffix = changeme

[storage-policy:0]
name = level1

[storage-policy:1]
name = level2
default = yes

[storage-policy:2]
name = level3
deprecated = yes
```

Once the storage policies are declared, they can be used to create builder files. For each storage policy (storage-policy:N), an *object-N.builder* file will be created.

Creating the Ring Builder Files

With the devices ready and storage polices created, it is time to create the builder files. You need to create a minimum of three files: *account.builder*, *container.builder*, and *object.builder*. You will also create a builder file for each user-defined storage policy that you are implementing in your cluster.

As their names indicate, these are the files that are used to build the rings that the Swift processes use for data storage and retrieval.

The builder files are some of the most critical components of the cluster, so we will take a closer look at their creation.

The create command

Think of a builder file as a big database. It contains a record of all the storage devices in the cluster and the values the ring-builder utility will use to create a ring.

The help menu for `swift-ring-builder` shows the format for the `create` command as:

```
swift-ring-builder (account|container|object|object-n).builder create
<part_power> <replicas> <min_part_hours>
```

So the commands we will be running are:

```
swift-ring-builder account.builder create <part_power> <replicas>
<min_part_hours>
swift-ring-builder container.builder create <part_power> <replicas>
<min_part_hours>
swift-ring-builder object.builder create <part_power> <replicas>
<min_part_hours>
swift-ring-builder object-n.builder create <part_power> <replicas>
<min_part_hours>
```

The three parameters the `create` command takes are:

`part_power`
: Determines the number of partitions created in the storage cluster

`replicas`
: Specifies how many replicas you would like stored in the cluster

`min_part_hours`
: Specifies the frequency at which a replica is allowed to be moved

These are critical parameters for a cluster, so let's dig a bit more deeply into each of these configuration settings before using them.

Partition power

The total number of partitions that can exist in your cluster is calculated using the *partition power*, an integer picked during cluster creation.

Don't change the partition power after the cluster is created. A change will result in the reshuffling of every single thing in the cluster. That much data in flight could create vulnerabilities, and the data will be inaccessible for some period of time before the system is repartitioned and the data is moved to where it should be.

The formula to calculate the total number of partitions in a cluster is:

$$\text{total partitions in cluster} = 2^{\text{partition power}}$$

For example, if you choose a partition power of 15, the number of partitions your cluster can support is $2^{15} = 32{,}768$. Those 32,768 partitions are then mapped to the available drives. Although the number of drives in a cluster might change, the number of partitions will not.

If your first thought is to choose a very large number, your instinct would be rewarded. Rings are relatively small compared to memory available on modern systems, so it is best to err on the large side. However, you should keep in mind several things if you choose a large number of partitions. Replication might take longer because fewer files will be grouped together in each partition for replication checks. Also, lookups take a fraction longer because the ring gets that much bigger. Lastly, a larger number of partitions means it takes longer to build the ring when making future changes.

To choose the partition power, estimate the maximum number of drives you expect your cluster to have at its largest size. (It might help to have a crystal ball handy.) In general, it is considered good to have about 100 partitions per drive in large clusters.

If you can make that prediction, you can calculate the partition power as follows:

$$\log_2 \ (100 \times \text{maximum number of disks})$$

Let's look at an example for a large deployment of 1,800 drives that will grow to a total of 18,000 drives. If we set the maximum number of disks to 18,000, we can calculate a partition power that would allow for 100 partitions per disks:

$$\text{partition power} = \log_2 \ (100 \times 18,000) \approx 20.77$$

So we judge that a good partition power for this example is 21.

Even if you guess wrong, there is still recourse—it's always possible to stand up another object storage cluster and have the authentication system route new accounts to that new storage cluster.

Replicas

The more replicas you have, the more protected you are against losing data when there is a failure. Distributing replicas across data centers and geographic regions protects you even more against hardware failures. The replica count affects the system's durability, availability, and the amount of disk space used. For example, if you have a replica count of three, then each partition will be replicated for a total of three copies. Each of the three replicas will be stored on a different device in the cluster for redundancy. When an object is put into the cluster, its hash will match a partition and be copied to all three locations of that partition.

You set the replica count for the cluster in each of the builder files using the `replicas` parameter. When you build a Swift ring, the value of `replicas` is how many copies of the partition will be placed across the cluster. It is set as part of the ring-building process to any real number, most often 3.0. In the less-common instance where a non-integer replica count is used, a percentage of the partitions will have one additional replica; for instance, a 3.15 replica count means that 15% of the drives will have one extra replica for a total of 4. The main reason for using a fractional replica count would be to make a gradual shift from one integer replica count to another, allowing Swift time to copy the extra data without saturating the network.

Part of partition replication includes designating handoff drives. This means that when a drive fails, the replication/auditing processes will notice and push the data to handoff locations. This dramatically reduces the MTTR (mean time to repair) compared to standard three-way mirroring or RAID. The probability that all replicated partitions across the system will become corrupt (or otherwise fail) before the cluster notices and is able to push the data to handoff locations is very small, which is a main reason why we say that Swift is durable. Depending on the durability guarantees you require and the failure analysis of your storage devices, you can set the replica count appropriately to meet your needs.

Minimum part hours

While a partition is being moved, Swift will lock that partition's replicas for a period of time to prevent several from being moved simultaneously. Moving multiple replicas at the same time could risk making data inaccessible.

The minimum part hours, configured through the `min part hours` setting, ensures that only one partition's replica is moved at a time. It is best to set the hours to something greater than what it takes for the system to do a full partition replication cycle. A good default setting is 24 hours.

To tune the setting, look at the logs of each replicator on each object store. The log will say how long the replication cycle took. Set the minimum part hours to be comfortably out of reach of the longest replication time.

If the cluster experiences an unusual number of drive failures, or if you are making ring changes, it might be worth increasing the minimum part hours setting temporarily because replication times will be increasing. If they increase outside of the minimum part hours setting, you'll have an increased risk of unavailable data. This setting can be dynamically tuned at cluster runtime to optimize the rate at which ring changes can be made.

Running the create command

Now we are ready to create the builder files.

The commands we will be running are:

```
swift-ring-builder account.builder create <part_power> <replicas> <min_part_hours>
swift-ring-builder container.builder create <part_power> <replicas> <min_part_hours>
swift-ring-builder object.builder create <part_power> <replicas> <min_part_hours>
swift-ring-builder object-n.builder create <part_power> <replicas> <min_part_hours>
```

Now that we understand more about the values needed for `part_power`, `replicas`, and `min_part_hours`, please select your values and run the `create` command. Here for account, container, and object we use a `part_power` value of 17, `replicas` value of 3, and `min_part_hours` value of 1.

For our storage policies, these values may be different. For this example, we will have storage policy 1 provide increased durability by setting its replica count to four. So we would use a `part_power` value of 17, `replicas` value of 4, and `min_part_hours` value of 1.

For storage policy 2, which we designated as deprecated, we will use the default settings. In general, a storage policy will become deprecated after having been in use by the cluster, so there would be an existing ring. Since that is not the case here, we need to be sure one is created for storage policy 2, as later in this installation the proxy server process will try to load it. The proxy server process loads deprecated policies because they are still able to be accessed.

```
cd /etc/swift
swift-ring-builder account.builder create 17 3 1
swift-ring-builder container.builder create 17 3 1
swift-ring-builder object.builder create 17 3 1
swift-ring-builder object-1.builder create 17 4 1
swift-ring-builder object-2.builder create 17 3 1
```

You'll now see *account.builder*, *container.builder*, *object.builder*, *object-1.builder*, and *object-2.builder* in the directory. There should also be a backup directory, appropriately named *backups*.

Don't lose the builder files

Be sure not to lose these builder (*.builder*) files! Keep regular backups of them.

To take some mystery out of what was just created, let's open an interactive Python session and show what is in an *object.builder* file. The contents are a Python data structure that you can view using a `pickle` file. Some of the fields will be familiar.

```
$ python
>>>
>>> import pickle
>>> print pickle.load(open('object.builder'))
{
  '_replica2part2dev': None,
  '_last_part_gather_start': 0,
  'in_part_hours': 24,
  'replicas': 3.0,
  'parts': 262144,
  'part_power': 18,
  'devs': [],
  'devs_changed': False,
  'version': 0,
  '_last_part_moves_epoch': None,
  '_last_part_moves': None,
```

```
    '_remove_devs': []
}
```

Adding Devices to the Builder Files

Our next goal is to add the drives, their logical groupings (region, zone), and weight. This part of the configuration serves two purposes:

- It marks failure boundaries for the cluster by placing each node into a region and zone.
- It describes how much data Swift should put on each device in the cluster by giving it a weight.

With the builder files created, we can now add devices to them. For each node, the storage device in */srv/node* will need an entry added to the builder file(s). If a drive is meant to be dedicated storage for a certain data type, it does not have to be added to the other ring builder files. For example, if you have a pair of SSDs that will handle all account and container data, you would add those drives to the account builder file and to the container builder file but not to the object builder file(s).

Entries for devices are added to each file with this format:

```
swift-ring-builder add account.builder <region><zone>-<IP>:6002/<device>
<weight>
swift-ring-builder add container.builder <region><zone>-<IP>:6001/<device>
<weight>
swift-ring-builder add object.builder <region><zone>-<IP>:6000/<device>
<weight>
swift-ring-builder add object-n.builder <region><zone>-<IP>:6000/<device>
<weight>
```

Let's take a closer look at the information provided before we add the drives.

Region

Swift allows a physically distinct part of the cluster to be defined as a region. Regions are often defined by geographical boundaries; for example, several racks of servers (nodes) can be placed in higher-latency, off-site locations. When a multi-region cluster receives a read request, Swift will favor copies of the data that are closer, as measured by latency. As explained in "Swift Architecture" on page 24, you can configure how replicas get distributed throughout a multi-region cluster using write affinity.

There are no restrictions on the value you choose for the name of your region label. We will use r1 in this chapter to indicate region 1.

Zones

Within regions, Swift allows you to create availability zones to isolate failures. The goal of zones is to allow the cluster to tolerate significant outages of large hunks of storage servers. An availability zone should be defined by a distinct set of physical hardware whose failure will be isolated from the rest of the cluster.

In a large deployment, availability zones might be defined as separate facilities in a large data center campus. In a single data center deployment, the availability zones might be different rooms. For a handful of racks in a data center, each rack could represent a zone. Typically, deployments create isolated failure boundaries within a data center by segmenting the power source, the network that is serving each zone, or both.

There are no restrictions on the value you choose for the name of your zone label. We will use z1 in this chapter to indicate zone 1.

IP

You need to specify the IP address of the node for each device. This should be on the network segment designated for internal communication that will allow the nodes in the cluster to communicate with each other via rsync and HTTP.

Port

Each of the account, container, and object server processes can run on different ports.

By default:

- The account server process runs on port 6002.
- The container server process runs on port 6001.
- The object server process runs on port 6000.

Weight

Each device in the system has a weight. As described in "Distribution of Data" on page 37, the weight is a number that determines the relative number of partitions a device (drive) will have. It is set as part of the ring-building process. Because this is a relative number, it's up to the operator to configure the weights that will be used to represent each drive.

For example, if when starting out each drive is the same size, say 2 TB, you could give each drive a weight of 100.0, so that they all have the same likelihood of receiving a replica of a partition. Then, when it's time to add capacity and 3 TB drives are available, the new 3 TB drives would receive a weight of 150.0 because they are 50% larger. With this weight, each 3 TB drive would recieve 1.5 times as many partition replicas as one of the 2 TB drives.

Another, often simpler, strategy is to use the drive's capacity as a multiplier. For example, the weight of a 2 TB drive would be 200.0 and a 3 TB drive would be 300.0.

Adding Drives

Now that we've covered the parameters you need to specify when adding devices, we'll go ahead and add our devices to the builder files.

The following adds the first device (d1) to the builder files:

```
swift-ring-builder account.builder add r1z1-127.0.0.1:6002/d1 100
swift-ring-builder container.builder add r1z1-127.0.0.1:6001/d1 100
swift-ring-builder object.builder add r1z1-127.0.0.1:6000/d1 100
swift-ring-builder object-1.builder add r1z1-127.0.0.1:6000/d1 100
swift-ring-builder object-2.builder add r1z1-127.0.0.1:6000/d1 100
```

Then we add the next device (d2) to the builder files:

```
swift-ring-builder account.builder add r1z1-127.0.0.1:6002/d2 100
swift-ring-builder container.builder add r1z1-127.0.0.1:6001/d2 100
swift-ring-builder object.builder add r1z1-127.0.0.1:6000/d2 100
swift-ring-builder object-1.builder add r1z1-127.0.0.1:6000/d2 100
swift-ring-builder object-2.builder add r1z1-127.0.0.1:6000/d2 100
```

Continue this pattern for each device that is being added to the cluster.

Building the Rings

Once all the devices have been added, let's create the ring files. The `rebalance` command creates an actual ring file used by Swift to determine where data is placed. The command will need to be run for each ring that you wish to create.

Once the rings are created, they need to be copied to the */etc/swift* directory of every node in the cluster. No other action will be needed after that, because Swift automatically detects new ring data every 15 seconds.

When a node that was down comes back online, be sure to provide any new ring files to it. If the node has a different (old) ring file, it will think that data isn't where it should be and will do its part to move it back to where it's "supposed" to be.

Here we run the commands to create the four rings:

```
cd /etc/swift
swift-ring-builder account.builder rebalance
swift-ring-builder container.builder rebalance
swift-ring-builder object.builder rebalance
swift-ring-builder object-1.builder rebalance
swift-ring-builder object-2.builder rebalance
```

As the command runs, each device signs up for its share of the partitions. During the build process, each device declares its relative weight in the system. The rebalancing process takes all the partitions and assigns them to devices, making sure that each device is subscribed according to its weight. That way a device with a weight of 200 gets twice as many partitions as a device with a weight of 100.

This rebalancing process also takes into account recent changes to the cluster. The builder files keep track of things such as when partitions were last moved and where partitions are currently located. This ensures that partitions do not move around if they've already been moved recently (based on what `min_part_hours` is set to) and that partitions are not reassigned to new devices unnecessarily.

Once the rebalance is complete, you should see the following additional files in */etc/swift*:

- *account.ring.gz*
- *container.ring.gz*
- *object.ring.gz*
- *object-1.ring.gz*
- *object-2.ring.gz*

Copy these files to the */etc/swift* directory of every node in the cluster.

Configuring Swift Logging

Next, we will configure RSyslog to start logging for Swift. In this example, we'll direct all the log files to a single location.

Swift uses RSyslog to help it manage where log messages go. In this example, we will set all the server processes to go to a single log for Swift. In each configuration file there is a setting called `log_name`. By default, all are set to `swift`.

Additionally, you can configure external logging and alerting.

Creating the Log Configuration File

Create a configuration file named *0-swift.conf* in the */etc/rsyslog.d* directory. It will contain one line:

```
local0.* /var/log/swift/all.log
```

Since we just created a script that will tell the system to log the *all.log* file in the directory */var/log/swift*, we will need to create that directory and set the correct permissions on it.

This command will create the directory the log files will be created in:

```
mkdir /var/log/swift
```

You also need to set permissions on the directory so the log process can write to it. For instance, the following commands do this on Ubuntu:

```
chown -R syslog.adm /var/log/swift
chmod -R g+w /var/log/swift
```

The same procedure on CentOS looks like this:

```
chown -R root:adm /var/log/swift
chmod -R g+w /var/log/swift
```

Restarting Rsyslog to Begin Swift Logging

To start logging with the new Swift settings, restart RSyslog with the following command:

```
service rsyslog restart
```

Configuring a Proxy Server

The proxy server process, as explained in "Server Processes" on page 27, is the connection between your Swift cluster and the outside world. This server process:

- Accepts incoming HTTP requests
- Looks up locations on the rings
- Interacts with the authentication/authorization middleware
- Forwards requests to the right account, container, or object server
- Returns responses to the originating requester

Your proxy server should now be up and running.

Setting the Hash Path Prefix and Suffix

The first configuration change to make is to set arbitrary, hard-to-guess strings as the `swift_hash_path_prefix` and `swift_hash_path_suffix` settings in */etc/swift/swift.conf*.

You add these strings to the pathnames in order to prevent a denial-of-service (DOS) attack. If someone knows the hash path suffix and prefix, he could determine the actual partition where objects would be stored. An attacker could generate containers and objects with that partition and repeatedly put large files to the same partition until the drive was full.

Edit the *swift.conf* file in the */etc/swift/* directory and add a unique string to `swift_hash_path_prefix` and `swift_hash_path_suffix`:

```
# swift_hash_path_suffix and swift_hash_path_prefix are used as part of the
# the hashing algorithm when determining data placement in the cluster.
# These values should remain secret and MUST NOT change
# once a cluster has deployed.
[swift-hash]
swift_hash_path_suffix = RzUfDdu32L7J2ZBDYgsD6YI3Xie7hTVO8/oaQbpTbI8=
swift_hash_path_prefix = OZ1uQJNjJzTuFaM8X3v%fsJ1iR#F8wJjf9uhRiABevQ4
```

We recommend selecting random strings of at least 32 characters for the prefix and suffix, which should be different.

You can generate a 32-character string fairly easily using a number of different methods. One option might be to run:

```
head -c 32 /dev/random | base64
```

Once you have two different strings saved, be sure to keep them secret. These make the partition path reasonably unguessable.

Starting the Proxy Server

Now start up the proxy server process:

```
swift-init proxy start

Starting proxy-server...(/etc/swift/proxy-server.conf)
```

If you get an error ending with `KeyError:` *`getpwnam(): name not found: swift`* it means that a user named `swift` hasn't been created. Fix this as shown in "Swift user" on page 126.

Setting up TempAuth Authentication and Authorization with Swift

This section covers setting up TempAuth and creating an account on the Swift cluster with it. TempAuth lets you specify accounts in configuration files.

Starting memcached

`memcached`, short for "memory cache daemon," is a process that stores data in memory for fast retrieval. More information can be found at the project's website (*http://memcached.org*). Although the project's official name includes the "d," we will adopt the common convention of referring to the service as "Memcache," and to the daemon itself as `memcached`.

The TempAuth middleware stores tokens in Memcache. If the memcached process is not running, tokens cannot be validated, and accessing Swift generally becomes impossible.

On non-Debian-based Linux distributions, you need to ensure that memcached is running:

```
service memcached start
chkconfig memcached on
```

Adding Users to proxy-server.conf

If you look in the file */etc/swift/proxy-server.conf*, you can find the section that describes TempAuth:

```
[filter:tempauth]
use = egg:swift#tempauth
# You can override the default log routing for this filter here:
...
# <account> is from the user_<account>_<user> name.
# Here are example entries, required for running the tests:
user_admin_admin = admin .admin .reseller_admin
user_test_tester = testing .admin
user_test2_tester2 = testing2 .admin
user_test_tester3 = testing3
```

With TempAuth, users are defined in the configuration file itself with the format:

```
user_$SWIFTACCOUNT_$SWIFTUSER = $KEY [group] [group] [...] [storage_url]
```

You can create a user and account of your own, by adding a line under the default TempAuth account with the correct information:

```
...
user_test_tester3 = testing3
user_myaccount_me = secretpassword .admin .reseller_admin
```

An optional parameter for the user entry would be to explicitly add the storage URL with port 8080 to the end of the line. This might be needed in some cases, depending on your particular configuration:

```
user_myaccount_me = secretpassword .admin .reseller_admin <storage URL:8080>
```

Two configurations must also be set for the account. Locate and set the allow_account_management and account_autocreate options to true in the file:

```
allow_account_management = true
account_autocreate = true
```

See the SwiftStack blog (*http://swiftstack.com/blog/2012/01/04/swift-tempauth/*) for more details on TempAuth configuration.

Starting the Servers and Restarting the Proxy

To access user accounts, the account server process must be started. Now is also a good time to start the container and object server processes. When the proxy server is unable to reach one of the other main server processes, it will return a `503 Service Unavailable`.

```
swift-init account start
Starting account-server...(/etc/swift/account-server.conf)

swift-init container start
Starting container-server...(/etc/swift/container-server.conf)

swift-init object start
Starting object-server...(/etc/swift/object-server.conf)
```

Then, because we have changed the proxy server process configuration, we will restart the proxy server process:

```
swift-init proxy restart

Signal proxy-server  pid: 5240  signal: 15
proxy-server (5240) appears to have stopped
Starting proxy-server...(/etc/swift/proxy-server.conf)
```

Keep in mind that TempAuth is appropriately named as a temporary auth system. Although we are using it here as a quick way to auth with our new Swift cluster, it has several drawbacks that make it less than ideal for production. The first, as you see, is that the proxy server processes must be restarted when adding or removing accounts, and the second is that the credentials are stored in plain text. For more information on auth options with Swift, see Chapter 13.

Account Authentication

Now let's authenticate the account that was added to TempAuth in Swift using cURL:

```
curl -v -H 'X-Auth-User: $SWIFTACCOUNT:$SWIFTUSER' -H 'X-Auth-Key: <password>' \
    <AuthURL>
```

Pass in the `$SWIFTACCOUNT:$SWIFTUSER` using the `X-Auth-User` header, and the password using the `X-Auth-Key` header. If you are successful, the response headers will include the `X-Storage-URL` and `X-Auth Token`.

Sending in the authentication:

```
curl -v -H 'X-Auth-User: myaccount:me' -H 'X-Auth-Key: secretpassword' \
http://localhost:8080/auth/v1.0/
```

You should get a response similar to:

```
* About to connect() to localhost port 8080 (#0)
*       Trying ::1... Connection refused
```

```
*       Trying 127.0.0.1... connected
* Connected to localhost (127.0.0.1) port 8080 (#0)
> GET /auth/v1.0/ HTTP/1.1
> User-Agent: curl/7.19.7 (i486-pc-linux-gnu) libcurl/7.19.7 OpenSSL/0.9.8k
    zlib/1.2.3.3 libidn/1.15
> Host: localhost:8080
> Accept: */*
> X-Auth-User: myaccount:me
> X-Auth-Key: secretpassword
>
< HTTP/1.1 200 OK
< X-Storage-Url: http://127.0.0.1:8080/v1/AUTH_myaccount
< X-Storage-Token: AUTH_tk265318ae5e7e46f1890a441c08b5247f
< X-Auth-Token: AUTH_tk265318ae5e7e46f1890a441c08b5247f
< X-Trans-Id: txc75adf112791425e82826d6e3989be4d
< Content-Length: 0
< Date: Tue, 21 Mar 2013 22:48:40 GMT
<
```

If the connection is refused, verify that it was attempting to connect on port 8080 of the localhost address.

The HTTP response contains the `X-Auth-Token`:

```
< X-Auth-Token: AUTH_tk265318ae5e7e46f1890a441c08b5247f
```

It will be stored in Memcache so that future storage requests can authenticate that token. Again, to take some mystery out of what we are creating, let's open an interactive Python session and show what the entry in Memcache looks like:

```
python
>>> import swift.common.memcached as memcached
>>> memcache = memcached.MemcacheRing(['127.0.0.1:11211'])
>>> print memcache.get('AUTH_/user/myaccount:me')
AUTH_tk58ad6d3ca1754ca78405828d72e37458
>>> print memcache.get(
...     'AUTH_/token/AUTH_tk58ad6d3ca1754ca78405828d72e37458')
[1394158570.037054, 'myaccount,myaccount:me,AUTH_myaccount']
```

Verifying Account Access

Now you're ready to make your first request. Here we will attempt to list the containers in the account. The system should return a response of `204 No Content` because we have not created any containers yet:

```
curl -v -H 'X-Storage-Token: AUTH_tk58ad6d3ca1754ca78405828d72e37458' \
    http://127.0.0.1:8080/v1/AUTH_myaccount/
```

```
* About to connect() to 127.0.0.1 port 8080 (#0)
*       Trying 127.0.0.1... connected
* Connected to 127.0.0.1 (127.0.0.1) port 8080 (#0)
> GET /v1/AUTH_myaccount HTTP/1.1
> User-Agent: curl/7.19.7 (i486-pc-linux-gnu) libcurl/7.19.7 OpenSSL/0.9.8k
   zlib/1.2.3.3 libidn/1.15
> Host: 127.0.0.1:8080
> Accept: */*
> X-Storage-Token: AUTH_tk215c5706a61048c09819cd6ba60142ef
>
< HTTP/1.1 204 No Content
< X-Account-Object-Count: 0
< X-Account-Bytes-Used: 0
< X-Account-Container-Count: 0
< Accept-Ranges: bytes
< X-Trans-Id: txafe3c83ed76e46d2a9536dd61d9fcf09
< Content-Length: 0
< Date: Tue, 21 Jun 2011 23:23:23 GMT
```

If the connection is refused, verify that it was attempting to connect on port 8080 of the localhost address.

Congratulations, you've created an account in Swift!

Creating a Container

Accounts and containers are just SQLite databases. For each account, there is an account database that contains a listing of all the containers in that account. For each container, there is a container database that stores a listing of all of the objects in that container. Each of these databases is stored in the cluster and replicated in the same manner as the objects.

To create a container in an account, we will use the HTTP verb PUT and append the new container name to the end of the storage URL.

Using the auth token from before, run the following command to create a container called *mycontainer*:

```
curl -v -H 'X-Storage-Token: AUTH_tk58ad6d3ca1754ca78405828d72e37458' \
       -X PUT http://127.0.0.1:8080/v1/AUTH_myaccount/mycontainer
```

You should see something similar to:

```
201 Created
Success!
```

Here's what is happening behind the scenes:

- The proxy server process sends a request to the account server process to update the account database with a new container
- The proxy server process sends a request to the container server process to create the container database record

What's interesting here is that these account/container databases are simply SQLite databases. In the following example we open the path to one of those account databases with SQLite, list the tables, select the `account_stat` table, and view the contents. Because we only have one container, it will return the single row with information about the container:

```
sqlite3 /srv/node/d2/accounts/497/e15/7c7d7a8558f1774e7f06d95094136e15/7c7d7a855
8f1774e7f06d95094136e15.db

sqlite> .tables
account_stat   container   incoming_sync   outgoing_sync   policy_stat
sqlite> select * from account_stat;
AUTH_admin|1308715316.66344|1308715316.64684|0|0|0|0|
00000000000000000000000000000000|ccfa951a-82a5-42fc-96c1-7c3e116e6e2e||0|
sqlite> .quit
```

Uploading an Object

Now let's use the Swift command-line interface (covered in Chapter 4) to upload a file. The command will look like this:

```
swift -A <AUTH_URL> -U <account:username>  -K <password> upload \
        <containername> <filename>
```

Notice that the verb is `upload`, but remember that it is still a `PUT` request when the `swift` command sends it to the storage URL. Also notice that the container and file names are at the end of the request, separated by a space.

Let's try to upload a file:

```
swift -A http://127.0.0.1:8080/auth/v1.0/ -U myaccount:me -K secretpassword \
  upload mycontainer some_file
```

The request is received by the cluster. First, the cluster figures out where this data is going to go. To do this, the object storage location (account name, container name, and object name) is used with the object ring to locate the nodes with the correct replica partitions. Once the partitions are located, the data is sent to each storage node, where it is placed in the appropriate partition. However, a quorum is required! At least two of the three writes must be successful before the client is notified that the upload was successful. Next, the container database is updated to reflect the new object in it.

Starting the Consistency Processes

As discussed in Chapter 3, many consistency processes need to run to ensure that Swift is working correctly. This section will cover:

- Configuring and turning on rsync
- Starting the replicator processes
- Starting the other consistency processes

Configuring rsync

On Ubuntu:

Edit or create the *etc/default/rsync* file; add `RSYNC_ENABLE=true` on one line:

```
RSYNC_ENABLE=true
```

On Centos:

```
sudo setenforce Permissive
sudo setsebool -P rsync_full_access 1
sudo chkconfig rsync on
```

Edit or create the */etc/rsyncd.conf* file, adding in the following Swift information:

```
uid = swift
gid = swift
log file = /var/log/rsyncd.log
pid file = /var/run/rsyncd.pid

[account]
max connections = 25
path = /srv/node/
read only = false
lock file = /var/lock/account.lock

[container]
max connections = 25
path = /srv/node/
read only = false
lock file = /var/lock/container.lock

[object]
max connections = 25
path = /srv/node/
read only = false
lock file = /var/lock/object.lock
```

Now it is time to start the rsync service on Ubuntu:

```
service rsync start
```

On other xinetd-based systems, simply run (Centos):

```
sudo service xinetd restart
```

After the restart, you should test that rsync is running with these debugging commands:

```
rsync localhost::
rsync localhost::account
rsync localhost::container
rsync localhost::object
```

Starting the Remaining Consistency Processes

Consistency services can be started individually for a process. Start the replicators as follows:

```
swift-init account-replicator start
swift-init container-replicator start
swift-init object-replicator start
```

Alternatively, the consistency services can be started all at once using the the `swift-init` command with an `all` option:

```
swift-init all start
```

Running the command as this point will start up the auditor, the updater, and the account reaper. If we had not already started the replicators, it would have started them as well.

At this point, all the Swift processes should be running and OpenStack Swift should be fully installed.

Conclusion

Congratulations! Installation is half the battle and if you have followed along this far, you likely have your very own Swift cluster up and running. We hope going through this installation has given you some perspective and understanding of the parts that cooperate to make Swift work. In the next chapter, we'll look at how to make these processes easier by using SwiftStack's installation features.

CHAPTER 10
Installing SwiftStack

Amanda Plimpton

This chapter looks at how to install SwiftStack, which automates the installation and management of OpenStack Swift clusters. SwiftStack includes an unmodified version of OpenStack Swift, along with proprietary software components for deployment, integration (with authentication, billing, and external monitoring systems), and management of one or more Swift clusters. Some of the additional components are outlined in Chapter 2. Further details can be found at the SwiftStack site (*http://swiftstack.com/product*).

SwiftStack Controller and Node Overview

A key characteristic of SwiftStack is that it decouples the control, management, and configuration of storage nodes from the physical hardware. Although the actual storage services run on the servers where OpenStack Swift is installed, the deployment, management, and monitoring are conducted out-of-band by a separate storage controller. This storage controller can manage one or more clusters, which allows operators to manage multiple, geographically distributed storage clusters. Operators are able to use a single management system to dynamically tune clusters to optimize performance, respond to hardware failures, and upgrade clusters while they are still running—all driven programmatically for the entire storage tier, independent of where the storage resources are deployed.

Before we move on to installation, we should briefly describe the two main components: the SwiftStack Controller and the SwiftStack Node.

SwiftStack Controller

The SwiftStack Controller provides the management plane for one or more clusters with OpenStack Swift. As an out-of-band management system, the SwiftStack Controller decouples control from the actual storage nodes and can manage storage nodes remotely over the Internet or be deployed on-premises next to the storage cluster. For an operator, the Controller provides a browser-based interface for easier control and management of clusters.

Users sign in to the Controller's web interface and go to their cluster page. From there they can change cluster settings, add or remove capacity, or address notifications of component failures.

It all starts with the creation of a company's account, called the organization, on the Controller. Once an organization is created on the Controller, users can be added. These SwiftStack Controller users, depending on their permissions, can:

- Create more SwiftStack Controller user accounts for their organization
- Create and configure their cluster(s)
- Quickly and easily add or remove nodes and drives from their cluster(s)
- Create users for their cluster(s) using the SwiftStack auth system
- Configure an external auth (LDAP, Keystone) for their cluster(s)
- Tune and enable or disable middleware for their cluster(s)
- View the monitoring and health data for their cluster(s)
- Perform rolling upgrades of the Swift version on their nodes with no downtime

To understand how the SwiftStack Controller works, let's review some of the key features.

Deployment automation

As seen in Chapter 9, each device is formatted, mounted, and added to the ring builder files according to their physical location and size. SwiftStack automates this storage provisioning.

On a SwiftStack Node, agents identify the available devices. The SwiftStack Controller receives this inventory and displays it to the cluster operator, who can then configure and manage these devices on each node. The devices themselves get a unique SwiftStack identifier so that inventory can be kept and devices can be consistently remounted in the event that they get reshuffled in the same system, or are placed in an entirely new chassis.

Once the Controller has established a connection with a specific SwiftStack Node, the cluster operator can initiate several different setup and deployment tasks via the Controller's interface, including:

- Configuring network interfaces

- Configuring nodes and formatting drives
- Deploying account, container, and object rings
- Configuring availability zones and regions based on hardware topology

On large clusters, operators might prefer to automate this process by writing scripts based on command-line commands or integrating it with configuration management tools, such as Chef or Puppet.

Ring management

The SwiftStack Controller keeps track of all the devices and provides an interface for cluster operators to add or remove capacity. When these capacity changes require the generation of new rings, the SwiftStack Controller will create the rings and copy them to each node in the cluster. This means that when it's time to add more storage capacity, it can be done safely without interruptions. Likewise, data can be slowly migrated off a failing drive or a decommissioned node.

Node and cluster monitoring

The SwiftStack Controller provides the metrics you need to make informed decisions to properly manage and scale your cluster. It provides alerts on drive failures, node failures, and any other issues it detects.

The SwiftStack Controller also collects hundreds of data points on each node and accurately aggregates data from multiple systems into a single cluster-wide view that allows you to zoom in on events across a specific timeframe to gain insight. It will generate reports, including a report for capacity planning and a report on storage use for chargeback and billing.

SwiftStack monitoring can also be integrated with Ganglia, Nagios, and other monitoring tools.

SwiftStack Node

As of this writing, there are installers for SwiftStack Node software for CentOS/Red Hat Server 6.3, 6.4, or 6.5 (64-bit) and for Ubuntu 12.04 LTS Precise Server (64-bit).

Installing the SwiftStack Node software on a machine is a simple process that will install the following:

- Latest stable version of OpenStack Swift
- Dependencies needed for Swift
- SwiftStack management agents for monitoring Node health and communication with the Controller

- SwiftStack integrations for Swift, including authentication modules for systems such as LDAP
- SSL termination
- SwiftStack load balancer

Once installed, the Node's configuration takes place on the SwiftStack Controller web interface. There, a cluster operator can enter the networking details and designate the Node to have proxy services, storage (account, container, object) services, or both running on it.

Once the Node is added to the cluster from the Controller, its services are started and it becomes a fully functional member of the cluster. It behaves the same as a typical Swift node but also has those SwiftStack processes that run in the background for SwiftStack management and communication.

Among these processes are the SwiftStack agents that establish a VPN connection with the Controller. With this connection, a cluster operator can manage the Node via the Controller. The Node accepts only a limited number of commands from the Controller, specifically:

- Pushing new configuration files
- Activating new configurations
- Querying devices for drive discovery/inventory synchronization
- Formatting devices
- Unmounting devices
- Querying for network interfaces
- Querying for general system information (RAM/hostname/CPU core count)

At no point does the Controller have access to the data stored on a SwiftStack Node.

Creating a Swift Cluster Using SwiftStack

In Chapter 9, we walked through the numerous steps of installing Swift on a node. We installed Swift on only one machine, so we essentially created a one-node cluster for demonstration purposes. We will set up one node here as well, using SwiftStack, and you will quickly see that these steps are handled differently.

For the following example we use a SwiftStack Controller provided as a service over the Internet. rather than an on-premises Controller.

For those running an on-premises SwiftStack Controller, wherever you see *https://platform.swiftstack.com* in the following example, replace it with the hostname for your private controller, e.g., *https://swiftstack-controller.private.example.com*.

Creating a SwiftStack Controller User

As mentioned earlier, once a company has established an organization account on a Controller, SwiftStack Controller users can be added.

A cluster operator will use a SwiftStack Controller user account with the correct permissions set to add a node to the Controller. Creating a user is a simple task that the person or team in your organization with a SwiftStack Controller administrator account can perform.

Once you have a SwiftStack Controller user account in your organization, you are ready to proceed.

Installing the SwiftStack Node Software

The machine on which you will be installing the SwiftStack Node software needs:

1. A plain installation of CentOS/Red Hat Server 6.3-6.5 (64-bit) or Ubuntu 12.04 LTS Precise Server (64-bit) on it
2. Access to its SwiftStack Controller for the initial download of the SwiftStack Node software. This initial claim process and configuration requires communication over HTTPS (port 443).

All installation commands need to be performed as root.

As a good security practice and to learn what commands are being run during the installation, use the following to display the commands in the install script:

```
curl https://platform.swiftstack.com/install
```

Review the commands and when you ready to install, pipe the command into the bash shell, which downloads the install script and executes it:

```
curl https://platform.swiftstack.com/install | bash
```

Once the software is installed, the new Node contacts the Controller via HTTPS (port 443). If successful, the Node receives a unique identifier from the Controller. The Node then constructs a *claim URL* and displays it in the terminal. This confirms the installation process is complete.

```
+--------------------------------------------------------------------------+
|                                                                          |
| Your claim URL is:                                                       |
| https://platform.swiftstack.com/claim/dda53021-8da3-11e2-9108-000c29f59d7 |
|                                                                          |
|                                                                          |
+--------------------------------------------------------------------------+
```

With installation complete, the SwiftStack Node will open a secure VPN connection to the Controller over UDP (port 1194). This only allows outgoing connections from the Node over the VPN connection—no connections are allowed to the Node from the Controller.

Claiming a New Node

Once the claim URL is displayed, you should open a web browser and sign into the Controller with your SwiftStack Controller user account.

Once signed in, you can copy and paste the claim URL in the browser. The Node and Controller will attempt contact. When the Node is seen by the Controller, it will display a Claim Node button that you should click (Figure 10-1).

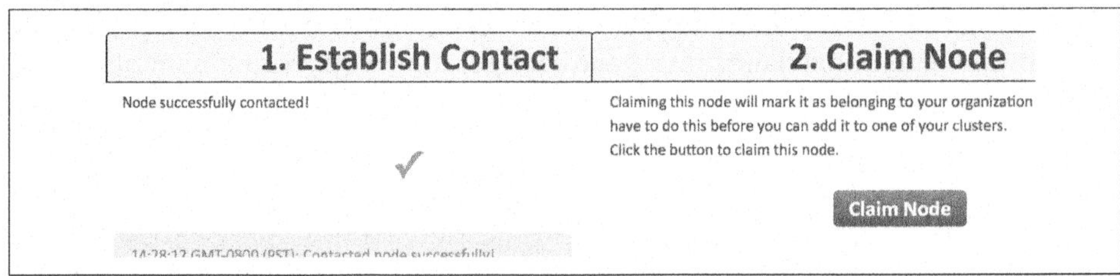

Figure 10-1. Claiming the Node on the Controller

The Node and Controller will be using the secure VPN connection initiated by the Node to communicate. The Node's VPN connection will need to be able to communicate out over port 1194, the VPN (UDP) Communications channel.

Creating a Cluster

After you click the Claim Node button, the Controller will prompt you to create a new cluster (Figure 10-2). If there is a preexisting cluster, you will also have the option to select that cluster.

To create a cluster, provide the cluster's name and outward-facing IP address. You can optionally also specify its hostname, SSL, NTP, and other advanced Swift options.

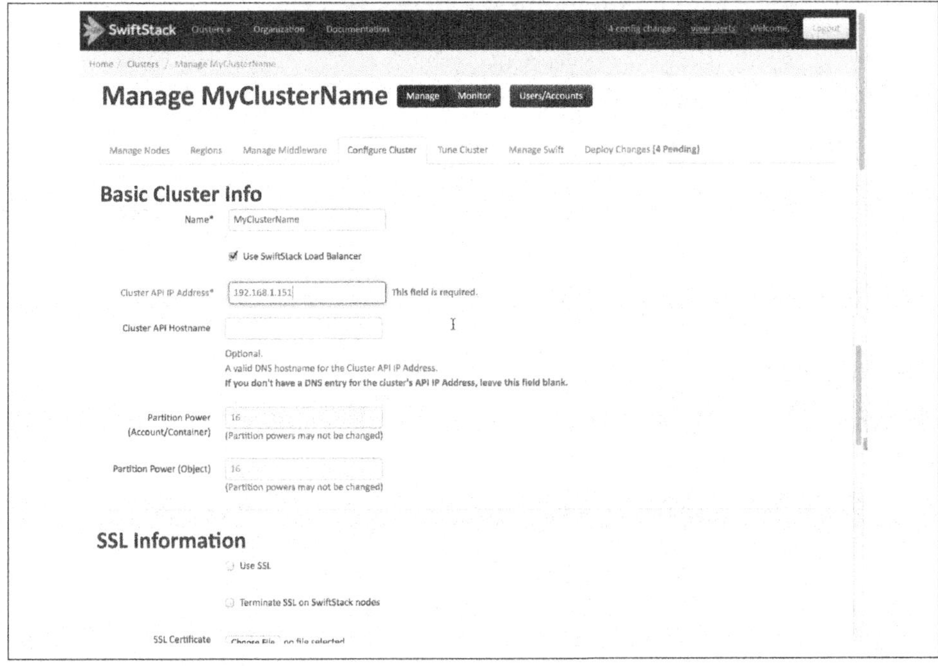

Figure 10-2. Creating a new cluster

Ingesting a Node

With the cluster created, the page will open to the Manage Nodes tab. You can select the region and zone for the new Node and then click on the Ingest Now button (Figure 10-3).

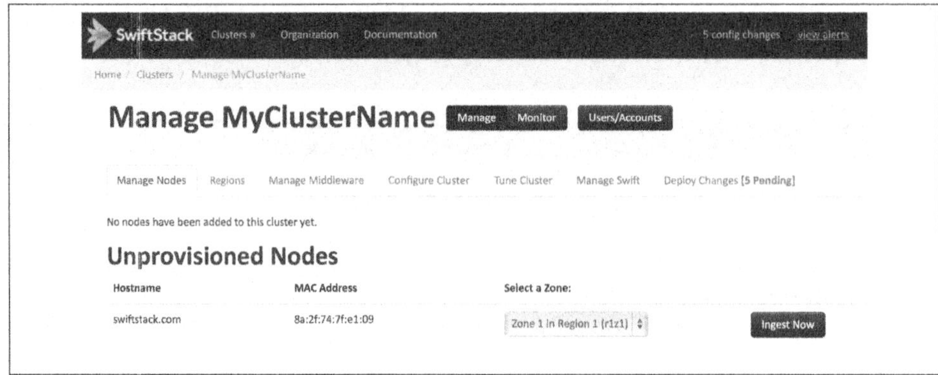

Figure 10-3. Screen to manage a new cluster

Enabling a SwiftStack Node

Once ingested, the Node will need to be enabled via the Enable tab (Figure 10-4).

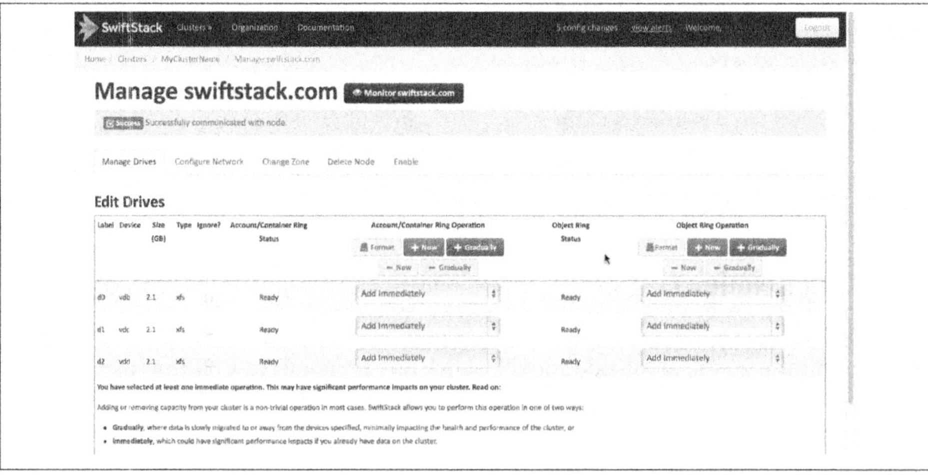

Figure 10-4. Enabling the Node

Provisioning a SwiftStack Node

Once the Node is enabled, click on the Drives tab. You can start provisioning the Node by clicking on the Format button. All available drives will be marked for formatting; you can then click the Change button to begin formatting the drives (devices). Formatting drives could take a few minutes to complete.

Once the drives are formatted, add them to the cluster using the +Now button for both the Account/Container Ring Operation and the Object Ring Operation. Any drive can be assigned to store account/container data, but SwiftStack generally recommends using faster media such as SSDs to ensure that account and container listings are quick (Figure 10-5).

For large, multinode deployments, scripts are available to automate the provisioning of large numbers of nodes.

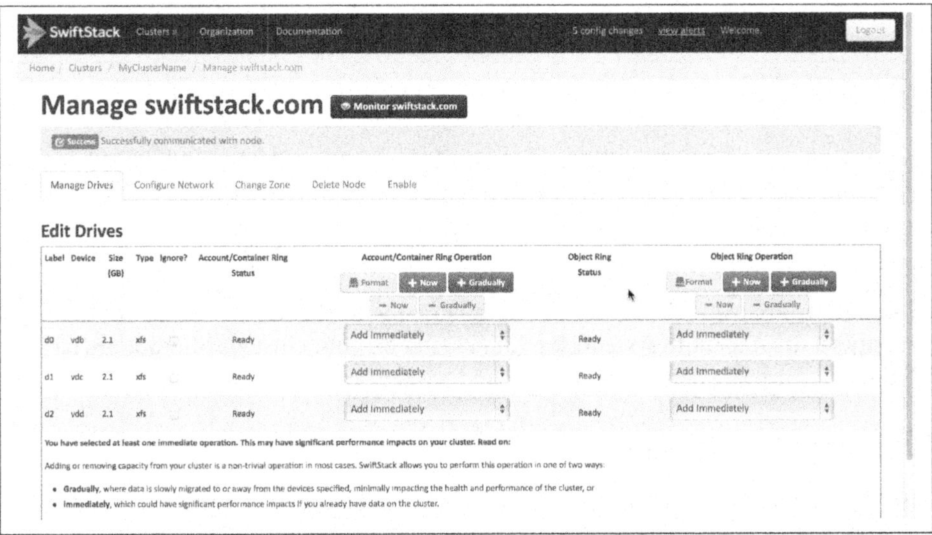

Figure 10-5. Configuring drive roles

Adding Swift Users

The next step is to add a user for the cluster. In Chapter 9 we did this by editing the TempAuth section of the proxy configuration file.

Here we are adding a user through the Controller using the SwiftStack auth system. Go to the Create a New User page (Figure 10-6) and provide the desired username, password, and permission level for the user account.

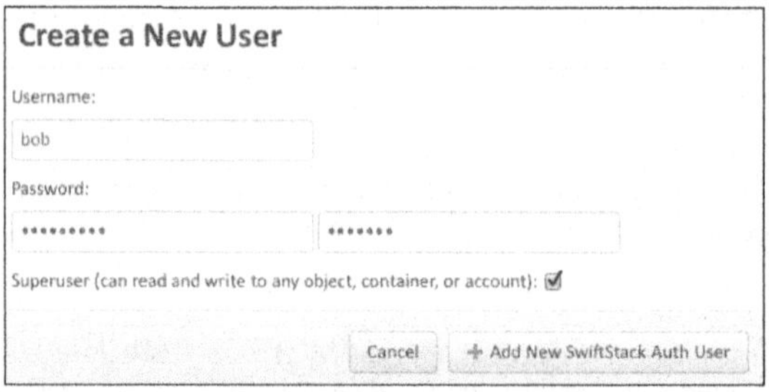

Create a New User

Username:

bob

Password:

Superuser (can read and write to any object, container, or account):

Cancel

Add New SwiftStack Auth User

Figure 10-6. Creating a user account

The authentication system built into SwiftStack is a fast, flat file that is deployed on each Node with hashed passwords. Although it does require a configuration push out to the cluster, it does not require a proxy restart. Users can also be added programmatically through a REST API function.

Although we are using the SwiftStack auth here, the SwiftStack Controller can be used to easily set up other auth systems for your cluster on your cluster's Middleware tab. See Chapter 13 for more details about Swift and authentication systems.

SwiftStack Middleware

The cluster will have a Manage Middleware tab that provides different middleware options and configurations. Several middleware packages are enabled by default for a new cluster, including Static Web, TempUrl, FormPost, Name Check, and Swift Web Console. More information about Swift and SwiftStack middleware options can be found in Chapter 14.

Figure 10-7. Managing middleware

Deploying to Cluster

With all the configurations set for your new cluster, it is time to apply them to the cluster. The Controller will display the Deploy SwiftStack Cluster page (Figure 10-8).

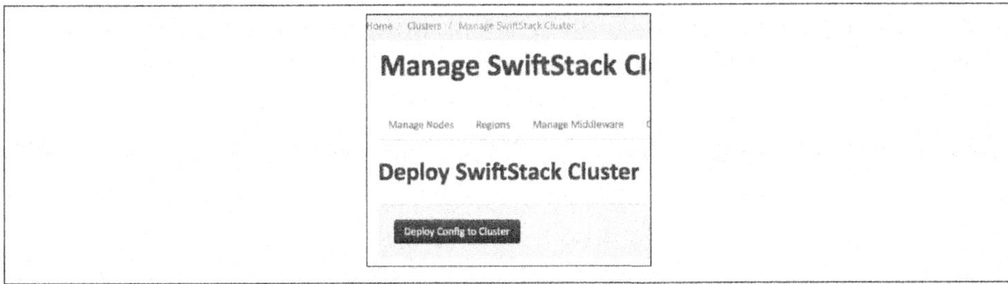

Figure 10-8. Deploying the cluster

Once you click the Deploy Config to Cluster button, the cluster:

- Adds appropriate devices and nodes into the Swift builder files
- Creates the Swift rings
- Adds any additional user accounts that have been created or modified
- Creates new Swift configurations based on the changes made to the network and tuning tabs
- Provides the new configuration files, and restarts processes when necessary, for each node in the cluster

While the cluster is applying all these configurations, a "Pending Jobs" status message is displayed. When the configuration deployment is done, a "Job Finished" status message is displayed and your SwiftStack cluster will be accessible at the IP address you specified (Figure 10-9).

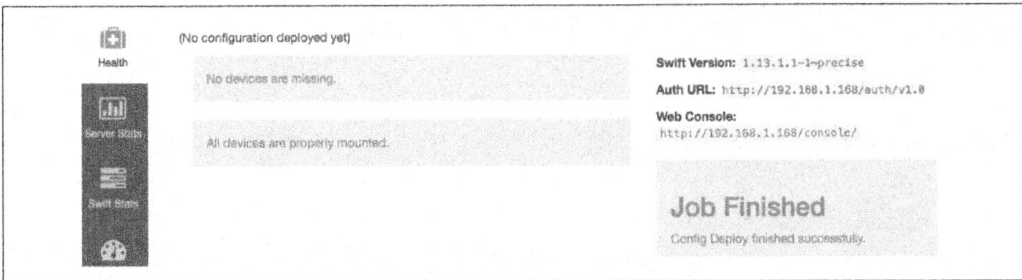

Figure 10-9. Job Finished message

Creating a Container and Uploading an Object via Web Console

Although you can use the command line to create a container on the node as we did in Chapter 9, let's use the web console instead to show additional capabilities of the Swift-Stack Controller.

Installed on the SwiftStack Node will be a built-in web console for storage users to upload, download, and manage data. After the configuration deployment is completed, the Controller will display a link to the web console.

Once you sign in to the account to which you want to upload an object, you can easily create a container by typing in its name, shown in Figure 10-10 as `MyContainer`, and clicking the OK button.

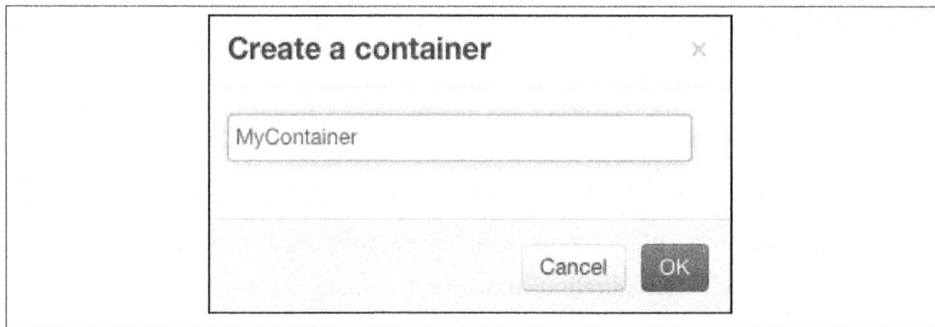

Figure 10-10. Creating a container

Now you can upload files by dragging and dropping them (Figure 10-11), or using the upload button.

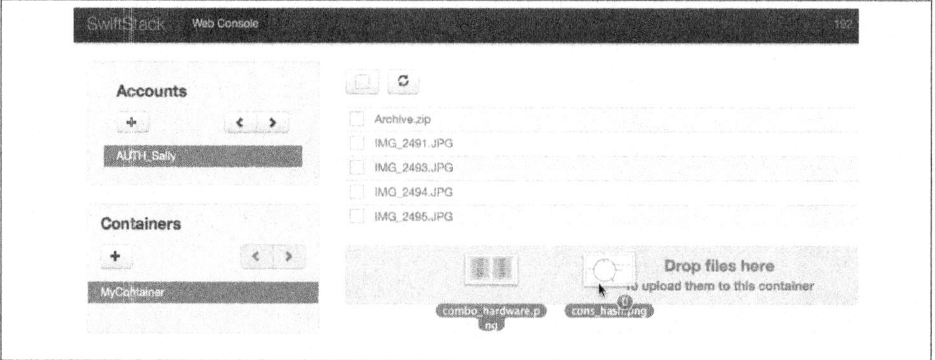

Figure 10-11. Uploading files

Conclusion

Congratulations! You have now seen a cluster installation from source and from SwiftStack. At this point you should be starting to see how the pieces of Swift fit together and some of its power. We have seen a number of options and features during these installations, but we have more to go. Coming up in the next chapters is more information about Swift settings, middleware, testing, and tuning. We will also cover what to do when—not if—hardware fails.

PART IV
Planning a Swift Deployment

This part offers guidance on various deployment considerations: choosing the right hardware and network layout, configuration, and operational issues such as allocating storage and monitoring.

CHAPTER 11

Hardware for Swift

Martin Lanner
Amanda Plimpton

In this chapter, we'll look at the basic hardware requirements for deploying a Swift cluster. As with most deployments, Swift requires up-front planning, validation, and testing to ensure that you select a suitable hardware configuration for your intended workload. This chapter focuses on the hardware that Swift runs on; we'll cover planning a deployment in the next chapter.

One of the *advantages* of Swift is that it can run on a wide range of hardware configurations, from commodity hardware to commercial hardware solutions. Indeed, SwiftStack works with several vendors who provide options from qualified chassis by major OEM (original equipment manufacturer) partners all the way through to pre-integrated racks from recommended VARs (value-added resellers).

At the same time, one of the *challenges* of Swift is that it can run on such a wide range of configurations. There are many options, and we shy away from offering definitive specifications about what hardware you need for your deployment, because these depend so heavily on use, workload, and availability.

What you plan to use your cluster for will determine the hardware configuration you should have. It's important to use a configuration that provides the ideal balance of I/O performance, capacity, and cost for your workload. For instance, customer-facing web applications with a large number of concurrent users will have a different profile than applications primarily used for data archiving and backups.

The hardware available to meet your requirements and budget will vary. As new hardware comes to market, specific components become obsolete and are succeeded by newer models, so specific recommendations for any given part might change. This is one of the benefits of Swift compared with storage systems that dictate the exact model of hardware, locking you in. With Swift, you can use standard hardware from almost any vendor, and if at any time you would like to change vendors or take advantage of newer, better, or less expensive hardware, you can easily do so. No expensive forklift upgrade needed!

As a result, we will talk about the general needs of a Swift cluster and provide some sample hardware specifications that should be viewed as a starting point, to be modified and tuned for your specific needs and expected workload. The two primary hardware considerations are the systems you use for nodes, and the networking required to allow the nodes to communicate.

Node Hardware Specifications

As you might recall from Chapter 3, several processes run on nodes. It is the Swift servers (proxy, account, container, and object) that will have the most influence on specific hardware requirements for specific nodes.

There are four main hardware components to consider:

- Central processing unit (CPU)
- Random access memory (RAM)
- Drives (HDD and SSD)
- Network cards (NIC)

Do not use parity-based RAID

Swift replicates data across disks, nodes, zones, and regions, so there is no need for the data redundancy provided by a RAID controller. Parity-based RAID, such as RAID5, RAID6, and RAID10, harms the performance of a cluster and does not provide any additional protection, because Swift is already providing data redundancy.

Let's take a closer look at each hardware component.

CPU

OpenStack relies on a 64-bit x86 architecture and is designed for commodity hardware.

In general, it is best to use fairly powerful CPUs, especially if they are going to be handling proxy requests. At this writing, CPUs with clock frequencies in the 2-2.5 GHz range are a good starting point. Generally, CPU power primarily matters in the proxy, but also in cases where object nodes are very densely populated with many disks. Here we have outlined some conditions and configurations that warrant the need for more CPU power:

Running proxy servers
: Nodes running proxy server processes will make greater demands on the CPU. If you plan to do SSL termination on the proxy nodes, CPU use will be even greater. The proxy node workload tends to be CPU-bound because it doesn't do any disk I/O; instead it shuffles around network data as it forwards client requests to other servers and returns their results. Thus, we recommend loading up your proxy servers with as much processor power as you can afford, especially if you need to support lots of small objects, many users, and high concurrency.

Lots of storage
: For very dense storage nodes, getting more powerful CPUs is also recommended. Object nodes will run services to field incoming requests from the proxy nodes, as well as handle replication, auditing, and other processes to ensure durability.

Of course, there are other considerations, too. One of the core ideas behind Swift is to distribute data as widely as possible to reduce risk. Similar to the as-unique-as-possible principle, when it comes to proxy nodes, you also want to make sure you have enough of them to reduce your risk of failure in the system. Now, let's assume you'll be building a small cluster and you've decided to run the proxy server process on dedicated hardware. Because you want to ensure that you don't have a single point of failure, you will need at least two proxy nodes. Based on some testing and benchmarking you've done of the anticipated workload, let's further assume you've come to the conclusion that you will need 24 GHz of total CPU to start. Getting to 24 GHz of CPU can be done in many different ways. We will provide two examples:

Example 1: Two proxy servers
: You can use two proxy servers with 6 * 2.0 GHz cores, which would provide you a total of 24 GHz, as follows:

$$2 \text{ nodes} \times 6 \text{ cores} \times 2.0 \text{ GHz} = 24.0 \text{ GHz}$$

Example 2: Three proxy servers
: You can use three proxy servers with 4 * 2.0 GHz cores, which would also provide you with a total of 24 GHz of CPU power:

$$3 \text{ nodes} \times 4 \text{ cores} \times 2.0 \text{ GHz} = 24.0 \text{ GHz}$$

So, what's the difference here? Well, we generally have two considerations in this scenario: (1) the additional cost of buying three versus just two servers to run as dedicated proxy nodes, and (2) the benefit of having three versus only two proxy nodes. Clearly, from a perspective of minimizing risk, getting three nodes would be beneficial. However, getting three proxy node servers will most likely increase the cost of the overall solution. In the end, it's up to you, the deployer of the system, to decide what the best solution is. It might be that you have a limited budget and therefore have to go with the two-node solution. Conversely, your situation might be more sensitive to potential outages and the potential of causing unavailability or network limitations in case you lose a proxy node.

Calculating CPU cores

The ratio of CPU cores to disks and workload can vary greatly depending on your use case, expected workload, and budget. Generally speaking, a high-throughput, high-concurrency web application that handles mainly small files will be more CPU intensive than a node used for backup or archiving. In high-concurrency scenarios, the proxy server process will require a fair bit of CPU, while low concurrency and larger files will need less processing power. Under conditions of very high concurrency, you might need a ratio close to 2 cores: 3 drives in the system. At the other end of the spectrum, with low concurrency and few files, you might be able to get away with as a low as 1:4 ratio of cores to drives.

To determine how many CPU cores you'll need, you should know how many drive bays there are in the chassis of the server and what clock rate (GHz) the cores will be running at. Use the ratio of cores to drives as the integer to multiple by (e.g., 1:2 ration would be 1/2); this value would likely be between 1/2 and 2/3.

CPU calculation formula

$$\frac{\text{total drives in chassis} \times \dfrac{\text{cores} \cdot \text{GHz}}{\text{drives}}}{\text{GHz of cores}}$$

This CPU calculation formula helps you decide whether using three cores at 2.0 GHz or two cores at 3.0 GHz makes sense (given budget, materials, and other constraints) for your configuration. (Obviously, given that most clock rates are not whole numbers, you will have to decide whether you want to round up or down on the number of cores.)

Let's look at some examples.

In the first example, let's say we want to buy a server with a 36-drive chassis and 2.44-GHz processors (cores). Assuming a desired core:drive ratio of 1:2, we would need our server to come with at least seven 2.44-GHz processors.

$$\frac{36 \text{ drives} \times \dfrac{1}{2} \dfrac{\text{core} \cdot \text{GHz}}{\text{drive}}}{2.44 \text{ GHz}} \approx 7.37 \text{ cores}$$

The same server, but with 2.0 GHz CPUs, would need 9 cores:

$$\frac{36 \text{ drives} \times \frac{1}{2} \frac{\text{core} \cdot \text{GHz}}{\text{drive}}}{2 \text{ GHz}} = 9 \text{ cores}$$

On the other hand, fewer drives means you don't need as many processors. A server 2.44-GHz CPUs but only 11 drives would need only two to three cores:

$$\frac{11 \text{ drives} \times \frac{1}{2} \frac{\text{core} \cdot \text{GHz}}{\text{drive}}}{2.44 \text{ GHz}} \approx 2.25 \text{ cores}$$

In calculating the CPU cores, it's not always as simple as applying core-to-drive ratios for any given use case and workload. Real world calculations must also take into consideration things like the GHz frequency of each core, price, and availability.

For a more scientific approach to a specific deployment, you might want to calculate the total amount of processing power available with a given CPU and its clock speed. By calculating various hardware configurations it is possible to narrow down the best price for the optimal amount of processing power.

To calculate the total processing power, multiply the sockets times the number of cores times the GHz frequency.

$$\text{sockets} \times \text{cores per socket} \times \text{GHz of cores} = \text{total GHz per node}$$

For example, if you are considering a system with two eight-core CPUs running at 2.4 GHz with a cost of $1,300/socket, you would have:

$$2 \text{ sockets} \times 8 \text{ cores} \times 2.4 \text{ GHz} = 38.4 \text{ GHz per node}$$

If you then considered a system with two six-core CPUs running at 3.0 GHz at a $1,000/socket, you would have:

$$2 \text{ sockets} \times 6 \text{ cores} \times 3.0 \text{ GHz} = 36 \text{ GHz per node}$$

Granted, prices of CPUs vary and in some cases you might not even have an option to specify what CPU goes into a server. However, in many situations, if you do the math, you might be able to save considerably by optimizing around the CPU selection.

RAM

In addition to supporting the Swift processes, system RAM caches the XFS inodes and works as a buffer cache to quickly serve frequently accessed objects. In general, we would suggest at least 1 GB of RAM per drive. However, just like with everything else, the amount of RAM you need depends on your needs and the configuration of other hardware. The size of hard drives and the average size of objects stored dictates the amount of RAM you need. Being able to hold all inodes in RAM would provide ultimate performance. However, in most cases that's not necessary and would be cost prohibitive, as you could end up needing very large amounts of RAM.

Following the above logic, the more inodes you can cache, the faster your cluster will run. The default XFS inode size is 256 bytes. In addition to objects taking up inodes, so do the *hash_dir*, the *suffix_dir*, and the *partition* directories on disk. All in all, the system needs at least 1 KB of RAM per object. Thus, the size of your disks and the average size of your objects will determine how much RAM your nodes will need.

For example, consider nodes with:

- 36 drive bays
- 4 TB disks
- Average object size of 50 KB
- Disks approximately 50% full

In such a scenario, each node would store approximately 1.5 billion objects. Hence, to store all the inodes in RAM for 1.5 billion 50 KB objects, you would need almost 1.4 TB of RAM in each server. Obviously, most people probably won't need this much.

To contrast the previous example, consider the following situation:

- 60 drive bays
- 4 TB disks
- Average object size of 25 MB
- Disks about 90% full

In this scenario you would store fewer than 9 million 25 MB objects on each node. As a result, that would only require roughly 9 GB of RAM to store every inode in RAM.

As you can see, the RAM requirements can vary wildly. Caching every inode in RAM is typically not necessary, unless you need your cluster to operate at insane speeds. And even if you do, you would likely face other bottlenecks that would limit cluster speed, such as the network.

In summary, if you know your anticipated average object size, and a rough idea of the request patterns, you should be able to come up with a good estimate of how much RAM you will need. At least 1 GB of RAM per disk is probably a good starting point. But, as you can tell, more RAM will only benefit the cluster. In the end, RAM is relatively inexpensive compared to the other components in a server. Therefore, if you put extra

RAM in your nodes, it is many times a good investment, especially if you take into consideration what it would cost you in labor to upgrade all your nodes with more RAM after you've put them into production.

It's also worth mentioning that nodes that run proxy server processes, and especially ones that are part of a cluster with high concurrency, will need more RAM to handle large amounts of simultaneous connections.

Drives

All nodes require a drive for the operating system. It is common to see a pair of drives deployed using RAID1 for the operating system (OS) in order to prevent a single drive failure from taking out an entire node. This is typically the only time you'll use RAID in a Swift node. Still, in large-scale clusters with many, many nodes, where every penny is counted to optimize for cost, it's not uncommon to see the operating system put on a single disk, with no redundancy. After all, if you have hundreds of nodes and you lose one node for some time, you've only lost a percent or a fraction of a percent of your capacity. Depending on your sensitivity to failures, which should be tightly coupled with the size of your cluster, you can use desktop- or enterprise-grade drives for the OS disk. The OS doesn't take much space, so you can use the smallest drive you can get. If using regular hard disks for the OS, it's typically hard to find disks smaller than 250 GB. Sometimes it can be more cost effective to buy a small SSD, which many times can also be less failure prone than a regular hard drive.

After the OS drive(s), additional drives might be needed depending on which role the node will play in the cluster, and subsequently which processes will be running on the node.

- Proxy
  - Proxy servers do not require additional drives.
- Account/container
  - If you run account and container services on the same nodes as object service, you can use the same SATA disks for all services on the node. However, we recommend storing account and container data on SSDs.
  - To speed up account and container lookups, again, we highly recommend using SSDs. Storing account and container data on SSDs will give your cluster a significant speed boost. This becomes especially important if your application uses only a few containers with many millions of objects in each container. Account and container data is stored in SQLite databases, keeping location data on containers and objects, respectively. Therefore, if you have the account/container data stored on standard hard disks, over time, your Swift cluster might slow down. This is because the process of looking up data locations takes much longer when using regular hard drives.

- Account and container data is treated just like object data, meaning it, too, is stored with the number of replicas specified for the cluster. Thus, if you use SSDs for account/container storage, you should of course have a minimum of three SSDs in your system, or whatever your replica count is set to, in order to take advantage of the as-unique-as-possible principle.
- Very large deployments might want to put the account and container server processes on several dedicated, high-performance nodes with SSDs.

- Object
  - SATA disks are the best price-performance choice for a Swift cluster. Standard desktop- or enterprise-grade drives are typically recommended.
    - At this writing, the best value is a 3 TB or 4 TB SATA drive. 6 TB disks have just become available, but their price makes them more expensive per terabyte compared with 3 TB and 4 TB disks.
    - Keep in mind that because Swift does not use RAID, each request for an object is handled by a single disk. Faster drives will increase the single-threaded response rates. Still, with enough disks in a system you will get enough input/output operations per second (IOPS) that 7200 RPM disks are normally the best choice.
    - We do not recommend using drives with power-saving features, sometimes called *green drives*, because Swift is continuously ensuring data integrity, and the chronic power down by the drive and power up by Swift might result in excess wear.
  - Chapter 12 shows how to calculate the number of drives needed to store objects.

Cluster Networking

When determining the networking hardware needed for a deployment, keep in mind that the deployment must integrate with the existing network as well as have its own requirements met. Individual network integration requirements will vary and will in most cases require consulting and collaboration with your network engineering team.

To determine the networking hardware needed, you can look at the requirements of the network segments that a Swift cluster can be configured with:

- Outward-facing network
  - For external (Internet and/or client) communication via API access
  - Used by the proxy and authentication services
  - If a load balancer is not being used, you'll need to consider how you will distribute client load between the available proxy servers

- Cluster-facing network
  - Used for internal node-to-node communication
  - Traffic on this network is not encrypted, so this network must be otherwise secured
- Replication network
  - Multi-region clusters will likely need a network segment for replication traffic
  - Even single-region clusters can benefit from a dedicated replication subnet
  - Traffic on this network is also not encrypted, so it, too, should be inaccessible by unauthorized clients
- Out-of-band node management
  - The internal network is used by the Intelligent Platform Management Interface (IPMI), Dell Remote Access Controller (DRAC), Integrated Lights-Out (iLO), or other hardware management system
- Cluster management
  - Similar to the the out-of-band network, if a central controller such as the SwiftStack Controller is used for cluster management, it is recommended that it be kept on a separate subnet.

The networks outlined above do not necessarily have to be tied to physical network interface cards (NICs). It's perfectly acceptable to VLAN them all on top of a single NIC or over two or more NICs bonded together. You can mix and match between the options in your implementation as well. It's up to you and your network and security teams. As long as you understand how Swift works and how it can use the various network options, you can come up with a good solution for your cluster.

Separate NICs for separate network segments

For small (and test) clusters, you might get away with using one flat network for all communication. For most other scenarios, it's a good idea to create separate subnets for each of the network segments.

Network Cards

Before getting into details of network segmentation and subnets, let's review the typical NICs.

When considering NICs, you have a set of network segments to consider:

- Outward-facing traffic (typically 10 GbE)
- Cluster-facing traffic (typically 10 GbE)

- Replication traffic (typically 10 GbE)
- Out-of-band node management (typically 1 GbE)
- Swift controller traffic: for SwiftStack or other cluster management solutions (typically 1 GbE)

Outward-Facing Network

The outward-facing interface is responsible for all communication with Swift clients. All proxy nodes will need to have an outward-facing NIC.

Because the outward-facing interface will be used by external resources, possibly including clients on the Internet, the outward-facing network should be firewalled to protect from external traffic on unauthorized ports.

The outward-facing NICs should be able to serve the anticipated workload of data ingest and requests from clients. Ultimately, your situation determines how much bandwidth you'll need. As a general guideline, workloads that include large files, such as virtual machine or database backups, will use more bandwidth, as it takes longer to read or write large objects from and to disk.

Load balancing can, to some extent, be provided by the proxy servers. But it's a good idea to use a dedicated load-balancing solution once the load-balancing capacity exceeds the capability of a single node. The type of load balancing you choose depends on your cluster workload.

Cluster-Facing Network

Proxy nodes will need to be able to talk to all the account, container, and object nodes. For this the cluster-facing network is used. The cluster-facing network is usually the segment that gets saturated first, if your use case is heavy on writes. The reason for this is that a write request of, let's say a 100 MB object, will be received on the outward-facing interface of the proxy and then be streamed out over the cluster-facing network in triplicate to the object servers. Subsequently, for every write the cluster-facing network will see three times the bandwidth of the size of the object to be written to disks in the cluster.

The cluster-facing network provides internal communication among nodes. *Top-of-rack* (ToR) switches allow communication between nodes in a rack, as well as to nodes in other racks in the cluster. As the name indicates, the ToR switch is generally placed in the top slot of a rack. In larger installations, aggregation switches are commonly implemented to allow communication among multiple ToR switches. On very small clusters, fewer switches are needed.

Replication Network

A segmented replication network isn't always necessary. However, you should always have a dedicated replication network when running multi-region clusters.

Under normal circumstances, the replication network sees less traffic going across it. Yet, the replication network is the network that will always see traffic, as the constant processes of auditing and replication are using the replication network. The replication network will definitely see heavy usage during capacity adjustments and when the cluster isn't quite healthy.

Multiregion clusters should have a network segment for replication traffic. When deploying a Swift cluster, the replication traffic between the storage nodes must be balanced against the client traffic to read and write data from those same servers. This becomes especially important in a multi-region cluster where a defining characteristic is that regions are separated by a network link that often has high(er) latency and low(er) reliability. Operators can use standard network management tools to ensure proper quality of service (QoS) and reliability on each of the networks and classes of traffic.

Out-of-Band Management

For server management purposes, most system administrators would like to have an out-of-band management NIC, by IPMI, DRAC or iLO, to provide node access if all other NICs become unreachable. The out-of-band management network only needs 1 Gbps of bandwidth.

Other Networking Connections

The complexity of your organization's network might dictate additional devices and configurations. Also, consider what other resources on the network the cluster might need to communicate with, such as the SwiftStack Controller or an authentication server like LDAP.

In the end, when determining your network requirements and selecting network cards, keep in mind that upgrading and retrofitting nodes from 1 Gb NICs to 10 GbE NICs would likely be cumbersome and costly. With an eye on expansion, scalability, and preventing networking from becoming a significant bottleneck, we often end up suggesting using 10 GbE NICs for the outward-facing, cluster-facing, and replication networks whenever possible and economically defensible.

Conclusion

In this chapter you've learned about some general hardware guidelines for nodes and some of the devices needed for the different network segments of a Swift cluster. As always, there's no one-size-fits-all solution, so be sure to carefully consider your use case and the optimal components for your needs. Still, as long as you don't make major, fundamental mistakes in your networking setup, the beauty of Swift is that it will allow for networking changes. Even if you configure your networking one way, you can relatively easily adjust it at a later time to meet expansion or segmentation needs. If you plan network changes carefully, you can make the changes without any cluster downtime.

CHAPTER 12

Planning a Swift Deployment

Martin Lanner
Amanda Plimpton

The previous chapter covered the individual hardware requirements and general networking needs of a cluster. This chapter aims to help you build out the requirements and specifications for your own deployment of Swift. In the end, we hope you'll be able to take advantage of Swift's flexibility to tailor a deployment that best meets your needs.

When planning an OpenStack Swift deployment, the first step is to define your workload and functional requirements. We will first look at some of the criteria that will help you think through your workload, requirements, and constraints. The rest of the chapter will then focus on system design and networking. System design will look at how many nodes will be needed, how services will be tiered, and what logical grouping of the nodes will best serve the needs of the cluster and take best advantage of Swift's features. Networking will focus on the different network segments that a Swift cluster might use.

Your Use Case

Every organization has its own intended usage and specifications for its Swift deployment. Influencing factors include storage capacity, access patterns, and geographic location.

Consider the following use cases for a Swift deployment:

- Software-as-a-service (SaaS) provider, storing application data and serving it with high availability to enterprise customers or end users worldwide
- General-purpose website, designed to support high-traffic loads
- Financial service, storing data with high durability and stringent compliance requirements

- Media/entertainment application, serving large volumes of data to many users
- Promising experimental project, which must be architected for data growth, concurrency, and low latency upon success
- Internal enterprise solution for storage and file sharing in a private cloud
- Cold-storage system, which is expected to grow rapidly and must meet durability requirements for legal or corporate policy compliance
- Public cloud storage provider

Each of these scenarios would use Swift in different ways and each has different requirements. For your deployment, you will similarly want to consider the following:

- Storage requirements
  - What is the initial desired storage capacity and scaling plan for data growth?
  - Data durability: how many replicas will you be storing?
  - What are the trade-offs between commodity hardware and proprietary systems?
  - Will you be using existing hardware?
  - Are there any compliance requirements for the storage and access of the data?
- Access patterns
  - How many users will concurrently access the system?
  - How frequently will they access the system, in requests per second per user?
  - Is request traffic typically consistent or bursty? How large a burst (in both requests per second and bytes per second) must the system support?
  - How low a latency is desired in servicing requests?
  - Is all data expected to be accessed uniformly?
- Geographical requirements
  - Where will the cluster be deployed?
  - Will your cluster be deployed to one geographical site, or multiple sites?
  - Where are the cluster's users?
  - What patterns of network latency (ping time) exist between the users' locations and the cluster's locations?
  - Are some users close and others far?

As you can tell, there are many questions about data location, data usage, and data access you should consider when determining the requirements and specifications of your deployment. The design process begins in earnest once you have evaluated your use case and estimated your deployment's workload, requirements, and constraints. Design starts with cluster size, then moves on to tiering services and then defining the logical groupings of your cluster.

System Design

System design begins with determining the size of your cluster. Size is a function of storage capacity and how many nodes you will need to meet that requirement. The primary factor determining node count is the number of drives, so the first step is to map your storage capacity to a drive count and then to a node count. Other considerations might affect the node count, but our recommended starting point is to determine the storage-based node requirement. The next steps will be to calculate the total storage needed and how many nodes are required to meet that storage need.

A word about hardware

In Chapter 11, we discussed the general hardware requirements of nodes. For your specific design the best components to buy are the ones that are lowest in cost and reliable enough for your needs.

How Many Nodes?

Swift storage nodes—the physical machines running account, container, and object services—are the foundation of your deployment. To determine how many Swift nodes you will need to store data in your cluster, you will first need to know (or have a best guess for):

- The usable capacity desired for your cluster
- Cluster replica count
- Preferred hard drive size
- Number of drive bays in the preferred server chassis

With that information, you can determine how many object storage nodes you will need by:

1. Calculating the total storage needed
2. Dividing by the size of the hard drives
3. Dividing by the number of drive bays in a chassis

Total storage

Total storage is the total capacity in gigabytes for storing data in your cluster. To calculate total storage, you need to take into account two factors: replica count and disk shrinkage.

With Swift, the standard replica count is three. Deployments that experience extremely high concurrency might benefit from a higher replica count and additional proxy nodes. As a result, the first step in determining usable capacity is to multiply the desired storage capacity of your cluster by the replica count. If you expect your cluster to store 250 TB of data and wish to set the replica count to three, you will need a total of 750 TB of storage. Replication ensures the durability and availability of data. The unique-as-possible placement of the replicas allows you to take advantage of lower cost drives while simply adding more or replacing any that fail without any loss of data or downtime.

Our recommended strategy accounts for "disk shrinkage" by multiplying the storage requirement by 1.087. Disk shrinkage is the difference between the raw storage capacity of a hard drive's disk and its usable capacity. Shrinkage occurs because of advertised drive sizes and filesystem formatting.

Drive manufacturers label their drives with decimal (base 10) values, and operating systems use binary values (base 2). However, the same acronyms (KB, MB, GB) are frequently used for both number sets. More precise naming would be:

- Decimal prefixes: kilo-, mega-, giga-, tera- (acronyms K-, M-, G-, T-)
- Binary prefixes: kibi-, mebi-, gibi-, tebi- (acronyms Ki-, Mi-, Gi-, Ti-)

By distinguishing between the two we make it easier to see the difference in drive size and storage capacity. For instance, a 1 GB drive has 1,000,000,000 bytes, but a computer that wants to store 1 GiB of data needs 1,073,741,824 bytes. This is because a binary kibibyte is actually 1,024 bytes, a binary mebibyte is actually 10,485,760 bytes, and so on.

That 1 GB drive would be completely full and the computer would still need to store 73,741,824 more bytes of data—over 7.3% of the total.

As mentioned, formatting a drive uses some of the storage space on the disk, depending on the filesystem. A comparison of filesystem overhead for different filesystem types can be found online (*http://bit.ly/rwm-jones*). XFS, the recommended filesystem for Swift, has a low overhead, at around 0.5% by this methodology. Between the decimal-binary conversion issue and filesystem overhead, total capacity loss can be about 8-9%. We use 8% for our calculations. To factor in this 8% loss you need to multiply your desired storage amount by 1/0.92, or 1.087.

Putting all the factors together then, the formula for calculating total storage needed is:

$$\text{usable capacity desired in GiB} \times \text{replica count} \times 1.087$$
$$= \text{total raw storage needed in GB}$$

Total drives needed

To calculate the number of hard drives (HD) you'll need, take your total raw storage number and divide by the desired HD size. At the time of this writing in 2014, 2 or 3 TB hard drives are commonly used for Swift nodes.

The formula for calculating the number of HDs you'll need looks like this:

$$\left\lceil \frac{\text{total storage}}{\text{HD size}} \right\rceil = \text{total number of HDs}$$

The "⌈" and "⌉" indicate the *ceiling function*, which rounds up to the nearest integer. (You can't buy 10.1 drives—you'll need to buy 11 in order to store all your data.)

Total servers (nodes) needed

Finally, determine the number of servers your storage nodes will need by dividing the number of HDs by the number of drive bays in the chassis. (You might have multiple chassis options, with different numbers of drive bays. Keep these options in mind to try alternate scenarios, but for now just use your preferred chassis.) So the formula is:

$$\text{total number of servers (nodes)} = \left\lceil \frac{\text{total number of HDs}}{\text{slots in chassis for storage drives}} \right\rceil$$

Note that we are counting the slots in the chassis for *storage* drives—you'll also need to account for an operating system, either on a drive in one of the bays, or via some other mechanism provided by the chassis.

Let's look at an example to see how you would use these formulas. For our example we will assume the following values:

- Desired usable capacity = 100 TiB
- Cluster replica count = 3
- Preferred hard drive size = 3 TB
- Number of hard drive slots per chassis = 36

How many nodes are needed to store 100 TiB of data given this configuration?

First, we determine the total storage needed:

1. Multiply the usable capacity desired by the replica count:

$$100 \text{ TiB} \times 3 \text{ replicas} = 300 \text{ TiB}$$

2. Then multiply by 1.087 to get the total raw storage needed in advertised drive size:

$$300 \text{ TiB} \times 1.087 = 326 \text{ TB}$$

3. Then divide by the advertised size of the hard drives:

$$\left\lceil \frac{326 \text{ TB total raw storage}}{3 \text{ TB per drive}} \right\rceil = \lceil 108.6667 \rceil = 109 \text{ drives}$$

4. The total number of storage nodes needed is then determined by dividing by the drive bays in the chassis:

$$\left\lceil \frac{109 \text{ drives}}{36 \text{ drive bays}} \right\rceil = \lceil 3.028 \rceil = 4 \text{ servers (nodes)}$$

So for this example, our options for our 100 TiB cluster are:

- Settle for a 99.3 TiB cluster and use three Swift object storage nodes completely filled with drives.
- Use four Swift object storage nodes, but put only 27-28 drives in each instead of 36.

What About the Account and Container Storage?

Our calculations so far address the storage needs of the objects. The data stored for account and container information typically is on the order of 1-2% of the size of the object data in the cluster. Our recommended best practice is to use fast drives such as SSDs, distributed evenly across failure domains (in this case, one drive on each of three servers). But as you see, the number of drives storing object data will dominate in determining the number of machines needed.

What now?

You've determined the number of nodes dictated by your storage requirements, under one set of assumptions. Soon enough, you'll probably go back, change some assumptions, and run some alternate scenarios. But let's see what we've learned from our work so far.

If you have a small number of nodes, say fewer than 5 or 10 (it's definitely a judgment call), you will almost certainly want to use an all-in-one tiering strategy. This gives you a proxy server process on each node. In most cases, this will be sufficient proxy capacity, but if you have a particularly high traffic load in proportion to your storage capacity, you might want more proxy server processes.

If you have a moderate node count, your deployment requirements will determine what tiering strategy is appropriate. In some cases, all-in-one tiering is fine for larger clusters, consisting of as many as 30 machines. However, beyond the smallest clusters, you really need to analyze your system for bottlenecks:

- If you haven't provisioned your networking appropriately, that is likely to be your system's weak point.
- If you have extremely high request traffic, you might be limited by the proxy server processes.
- The proxies might be limited by the object servers, in particular the drives. If all the drives are in constant use, you will need more drives in the system. Using a larger number of smaller drives can alleviate this pressure.
- Creating or deleting objects puts a load on the container servers. If your workload creates or deletes a large number of small objects, especially within a small number of containers, this might be a bottleneck.

If you have a bottleneck, the next section gives you some options to rebalance your system.

Design options

You might want to adjust the number of nodes without changing the storage capacity. Decreasing the node count can reduce hardware costs and rack count. Increasing the node count can yield smaller servers (1U or 2U instead of 4U), and more processing power per storage volume, which allows more proxy processes to handle incoming requests.

As a system designer, you have several "knobs" you might twiddle:

- Choose a chassis with fewer drive bays
- Choose a different drive size—two 2 TB drives read data faster than one 4 TB drive, but they take up more physical space
- Underfill the drive bays in each chassis—recommended for easy expansion!
- Add or remove nodes
- Select a tiering strategy (see the next section)

Tiering Node Services

At this point you should decide which, if any, of the Swift services on the nodes should be split off onto their own dedicated hardware. As you may recall, the four main server processes are proxy, account, container, and object.

Typical tiering configurations include:

- All-in-one node, a.k.a. combined node or PACO (proxy-account-container-object) node
  - All services are running on all nodes
  - Most cost-effective for small deployments
  - Maximum redundancy: when one machine fails, all other machines take up the slack
- Proxy-storage, a.k.a. proxy and account-container-object)
  - Supports heavy concurrent traffic loads with smaller data sets
  - Dedicated proxy machines handle external HTTP traffic
  - Proxies become a failure scenario; at least two proxy machines are required for redundancy
  - Proxies might be limited by drives on object servers, but this can be solved by increasing the replica count, thereby increasing the total drive count
- Proxy, account-container, object
  - Supports heavy traffic loads on very large data sets
  - Also supports special scenarios such as very large numbers of small files
  - Modifying objects puts load on the container servers, which can be pulled out into their own tier when they get large enough
  - Cost-effective only for specialized use cases or very large clusters

Once you know your system design requirements and you have analyzed a few hardware scenarios to see how many nodes you might have, you can choose one of the tiering strategies just described. Now it's time to decide how to group your cluster's hardware into regions, zones, and storage policies.

Defining Your Cluster Space

Place your nodes with two general goals in mind: isolating single points of failure, and avoiding bottlenecks. Regions, zones, and storage policies are three flexible ways to separate points of failure and choke points so that if one part of the cluster is unavailable, nothing is lost or unavailable.

Regions

Swift allows the parts of the cluster that are physically separate to be defined as regions. Regions are often defined by geographical boundaries. For example, a new region might be defined for several racks of servers (nodes) that are placed in a higher-latency, off-site location from the other nodes in the cluster. A cluster must have a minimum of one region, and as a result there are many single-region clusters where all the nodes belong to the same region. Once a cluster is using two or more regions it is considered a multi-region cluster.

Multi-region clusters (MRCs) have certain read and write behaviors. In particular, when an MRC receives a read request, Swift will favor copies of the data that are closer, as measured by latency. This is called *read affinity*.

Swift also offers *write affinity*, but not by default. By default, Swift attempts to simultaneously write data to multiple locations in a multi-region cluster, regardless of the region. This is well suited for low-latency connections where the write requests, data transfer, and responses can be fast.

In the case of a high-latency connection, it may be beneficial to turn on *write affinity*. With write affinity each write request creates the necessary number of copies of the data locally. Then the copies are transferred asynchronously to other regions. This allows faster write operations, at the cost of increased inconsistency between regions until the asynchronous transfers complete.

Swift allows you to configure a dedicated replication network for regions. Replication traffic between storage nodes would be transmitted over a separate network. This feature makes it possible to configure a cluster so that a sustained burst of background replication traffic does not block end-user access to the proxy nodes.

Two possible ways you may want to implement regions for your cluster are:

Off-site disaster recovery (DR)

Store one replica in a geographically distant data center apart from the other replicas, for disaster recovery purposes. One possible configuration is to place two replicas in a single region (the primary location) and use another region to hold a single replica (the offsite location).

When a client makes a request to the primary region, the read and write affinities will ensure the proxy server process prioritizes the storage nodes in its region over remote regions, allowing for higher throughput and lower latency on storage requests. For uploads, three replicas will be written in unique locations as usual, but the proxy node will select three locations in the same region. Then the replicators will asynchronously replicate one of the three copies to the offsite region.

Multi-region sharing
: Suitable for deployments where each geographic region will be accessed equally. This would be ideal for multi-region archiving and file sharing applications.

  Here, with read and write affinities enabled, the proxy process in a region will accept writes, and write three as-unique-as-possible copies within its region. Then, asynchronously, the object will be replicated to the other regions. Read requests go to a local region, and there will be an affinity to serve data from a storage node within that region.

Zones

Within regions, Swift allows availability *zones* to be configured to isolate failures. An availability zone should be defined by a distinct set of physical hardware whose failure would be isolated from other zones. In a large deployment, availability zones might be defined as separate facilities in a data center, perhaps separated by firewalls and powered by different utility providers. In a single data center deployment, the availability zones might be different racks. While there does need to be at least one zone in a cluster, it is far more common for a cluster to have many zones.

Swift will use the defined zones to attempt to place data in different failure domains, so that if a zone fails, the data remains available in another zone. In your deployment, you will want to create zones that account for these failure domains. Depending on the size of a cluster, a zone might be all drives on a node, all nodes behind the same switch, all nodes in a rack, or all nodes in a data center room.

Storage policies

Storage policies were still under development at this writing, but they will enable a Swift operator to define different storage strategies so that a single storage cluster can be used in multiple ways. A storage policy can span different regions or zones, various storage media, or varying replica counts. For example, one storage policy could be configured to distribute data across multiple regions, another could be configured for replica distribution in a single region, and a third could be deployed only on fast storage media such as SSDs. This powerful new Swift feature will require some research during the design process. We suggest the OpenStack Swift documentation as a good starting point.

Node Naming Conventions

It is good practice to name the nodes in a way that makes it simple to distinguish between proxy and storage nodes. For small clusters, giving the nodes hostnames such as `proxy1` or `storage1` is usually good enough. However, for larger clusters, it's good to have a more detailed naming convention schema. An example follows of how you might name nodes in a larger cluster:

- Data center (d)
- Rack (r) or zone (z)
- Node type: proxy (p) or storage (s)

Examples:

```
d1-z2-p3.example.com
d1-z2-s4.example.com
```

Authentication and Authorization

As your deployment planning progresses, one of the next considerations is how to grant access to the cluster. You will need to select a mechanism for authentication and authorization (collectively called *auth*). Many auth systems exist, ranging from simple files on disk to large-scale enterprise-grade systems such as LDAP. Swift allows you to choose an auth system that meets your needs. In selecting an auth system, consider the following questions:

- Security considerations
  - What is your security model? What are your protected assets? Who are the adversaries? What are the threat models? What remediations (e.g., auditing, immediate token revocation) need to be available?
  - Where are your security perimeters? (e.g., Are the nodes considered secure? If an auth system stores sensitive data on the nodes, will that weaken your security model?)
- Scalability considerations
  - How many users does your auth system need to support?
  - What latency is tolerable for an auth exchange?
  - How many concurrent login attempts do you expect?

Of course, if you have a scalable, robust, and secure auth system such as LDAP already deployed in your organization, there are many benefits to using that system. Happily, Swift supports many auth systems with different characteristics. For more details, consult Chapter 13.

With an auth service selected, the next step is to determine the networking and configuration considerations to ensure that your cluster can be reached by clients, communicate internally, and reach its preferred auth service.

Networking

With the size and configuration of the cluster addressed, the cluster's access and communication is next. Chapter 11 discussed the general hardware requirements for the networking, including switches, network interface cards (NICs), load balancers, and the networking segments used by the cluster. Here will we look at the network segments and some possible topologies. We advise you to work with your networking team to ensure that your deployment meets all network standards for your organization.

- Outward-facing network segment
  - All Swift clusters require an outward-facing network for external (Internet and/or clients) communication via API access.
  - Swift clients and external auth services communicate with the proxy over this network.
  - SSL is commonly terminated at the proxy server, which can communicate with the storage nodes in the clear over the trusted cluster-facing network.
- Cluster-facing network segment
  - Used for internal node-to-node communication.
  - Traffic on this network is not encrypted, so this network must be otherwise secured.
  - If you are using the multi-region cluster feature, this segment has additional replication bandwidth requirements unless a separate replication network is configured.
- Hardware management network segment
  - This internal network is used by the IPMI, iLO, or other hardware management system.

You will need to model cluster usage, estimating the average object size (or an estimated distribution of object sizes) and the number of requests per second. These figures can be multiplied to determine the required outward-facing network capacity.

For example, say that you want your cluster to support a long-term maximum of 100 requests per second (read plus write), and you estimate that your long-term average object size is 1 MB (1,000,000 bytes, rather than 1 MiB or 1,048,576 bytes). Remember to use the average object read or written, not the average object on disk, if they are different. If most of your requests are for the same subset of data, those object sizes should be weighted more heavily.

Multiplying 1 MB per request by 100 requests per second yields 100 MB per second, or 0.8 Gbps (gigabits per second) on your outbound network. For these requirements, a 1 Gbps uplink is technically adequate, but is cutting things a bit close after you add in auth requests, any system traffic such as OS upgrades, external monitoring, TCP overhead, congestion, and so on.

When determining the capacity needed for the network, keep in mind that each write of an object to a proxy server results in three writes to different storage servers. So to ingest 1 Gbps of data, the proxy server must be able to send 3 Gbps of data to the object servers.

Outward-Facing Network

When a client resolves the Swift cluster's hostname to an IP address, it is reaching the outward-facing network of the Swift cluster. Typically, that address will be a WAN IP address on a firewall or load balancer.

Firewall

A firewall (hardware or software) is always recommended when there is external traffic entering a network.

Load balancing

The type of load balancing you choose will depend on your use case and what your cluster workload will look like. Certainly, some amount of load balancing can be provided in software (such as the Linux Virtual Server) running on the proxy server machines, but as a cluster grows there is a point at which the cost-effective solution is to use dedicated load balancing. That solution could be anything from round-robin DNS using BIND, to HAProxy and other open source solutions, as well as commercial equipment from companies like F5 and A10.

If you are setting up a cluster with an external load balancer, you will need to set up your load balancer to divide the load between your proxy nodes.

For example, if you selected 192.168.50.0/24 as your outward-facing network, you would need to set up your load balancer to include the IP addresses of the proxy nodes in its load-balancing pool. You will also need to assign the load balancer a virtual IP address (VIP) on which it will respond. Here we will use 192.168.50.10 for the VIP. For this example, the IP addresses used would be as follows:

- 192.168.50.10 (load balancer VIP)
- 192.168.50.11 (proxy1, included in pool)
- 192.168.50.12 (proxy2, included in pool)

To ensure the external load balancer pulls failing nodes out of the load-balancing pool, configure the load balancer to use the proxy node's health check URL. The health check URLs in our example are:

- *http://192.168.50.11/healthcheck*
- *http://192.168.50.12/healthcheck*

Cluster-Facing Network

The cluster-facing network provides internal communication among nodes. You can configure consistency services, especially the object replication processes, to run on this network segment in order to ensure that replication traffic doesn't interfere with incoming or outgoing user traffic.

Replication traffic volume depends on many factors, including failure rates and the frequency of adding and removing drives. Swift features that offload work to the replication processes, such as global clusters or container synchronization, add significant replication traffic volume. (In these cases, a separate replication network is often desirable.) Depending on the size of the cluster, top-of-rack (ToR) and aggregator switches may need to be incorporated for this network segment.

Let's discuss the network configuration options. If we build on the earlier example, we would have an outward-facing network 192.168.50.0/24 and then select a cluster-facing network 192.168.51.0/24. If we have two proxy nodes and six storage nodes, we might assign the network interfaces as follows:

- proxy1
  - Outward-facing interface: 192.168.50.11
  - Cluster-facing interface: 192.168.51.11
- proxy2
  - Outward-facing interface: 192.168.50.12
  - Cluster-facing interface: 192.168.51.12
- storage1
  - Outward-facing interface: 192.168.50.21
  - Cluster-facing interface: 192.168.51.21
- storage2
  - Outward-facing interface: 192.168.50.22
  - Cluster-facing interface: 192.168.51.22
- storage3

  - Outward-facing interface: 192.168.50.23
  - Cluster-facing interface: 192.168.51.23
- storage4
  - Outward-facing interface: 192.168.50.24
  - Cluster-facing interface: 192.168.51.24
- storage5
  - Outward-facing interface: 192.168.50.25
  - Cluster-facing interface: 192.168.51.25
- storage6
  - Outward-facing interface: 192.168.50.26
  - Cluster-facing interface: 192.168.51.26

Incoming requests to the cluster will be routed through the load-balancing solution to the proxies and from the proxies to the storage nodes, as depicted in Figure 12-1.

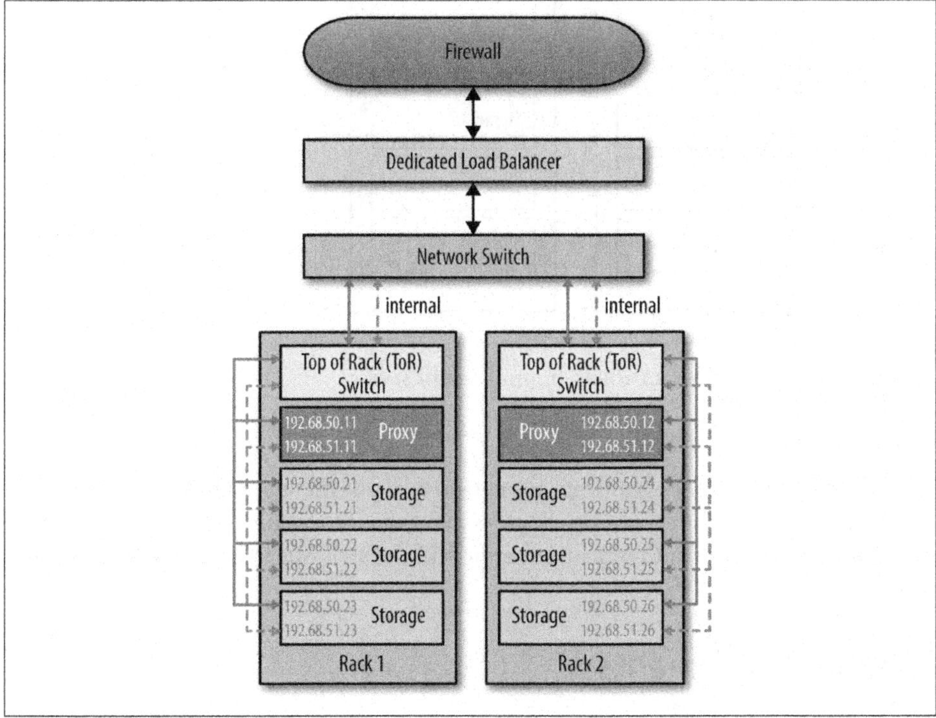

Figure 12-1. Layout with separate outward and cluster subnets

Hardware management network

This internal network is used by the IPMI, iLO, or similar services for hardware management. It is intended for hardware or emergency "out-of-band" communication.

When a hardware management network is used, all nodes need an additional NIC, most often a 1 GbE with one or two ports. The result is shown in Figure 12-2.

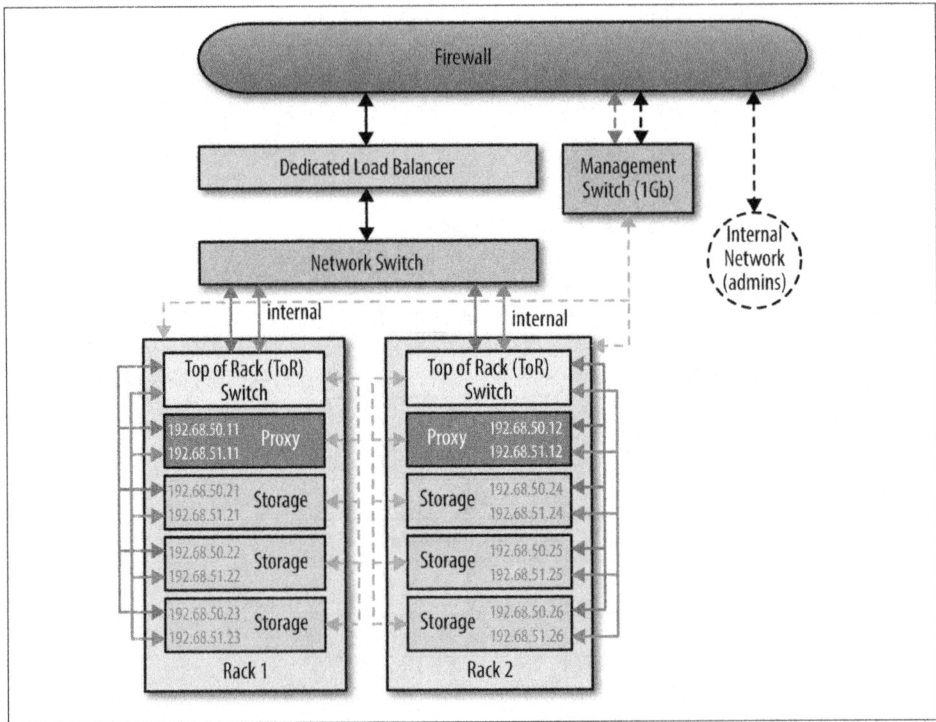

Figure 12-2. Layout with hardware management subnet

Other networking connections

The complexity of your organization's network might dictate additional devices and configurations. Other determining factors can include resources that might be used with the cluster, such as authentication services or the SwiftStack Controller.deployment planning

Sample Deployments

To review what we've covered so far, let's take a look at some sample deployments, and examine how they would be configured. As we have emphasized for the past two chapters, there is no one-size-fits-all configuration.

Small Cluster: Several Nodes

For a small deployment, in this case one with five nodes and a total of 50 TB of usable storage (150 TB raw drive capacity), you would likely be running all services on all nodes. This includes load balancing, proxy server, and object storage. This is automatically configured on the node through the SwiftStack installation and configuration process and does not require any additional setup by the operator.

Medium-Size Cluster: Multi-Rack

For a medium-size deployment with 6-12 storage nodes, you have a few options in configuring and deploying the cluster. At this scale, you could choose to run either a dedicated proxy/load-balancing tier of nodes, or run all the services on every node. If running a separate proxy tier, you need at least two dedicated proxy/load-balancing nodes for high availability. The proxy nodes should each contain two network interfaces, one for outward-facing API requests and one for the backend network connecting the storage nodes. On the other hand, if you are running all services on each node, be sure to verify that the overall network capacity is suitable for your workload.

Typically, a single network tier is used for small- and medium-size deployments. Either 1 GbE or 10 GbE switches can be used for this purpose, depending on the throughput that the cluster is expected to sustain.

Large Cluster: Multi-Region

For larger deployments, such as a cluster with 1 PB of usable storage, you should consider the following:

- A separate load-balancing tier might need to be used, depending on the request throughput.
- The proxy nodes will be set up in a separate proxy tier. In this example, there are eight proxy nodes.
- Each rack with storage nodes will be configured as a separate zone. In this example, there are 40 storage nodes, configured as a 4U chassis with 36 of the 3 TB drives. The zone can be configured in the SwiftStack Controller on the Node configuration page.
- A pair of aggregation switches with two links back to the frontend network/border network connects to the proxy tier and to each of the five ToR switches for each of the storage zones. All connections to the proxy tier and the zones are 10 GbE.
- Each rack with storage nodes has a pair of ToR switches. Each ToR switch connects to the aggregation network. Depending on the overall concurrency desired, a deployment can use either a 1 GbE or a 10 GbE network to the object stores. It's possible

to use a single, nonredundant switch, as the system is designed to sustain a zone failure.

Conclusion

In this chapter you've learned some of the questions you need to ask before planning your Swift deployment. You've also learned how to calculate the total storage needed and the number of nodes required.

Depending on your cluster size and particular needs, there are many options available for tiering and configuring your cluster. We discussed options for tiering the various node services (proxy, account, container, and object), and mentioned several tiering configurations and their applications.

Defining zones allows Swift to place data in different failure domains, for better availability and durability. Global clusters offer attractive capabilities for redundancy and distributed presence, but the high latency between data centers must be managed appropriately. In general, you should configure an outward-facing network (on which communication with end users occurs) as well as a cluster-facing network (on which the proxy communicates with storage nodes, and on which replication occurs).

Other deployment considerations include choice of auth system, load balancing, SSL termination, and sustainable naming conventions. We discussed networking considerations and suggested some network topologies. Finally, we walked through some example deployments.

In the next chapter we'll discuss the details of authentication and authorization (collectively known as auth), which will let you control how and by whom your Swift cluster will be accessed.

CHAPTER 13

Authentication and Authorization

Amanda Plimpton
Jon Solera

As you install and configure your cluster, you will probably need to integrate it with authentication and authorization systems. The OpenStack projects, including Swift, use a token-based protocol for both authentication and authorization. Authentication and authorization services are collectively referred as *auth*. To authenticate, the user provides credential information such as a username and password over HTTPS (or perhaps HTTP in the case of an insecure experimental cluster), and if the credentials are valid, the user receives a token that can be sent in with future requests as verification of her authentication.

In this chapter, we will start by examining how authentication works with Swift. Then we'll cover authorization, which uses previously generated authentication information to determine what you're allowed to do. We will also look at *access control lists* (ACLs), which let you grant access to individual containers or entire accounts. After this overview you will learn about some of the readily available auth services. Some of these are preloaded with Swift while others can be added through third-party middleware. In the final section, we explore access control in more detail.

Authentication

Swift does not require a specific default auth service. Instead, it allows administrators to plug one or more auth services into its framework. This flexibility lets you choose auth middleware components that meet your needs, and enable them in the proxy server configuration of your Swift cluster.

Swift comes with two types of auth middleware, TempAuth and Keystone Auth. TempAuth is not suitable for production use because it deliberately compromises security for the sake of convenience, but it might be acceptable for testing Swift. For production environments where your cluster needs to integrate with other OpenStack products such as Nova and Glance, the Keystone Auth system is better. There are also many popular third-party auth middleware components from which to choose. Some have been developed by the Swift community, while others are offered as proprietary auth middleware components as part of a vendor's Swift products. For example, some companies, such as CloudStack, have created auth middleware for their custom auth system (cs_auth), while other companies including SwiftStack have built out auth middleware for their products that leverage popular auth systems such as LDAP.

If your organization has auth needs that aren't covered by one of the existing auth systems, it is possible to create custom middleware for authentication and authorization. You can use TempAuth and Keystone Auth as informal templates for developing your own custom auth middleware. If you're interested in creating auth middleware, see Chapter 8 for more information on middleware development.

How Authentication Works

From the user's perspective, a successful authentication is one where he provides his information (generally username and password) to the auth URL for his Swift cluster, and gets an authentication token (auth token) and storage URL in return that allows him to access the storage location of his primary Swift account.

All auth requests are directed to an auth URL, such as *http://swift.example.com/auth/v1.0*, which must be known in advance. In other words, if you are told you have been given access to a Swift cluster, you will need to know the username, password, and auth URL. Once you send in an auth request, its processing will be delegated to the auth middleware.

Authentication is the process of presenting credentials and getting a token. A byproduct of authentication is that the primary storage URL for the account is returned as well. The auth middleware calls on its associated auth server (Authentication Request, in the outline below) to determine authentication. The auth server will process the request and then return the results to the middleware (Authentication Handling). The middleware can then pass the response back to the user (Authentication Response). When positive authentication is made, the auth server will also return authorization group information, which the auth middleware caches for later use (Authentication Handling and Figure 13-1).

1. Authentication Request
    a. The Swift proxy server process receives the request with the user's credential information and passes it to the Swift auth middleware.
2. Authentication Handling
    a. Each configured auth middleware component will check the request to determine whether its own (possibly external) auth system can verify user credentials that have the format presented.
    b. If the auth middleware doesn't recognize the format of the user's credentials, it takes no action.
    c. If the auth middleware recognizes the format of the user's credentials, it tries to verify them by calling on its auth system. An auth system might be an external service such as LDAP or Keystone, or a local utility such as a file of encrypted usernames and passwords. In either case, in this section we will refer to this source of truth as the *auth system*, distinct from the Python middleware component, which we call the *auth middleware*.
        i. After each auth system check, regardless of the outcome, the request passes to the next auth middleware until all have checked it.
        ii. If the auth system can't verify the credentials, it does nothing, allowing the request to pass on to the next auth system (if any).
        iii. If the auth system verifies the credentials, it will return positive verification as well as additional information about the account, including the storage URL and authorization information.
        iv. The middleware receives the verification from the auth system; if it is negative, no action is taken. If it is positive, the middleware creates an authentication token (auth token) and stores the relevant information.
3. Authentication Response
    a. Once the last auth middleware has checked the request, a response is returned to the proxy server process.
        i. If no auth middleware had a positive verification of the credentials, the proxy server process returns a `401 Unauthorized` response to the client.
        ii. If the auth middleware had a positive authentication, then the proxy server process returns the auth token and storage URL to the user in the HTTP response headers.

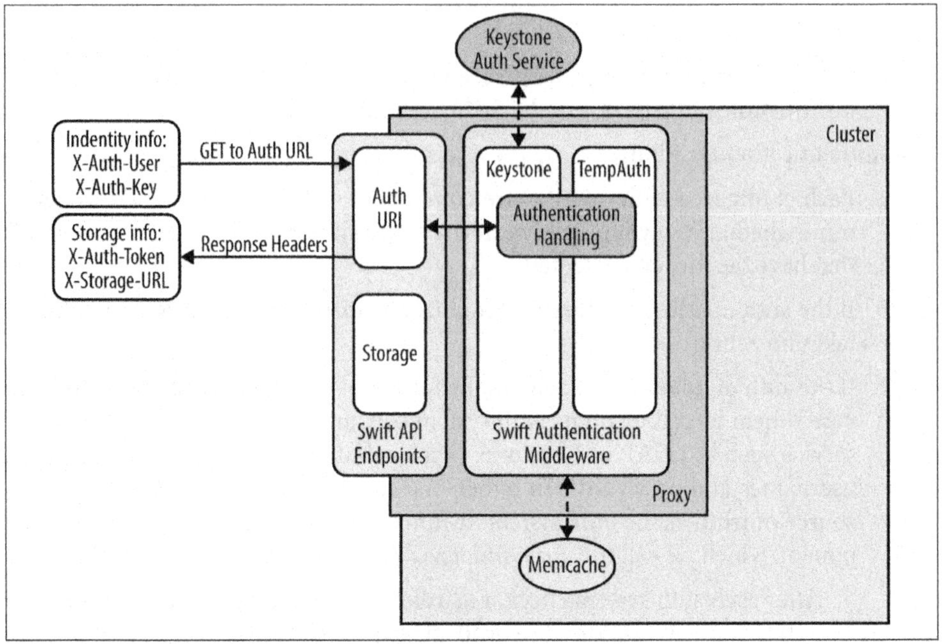

Figure 13-1. Authentication request, handling, and response

Let's examine further how authentication is handled.

Authentication Request

When users send authentication requests to the Swift cluster's authentication URL, they are interacting with Swift's authentication protocols rather than the protocols of any external auth system. Once received, the Swift proxy server process takes each request, passes the information into the middleware, and then returns the results of the authentication attempt back to the user. Users do not directly access the external auth services; all external auth transactions are handled by the Swift auth middleware.

Authentication URL

Swift uses the OpenStack authentication protocols, which currently have two versions. In Version 1 Auth (v1.0), the user provides credential information in the HTTP headers of a `GET` request, and then receives the authentication token, and storage URL, in the response headers. Version 2 Auth (v2.0) handles more sophisticated situations such as multiple storage URLs, and provides authentication via `POST` requests. Both versions are supported in the community, with each auth middleware package determining which protocols to support. However, for our purposes in discussing auth in Swift, we will focus on the simpler Version 1 protocol.

An auth URL has the following format: *http(s)://<host>(:<port>)/<auth_version>*.

The host and port identify a proxy server (or collection of proxy servers) that will handle authentication requests.

The *auth version* will end with either *v1.0* or *v2.0*. Version 1 Auth will usually have the word *auth* in front of the *v1.0*, separated with a slash. So a typical Version 1 Auth URL looks like *https://swift.example.com/auth/v1.0*, where *auth/v1.0* is the auth version. However, in Version 2 Auth, typically there is no *auth/* in the version path, and an auth URL would look like *https://swift.example.com/v2.0*.

At this point we'd like to note the formatting differences between the auth URL and the storage URL. The two URL types look very similar, and sometimes people who are new to Swift will use the wrong URL with their request. Any auth attempts to a storage URL will fail as thoroughly as a storage request to an auth URL.

- Auth URLs
  - End with *v1.0* or *v2.0*.
  - Version numbers contain a period and a zero.
- Storage URLs
  - Contain the Swift API version, always *v1*.
    - There is currently only one version of the Swift API.
    - The Swift API version does *not* contain a period and a zero.
  - End with a storage location
    - Account (*/v1/accountname*), container (*/v1/accountname/containername*) or object (*/v1/accountname/containername/objectname*) storage location.

Here are some typical auth URLs:

- *http://swift.example.com/auth/v1.0*
- *http://swift.example.com/v2.0*

Here are some typical storage URLs:

- *http://swift.example.com/v1/AUTH_johnsmith*
- *http://swift.example.com/v1/AUTH_johnsmith/container*
- *http://swift.example.com/v1/LDAP_maryjones/container/object111*
- *http://swift.example.com/v1/ProjectZebra*
- *http://swift.example.com/v1/AUTH_backups*

Authentication credentials

Authentication requests sent to an auth URL must include the authentication credentials that need to be verified. With Version 1 Auth, those credentials would be a username, passed in using the `X-Auth-User` header, and a key (or password), passed in using the `X-Auth-Key` header. For example, a cURL command to authenticate might look like this:

```
USERNAME=alice
PASSWORD=my_secret_password
AUTH_URL=https://swift.example.com/auth/v1.0

curl -i -H "X-Auth-User: $USERNAME" -H "X-Auth-Key: $PASSWORD" $AUTH_URL
```

Some organizations prefer for the authentication username and Swift storage account name to be related, resulting in one account per user. (Recall from Chapter 5 that *users* are identities, while *accounts* are storage areas.) For example, user `alice` stores data in the account `AUTH_alice`, user `bob` stores data in the account `AUTH_bob`, and so on. Other organizations might want one account per project, or one account per software client, or some other scheme. An example would be an `AUTH_backups` Swift account, which could be accessed by many users. The relationship between the authenticated user and the Swift account is defined by a combination of Swift cluster policy and the choice of auth middleware. As a result, the authentication username is not necessarily related to the name of the Swift account the user is trying to access. (For instance, user `alice` might be accessing the account `AUTH_backups` or even `AUTH_bob`.)

The specific format of the auth URL, and which pieces of information are required for successful authentication, depend on the requirements of the particular auth system. One of the problems in categorically describing all auth middleware is that there's no "one way" to configure it. In the following examples we use TempAuth as one example of how the authentication process looks. Most of the other auth middleware options tend to use a similar design, but they will vary in the format of their auth URLs or in the format or content of the credentials they require. Administrators will have to provide their users with the correct formats for specific deployments.

In the following example, the `curl` command is used for authentication by passing in the username and key (password) to the auth URL:

```
# General format
$ curl -i -H "X-Auth-User: $USERNAME" -H "X-Auth-Key: $PASSWORD" "$AUTH_URL"

# Specific example
$ curl -i -H "X-Auth-User: acct1:bob" -H "X-Auth-Key: bobpassword" \
    https://swift.example.com/auth/v1.0/
```

Authentication Handling

When the proxy server process receives a request, it sends that request through the proxy's WSGI middleware pipeline, as designated by the ordering of the middleware pipeline in the proxy server's configuration file (*proxy-server.conf*). If no auth middleware is installed in the pipeline, nothing will take action to reject the request, and thus all requests will be allowed. (It is possible, but not recommended, to run a wide-open Swift cluster with no auth middleware at all.)

If exactly one of the pipeline's middleware components is auth middleware of some type (the common case), that component is responsible for responding to auth requests by checking credentials and providing an auth token, and for rejecting unauthorized storage requests. If the auth middleware doesn't explicitly reject a request, it is allowed.

It is possible to have multiple auth middleware components in the pipeline, but only if they are designed to work together. Because each component rejects an unauthorized request by default, they need to coordinate in order to communicate that the request is unknown to the first component, but accepted by the second. Multiple auth middleware components are unusual and beyond the scope of this book. Instead, we will focus on the common case of one auth middleware component.

On an incoming auth request, the auth middleware extracts the credentials (typically username and password) from the request, and attempts to authenticate the user. Auth middleware typically calls out to an external source to verify credentials, such as a file on disk or (more commonly) an external service such as a Keystone or LDAP server. Auth middleware then has the option of caching the results of the auth attempt, under whatever caching policy seems appropriate to the auth middleware developer.

If the auth request's credentials are found invalid by the external source, the auth middleware returns a `401 Unauthorized` response to the user. However, if the credentials were recognized and pass verification, the auth middleware prepares to return a successful response to the user. The auth middleware sends an additional request to the external source, retrieving *authorization* information for the user, typically a list of *authorization groups* that the user belongs to. It also retrieves the storage URL of the primary Swift storage account associated to that user. (In V2 Auth, multiple storage URLs can be returned.)

When all this information is received by the middleware, it performs a series of actions:

1. The authentication token is generated.
2. The authentication token and authorization information are copied into a cache (typically Memcache, an in-memory cache server). This allows verification of the token on future requests.
3. The token and storage URL information are returned to the user.

Creating the authentication token

Upon successful authentication, the auth middleware creates an authentication token (auth token), which is a cryptographically secure, opaque string using a format predefined in the middleware's configuration file. Although the exact format and expiration of the auth token depends on the configuration, there are some relatively consistent elements.

Most auth middleware use a *reseller prefix* when creating an auth token. This is highly recommended to help avoid conflicts with other auth systems. The standard format for a reseller prefix is a short, all-caps abbreviation (e.g., `KEY` for Keystone) followed by an underscore (e.g., `KEY_`).

For example:

TempAuth token
: `AUTH_`tk9a227572ba1841d98c248c5a9f7f3999

Keystone auth token
: `KEY_`tk9a227572ba1841d98c248c5a9f7f3999

Most auth tokens expire 24 hours after their creation, by default. It is considered a good security practice to expire tokens after a limited period, in order to limit the damage if a token is leaked. If a company determines that it needs a longer period before expiration, the `token_life` value can be modified in the middleware's configuration file.

After the auth token expires, a user needs to reauthenticate against the auth URL and get a new auth token. Because most auth systems treat expired tokens identically to invalid tokens, a client can tell that the token expired if a request with a previously good token now receives a `401 Unauthorized` response.

Copying auth token and authorization information in Memcache

With the auth token created, most auth middleware will copy the auth token, its expiry time, and the authorization group information into a cache, typically Memcache, on the same machine as the proxy server process. As with many of the auth middleware settings, where the information is stored can be configured differently from the default. However, most auth middleware uses Memcache.

Memcache (or `memcached`, from "memory cache daemon"), first mentioned in "Starting memcached" on page 139, is a distributed cache server designed to serve all requests from memory. By refusing to store anything on disk, it can provide very low latency. Many auth systems use Memcache to store tokens, identity information, and authorization group membership.

We will talk more about authorization later in this chapter. The important thing to know at this point is that when an auth system is returning authentication approval, it's also retrieving the authorization information for a user from its external source, and storing it in Memcache for later use. Most commonly the information is the list of the authorization groups to which the user belongs. In Swift, authorization privileges are attached to authorization groups, generally including the one-member group that is automatically created for each user.

Authentication Response

Once the authentication handling is completed, successfully or unsuccessfully, a response is generated and returned to the user. If no auth middleware had a positive verification of the credentials, the proxy server process returns a `401 Unauthorized` response to the client.

If the auth middleware had a positive authentication, the proxy server process returns a `200 OK` response, which includes the auth token and storage URL in the HTTP response headers.

The whole cycle of auth request, auth handling, and auth response is the auth exchange. Although it took several pages to describe, for the user it is a matter of viewing a handful of lines as shown in Example 13-1 using the `curl` command and the `swift` command.

Example 13-1. Auth exchange using the curl command

```
$ curl -i -H 'X-Auth-User: bob' -H 'X-Auth-Key: bobpassword' \
    https://swift.example.com/auth/v1.0
HTTP/1.1 200 OK
X-Storage-Url: https://swift.example.com/v1/AUTH_bob
X-Auth-Token: AUTH_tk7a44e147a2614fc680b7a755648204fa
Content-Type: text/html; charset=UTF-8
Set-Cookie: X-Auth-Token=AUTH_tk7a44e147a2614fc680b7a755648204fa; Path=/
X-Storage-Token: AUTH_tk7a44e147a2614fc680b7a755648204fa
Content-Length: 0
X-Trans-Id: tx6e580624e6804267881f3-005318ffc5
Date: Thu, 06 Mar 2014 23:08:08 GMT
```

This `curl` command contains only the auth exchange. Any storage requests would follow afterward, using the auth token received here. Example 13-2 presents another example auth exchange and storage request, this one using the `swift` command-line interface (CLI).

Example 13-2. Auth exchange and storage request using the swift command

```
$ swift -A https://swift.example.com/auth/v1.0 -U bob -K bobpassword stat -v
StorageURL: https://swift.example.com/v1/AUTH_bob
Auth Token: AUTH_tkb5bab9e25a274b4a853fe2587b5dc8f9
   Account: AUTH_bob
Containers: 0
   Objects: 0
     Bytes: 0
Content-Type: text/plain; charset=utf-8
X-Timestamp: 1375225766.50237
```

```
X-Trans-Id: tx88ac2ec242fd4af6a1e3d-0051f847a6
X-Put-Timestamp: 1375225766.50237
```

Because the `swift` command always combines one auth request and one storage request, we see the results of the auth request (the storage URL and auth token) as well as the results of the storage request (a `HEAD` request on the account `AUTH_bob`, which reveals that the account has 0 containers, 0 objects, and 0 bytes).

The value of the `X-Storage-Url` header (called the `StorageURL` when returned by the `swift` command) in the raw HTTP request is specifically the storage URL of the primary Swift account associated with the authenticated user. This value is the URL to which *storage* requests (not auth requests) are usually made, *after* authentication.

In general, the storage URL has no direct relationship with the auth URL. However, they are often so similar that users can confuse them, as seen here:

Auth URL

- Format: *http(s)://$HOST:$PORT/$AUTH_VERSION*
- Example: *http://swift.example.com/auth/v1.0*
- Note that "v1.0" or "v2.0" will require the ".0" (period zero) at the end of the URL; otherwise an error will occur. *v1* is not a valid format for the auth URL.

Storage URL

- Format: *http(s)://$HOST:$PORT/v1/$ACCOUNTNAME*
- Example: *http://swift.example.com/v1/AUTH_bob*
- The "v1" in the storage URL refers to Version 1 (v1) of the Swift *storage* API, not the auth version. There is currently only one version of the Swift storage API, so all storage URLs will contain "v1". Also note that the storage URL contains "v1", *not* "v1.0". The v1.0 used in some auth URLs has no relationship to the v1 in the storage URLs.

As previously mentioned in "How Authentication Works" on page 194, Swift handles authentication requests ("here are my credentials, give me a token") differently from storage requests ("here is my token, please store or retrieve my data"). In addition to those differences, note that the handling of auth requests is delegated to the auth middleware, while the handling of storage requests is the purview of core Swift. The cluster admin's choice of middleware determines how auth transactions are handled, while Swift manages storage in a standardized way.

Using the Auth Token in Storage Requests

Depending on which action is being taken with the account, the storage URL might require additional segments: *.../<container>* to operate on a container in the account, and *.../<container>/<object>* to operate on an object.

For instance, the following shows that if a user wants to access an object called *pic1.jpg*, its storage URL will be the account storage URL, *http://swift.example.com/v1/AUTH_bob*, with the *photos_container* container and object name appended to it.

http://swift.example.com/v1/AUTH_bob/photos_container/pic1.jpg

Every request being made to the storage URL must include the auth token using the (case-insensitive) `X-Auth-Token:` header. For example, here is the syntax to upload a file with *cURL*:

```
$ curl -i -X PUT -H "x-auth-token: AUTH_tkb5bab9e25a274b4a853fe2587b5dc8f9" \
    http://swift.example.com/v1/AUTH_bob/photos_container/pic1.jpg \
    -T /tmp/pic1.jpg
```

When a storage request is sent in, the Swift proxy server process sends the request to the auth middleware to verify the auth token, determine authorization for the user, and then evaluate whether the request is directed at a resource for which the user is authorized.

As mentioned earlier, the auth token and authorization group information will be in Memcache where it can be accessed for the verification. Let's now take a closer look at authorization.

Authorization

From the user's perspective, a successful authorization takes place when she is able to send a request to access the cluster and do something (such as upload an object or get a list of containers in an account) and it works.

Earlier we learned that authentication is used to verify who you are. But authentication only verifies *identity*—it confirms that a user is who she claims to be. Once Swift is sure who you are, it is the role of authorization to verify what you're *allowed to do*. Authorization determines which resources a verified user can access.

Authorization Examples

Let's say that you have successfully authenticated as user `bob`, and you have a token to prove that you are `bob`.

If your Swift cluster is set up so that each user is associated with exactly one account, you would expect there to be one particular account associated with user `bob`—an account named, for example, `AUTH_bob`. The storage URL for this storage account will be returned in the response to the auth transaction, along with the token. Perhaps that storage URL is *http://swift.example.com/v1/AUTH_bob.*

Here are some authorization questions to consider about your account:

- Can you as user `bob` read an object in that account? For example, can `bob` issue a `GET` request for *http://swift.example.com/v1/AUTH_bob/mycontainer/myobject*? It's difficult to imagine a scenario in which a user shouldn't be allowed to read data from his own account—but maybe user `bob` hasn't paid his bill, so his account has been deactivated.
- Can `bob` write a new object to a container in that account (e.g., issue a `PUT` request to *http://swift.example.com/v1/AUTH_bob/mycontainer/new_object*)? Probably yes—but maybe `bob` has exceeded his storage quota, and shouldn't be allowed to store new data until he has deleted some of his old funny cat pictures.
- Can `bob` read an object from a different account, such as *http://swift.example.com/v1/AUTH_alice/alice_container/alice_object_*? At a high level, we might hope that `bob` can't read data in an account owned by `alice`, unless she gives him permission to do so.
- What if `alice` has given `bob` permission to read any data in one of her containers? It certainly seems reasonable that granting `bob` read permission doesn't obligate `alice` to allow `bob` to write or delete data. We say more about container-level access later.

Swift addresses these and other authorization issues at the proxy server level, in cooperation with the auth middleware. You might recall that the auth middleware is responsible for authenticating the user and looking up the user's authorization groups. There is almost always one default group: auth systems typically create an authorization group that contains only the authenticated user, in addition to any other authorization groups. The proxy server itself is responsible for using the list of authorization groups to determine what level of access should be granted for the request, and thus whether the request is authorized or unauthorized.

How Authorization Works

Earlier in the chapter, we mentioned that many auth systems store the necessary authorization information in Memcache. Although authorization is a separate process from authentication, it is more efficient to only make one call to the external auth service. This way, Swift can confirm authentication of the user, and in the process retrieve authorization as well as identity information. This allows each subsequent user request to the storage URL to be authorized using the cached information, until the cache is refreshed.

The process of authorizing a storage request that is properly authenticated (has a valid token) follows these steps:

1. Storage request processing
   a. User sends in a storage request, containing a valid auth token, to the proxy server endpoint.
   b. The web server, which complies with the Web Server Gateway Interface (WSGI) specification, receives the request and extracts the important information such as the HTTP verb, the URL, and the headers. This information is stored in the WSGI request environment, a dictionary-like data structure described in "Introduction to WSGI" on page 101.
2. Token verification and authorization information lookup
   a. The request is passed to the Swift authentication middleware for token verification and authorization group lookup.
      i. Auth middleware verifies whether the token is valid and unexpired.
      ii. Auth middleware looks up the user information, both authentication and authorization, associated with this token from Memcache.
      iii. Auth middleware copies the authorization groups and identity information into the WSGI request environment.
      iv. That data structure is passed down the middleware pipeline (via the standard WSGI mechanisms), where it eventually reaches the core proxy server code.
3. Authorization evaluated
   a. The core proxy server compares the list of authorization groups with the URL being addressed (and the HTTP verb being used), and determines whether the request is authorized.
      i. If the request is unauthorized, the proxy server process returns a `403 Forbidden` response.
      ii. If the request is authorized, the proxy server will now attempt to complete the request. It determines what resource is named in the request (account, container, or object) and makes another HTTP request to the appropriate resource server (account server, container server, or object server).
4. Storage request processed
   a. At this point, any of the three types of resources (accounts, containers, and objects) would be processed in analogous ways by its server. Let's say this is a container request. Assuming the cluster is configured to have the standard three replicas, the proxy server determines which three container servers to contact by using the container ring. The container ring maps the URI of the container

(e.g., */myaccount/mycontainer*) to a partition number, and looks up the location of all three nodes associated with the partition.

b. The proxy server process passes the request to the container server process on the three nodes. In the case of a read, a response from any one container server process is sufficient. In the case of a write, the proxy server process requires a quorum of two successful responses from the container servers.

5. Storage request response

    a. The core proxy server process responds to the client.

        i. If none of the replicas respond successfully to a read request, the proxy server starts querying handoff nodes. If the three primary replicas and three handoff nodes all return failure, the proxy returns a failure (e.g., `404 Not Found`) to the client.

        ii. If a write request receives fewer successful responses than required by the quorum, the proxy server asks the container ring for additional nodes (handoff nodes) running container servers that will store the data. In the case of a write or delete operation, the handoff nodes will eventually propagate the data back to the primary storage nodes, through the replicator consistency processes.

        iii. If not enough successful responses are received before a timeout elapses, the proxy server returns an error to the client.

    b. Once a quorum of successful responses is received, the proxy node will process the responses from the storage servers (removing internal data that should not be passed back to the user, etc.) and format a data structure representing an HTTP response.

    c. That data structure is passed back out through the middleware pipeline until it exits the outermost middleware, and the WSGI-compliant web server sends it to the client as an HTTP response with headers.

The major parts of this sequence are illustrated in Figure 13-2.

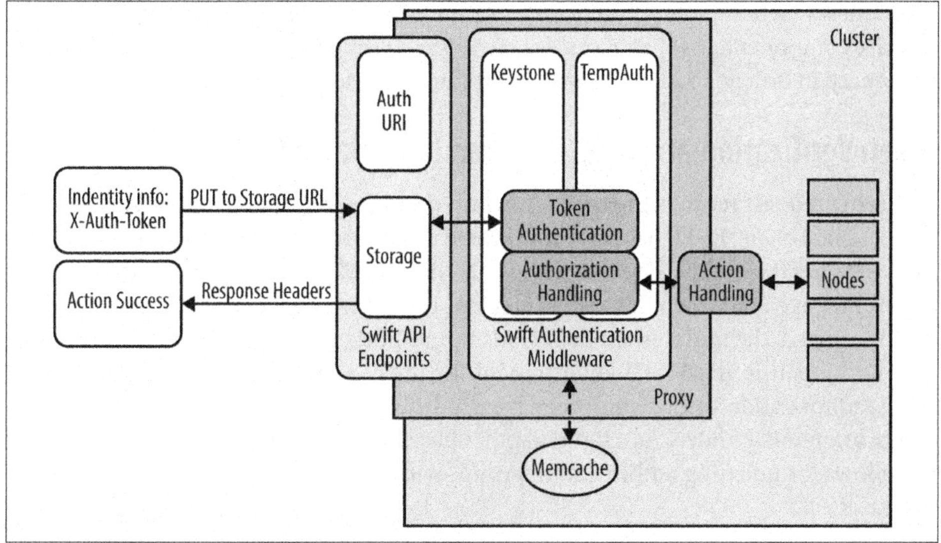

Figure 13-2. A request passing through authorization

As you can tell, there are many processes and components involved in authorization. Broadly, we can look at the authorization process as consisting of the initial storage request, the verification of the token by the proxy (via Memcache), the lookup of authorization group information in Memcache, and finally a comparison of the user's authorization groups against the authorization groups permitted to perform the requested operation on the resource (e.g., read the object).

Let's look at each of the major steps in more detail.

Storage Request Processing

Each time authenticated users want to send a request to a resource's storage URL, they provide the auth token and the HTTP method (e.g., `GET`, `PUT`) that they want to perform on the resource. One example would be creating a container called `tupperwarecontainer` in account `AUTH_bob`. That command using cURL might look like:

```
$ curl -i -X PUT -H "x-auth-token: AUTH_tkb5bab9e25a274b4a853fe2587b5dc8f9" \
    http://swift.example.com/v1/AUTH_bob/tupperwarecontainer
```

The request goes to the Swift API endpoint, where it is received by a WSGI-compliant web server running the Swift proxy code. First, the web server receives the request, and parses it into the WSGI request environment data structure. The WSGI request environment now contains the information that this is a `PUT` request, it was submitted with an `x-auth-token` header with the value `AUTH_tk...`, the URL was *http://swift.example.com/v1/AUTH_bob/tupperwarecontainer*, and other details. That WSGI request environment now passes through the middleware pipeline. At some point in the pipeline, the request reaches the first (often only) auth middleware component. That auth middleware component now has access (via the WSGI request environment) to all the data it will need in order to determine whether it can authenticate and authorize this request.

Token Verification and Authorization Information Lookup

When the request reaches the first Swift auth middleware, its auth token (the value of the `X-Auth-Token` HTTP header) is examined. If the prefix of the token (`AUTH_`, in this case) matches the middleware's reseller prefix (described in "Creating the authentication token" on page 200), then the token is looked up in Memcache. If the token is present and unexpired, the middleware then loads the authorization information from Memcache and sets it in the WSGI environment for the core proxy server to check against later. Authorization information may have a different cache expiration time than authentication tokens have. As a typical authentication cache expiration time is 24 hours, this allows for updating authorization groups without waiting a full day for the update to take effect.

The auth middleware populates the WSGI request environment with the user's authorization information, but the request is not authorized or refused as it passes through the auth middleware. Instead, that occurs in the core proxy server code. After passing through all the middleware, the updated WSGI request environment (including the list of authorization groups associated with the request's auth token) reaches the core proxy server code. The proxy server process is then ready to inspect the resource URL and HTTP method, and determine whether the request is authorized. However, the question of *how* to determine whether a request is authorized—how to use the authorization groups, where to find the resource's authorized groups, etc.—is a function that must live in the auth middleware code, not in the core proxy server. This is intentional: core Swift does not lock you into any particular auth system. Therefore, the core proxy server code must delegate authorization back to the auth middleware, even though the request has already passed through the auth middleware by the time it gets to the core proxy server.

To work around this obstacle, the middleware sets the `swift.authorize` value in the WSGI request environment so the proxy services will be able to trigger a callback later to perform the authorization for the specific request. The request is then passed to the next auth middleware. In addition to keeping auth concerns out of core Swift, another reason the authorization data is set but not used right away is that a second auth middleware further down the pipeline might modify that data and invalidate a previously set authorization.

Authorization Callback and Response

After the request has gone through the gauntlet of middleware, it is passed to the core proxy server code. The core proxy server will see a request that needs authorization, and trigger the callback via the WSGI environment's `swift.authorize` value. If the callback returns a positive response, the core proxy server will then process the request. If the callback returns a negative response, the core proxy server doesn't yet have confirmation that the request is allowed, but it isn't a final rejection. The core proxy server will add some additional information and do a callback with `swift.authorize` again. This second callback is referred to as the `delay_denial` authorization path. It is used in circumstances that require an additional data lookup. If Swift can authorize the request without the expense of the additional lookup, it will prefer to do that. If not, it must try the more expensive authorization path, via delayed denial. Delayed denial can be thought of as "This request doesn't look authorized, but I'm not yet positive, so I need to do more work."

The `delay_denial` authorization path is necessary when container-level authorization must be checked. For the `delay_denial` request, the proxy server fetches the container-level read and/or write access control metadata (`X-Container-Read`, `X-Container-Write`) from the container server. This additional data is then passed in during the second call to `swift.authorize`. If that second call returns positive authorization, the core proxy server code passes the request to the correct storage nodes that should handle the request. If the second authorization attempt still fails, the request is known with certainty to be unauthorized, and the proxy node returns a `403 Forbidden` response to the client.

Once the storage node has handled the request, it will return a success or failure to the proxy node. The proxy server process then sends that response back to the client.

Having discussed the mechanics of how Swift implements authorization and how the flow of control is handed off in the course of a request, we'll now address the higher-level question of what kinds of authorization can be granted.

Authorization and Access Levels

Swift supports access control at two levels: the account level and the container level. The responsibility for interpreting and enforcing access control rules falls to the authentication and authorization system, rather than to core Swift. However, the following access control patterns are defined in core Swift, and auth systems are generally expected to follow them.

Account-level access control grants privileges over an entire account. For example, account-level *read-only* access allows designated users to read anything (except privileged security-related metadata) in the account. Account-level *read-write* access adds the ability to create and overwrite objects, containers, and (unprivileged) metadata in the account. Account-level *admin* access, also known as *swift_owner* access, represents full privileges equivalent to ownership of the account.

Container-level access control grants privileges within a specific container. Because this type of access operates at the container level, a user might have certain permissions in some containers in another user's account, but different permissions (or no permissions) in other containers.

The access levels for containers are simply "read" and "write." Users might have container read access and be able to download any object within the container, or have container write access and be able to upload objects to the container, or have both read and write access to the container.

Container-level access control can also be used to grant permissions to unauthenticated users to read and/or write objects within the container. This anonymous access can be universal (users may read and/or write at any time) or based on the HTTP "Referer" [sic] header of a web-based request. You can use the latter to attempt to restrict access so that objects in the container are available only from a website that the owner controls, but this is more of a minor obstacle to interlopers than a real security measure. (Anyone can insert the Referer header, if the required Referer is known.)

Account-Level Access Control

Account-level access control is used to grant permission to access objects throughout the account, to create or delete new containers, or to access account metadata. It is also the best way to manage a cluster where accounts correlate with projects rather than with users. If each project has a Swift account, users who are project team members (or role identities for servers) might all have admin access to the account, or team leads might have admin access while others have read-write access, for example.

Account-level access control is governed by the `X-Account-Access-Control` header. The value of that header should be a JSON dictionary. For auth systems that follow the TempAuth model, that dictionary may have any combination of three keys: `read-only`, `read-write`, and `admin`. The value of any of these keys should be a JSON list of authorization groups who are permitted that level of access. Bear in mind that authorization groups are automatically created for individual users, under most auth systems, by using the auth system prefix. For example, user bob gets a default authorization group named AUTH_bob if the auth middleware's system prefix is AUTH_. Other authorization groups are defined by the auth middleware.

We describe the access levels in the following sections. Again, these descriptions technically only apply to TempAuth and auth systems like it, but the guidelines are the result of an extended discussion in the Swift community and are likely to apply to other auth systems that implement account-level access control.

Read-Only Access

Read-only access might sound restricted, but a user with read-only account-level access can download any object in the account, list objects in any container in the account, list all containers in the account, and view any unprivileged metadata about objects, containers, or the account itself.

Read-Write Access

Read-write account access confers all the privileges of read-only access, plus the ability to create objects, overwrite objects, create new containers, delete objects or (empty) containers, and set any unprivileged container or object metadata. Often this access level is powerful enough for most normal usage.

Admin Access

Admin account access grants full ownership of the account to the authorization groups in the list. A user with admin-level account access is a *swift_owner* of the account, with permission to do anything within that account.

Users with admin access can set account metadata, including privileged metadata such as the `X-Account-Access-Control` header. In other words, users with admin access may grant admin access to additional users, or revoke admin access from users.

JSON for Account Access Control

Because the `X-Account-Access-Control` header contains a JSON dictionary with keys corresponding to the access categories just described, the values of those keys are JSON lists with elements corresponding to the authorization groups that have been granted that access. So this header might look like this (it is a single line, but has been broken to fit the page):

```
X-Account-Access-Control:
  {"admin":["AUTH_alice","sysadmins"],"read-only":["AUTH_bob"]}
```

Note the missing `read-write` key in this example; missing keys are allowed. Although JSON is not the most complex format, it's still easy to make a typo or forget a closing brace or bracket, so it is generally a bad idea to construct these headers by hand. Swift's `common.middleware.acl` module provides a better mechanism:

```
from common.middleware.acl import format_acl
acls = {"admin": admin_list, "read-write": readwrite_list,
                             "read-only": readonly_list}
header = format_acl(version=2, acl_dict=acls)
```

If you write Python code to generate the ACL header value as shown, Python can provide syntax checking for you. On the other hand, if you manually generate a *cURL* command line, for example, there is no mechanism to check for typos.

Once the `X-Account-Access-Control` metadata is stored, designated users are granted the specified access.

Account-level access control requires version 2 of Swift's ACL syntax. Version 2 of the syntax provides many useful features, including Unicode support and forward compatibility with future versions. Container ACLs, described next, currently use version 1 of the ACL syntax.

Container-Level Access Control

Container-level access control is used to set up a container, or a fixed number of containers, as collaboration areas. When access needs to be granted only to specific containers or objects, the *container ACLs* may be set to allow this more granular access. This level of access is checked by the proxy during the authentication of a request only if the account-level access was not granted already. This avoids the somewhat expensive access control metadata retrieval, which is unnecessary when an account owner makes a request on her own account. Container ACLs might be sufficient for a Swift cluster where accounts are created in a one-account-per-user model. However, if accounts are not created one-per-user, account-level access control will definitely be required to grant access.

A user with *swift_owner* privileges on an account may grant container-level read or write access to a specific container by issuing a `PUT` or `POST` request to the container's URL with the `X-Container-Read` and/or `X-Container-Write` headers set. Note that the orthogonal `-Read` and `-Write` headers allow for read-only access (e.g., for a website) or write-only access (e.g., for an FTP-like file drop application, where clients should not see each other's uploads). A user would be required to be on both lists in order to gain read-write access.

The format of the container ACL is a comma-separated list of any combination of the following:

- Authorization groups: groups of which the user is a member (according to the auth system). For most auth systems, a user `alice` has a corresponding group `AUTH_alice` of which `alice` is the only member. In addition, `alice` might be a member of other authorization groups, as determined by the auth middleware.
- Referrers: domain names from which access is permitted regardless of username, preceded with `.r:`. (`.ref:`, `.referer:`, or `.referrer:` may be used as aliases for `.r:`; internally they are rewritten to `.r:` to save space.) Referrers may be added to the list with a leading minus sign to prohibit access rather than grant it; this allows

combinations like `.r:foo.com, .r:-untrusted.foo.com`. Asterisk wildcards are also permitted, the most common use being `.r:*` to grant global read access to a container.

- The keyword `.rlistings`, to indicate that clients should be allowed to retrieve a list of objects within the container (in addition to being allowed to retrieve the objects themselves by URL).

So a container ACL with a little of everything might look like this:

```
X-Container-Read: AUTH_alice,AUTH_bob,mygrp,.r:foo.com,.r:-bad.foo.com,.rlistings
```

Note that matching referrer ACL items later in a list override earlier ones, so it's necessary to specify `.r:foo.com,.r:-bad.foo.com` rather than the other way around!

Container ACL Examples

We'll now present a few examples of container ACLs and their uses. If you want to try these out, we recommend setting environment variables so you have to do less typing through these examples. The `swift` CLI respects the following environment variables automatically:

```
export OS_PASSWORD=your_password_here
export OS_AUTH_URL=http://localhost:5000/v2.0
export OS_USERNAME=admin
export OS_TENANT_NAME=admin
export OS_AUTH_TOKEN=AUTH_tkb5bab9e25a274b4a853fe2587b5dc8f9
```

For the `curl` examples, you might want to set your own environment variables, such as the following:

```
export TOKEN=AUTH_tk12345   # as retrieved with an auth request
export STORAGE_URL=https://swift.example.com/v1/AUTH_myaccount
```

ACLs can be set with the Swift CLI using a `POST` request with the read option (`-r`) and the write option (`-w`). For example, if you wish to allow the user called `bob` to read objects in the container `thiscontainer` in your own account, you can issue:

```
$ swift post -r 'bob' thiscontainer
```

Or using `curl`:

```
$ curl -H "X-Auth-Token: $TOKEN" -X POST -H "X-Container-Read: bob" \
    $STORAGE_URL/thiscontainer
```

When using a Swift account to serve up web pages from a container, you'll need to enable the StaticWeb middleware and allow referrers to reach the container. As with allowing requests based on authenticated Swift user identities (as shown above), allowing requests based on their HTTP referrer is also done using container ACLs. However, this type of access must be broader, as it isn't tied to an authenticated Swift user. To set up access based on the HTTP referrer, the syntax is `.r:` followed by a list of allowed referring domains. If you want to grant access to *all* referring domains (which is common if you want the container to be generally accessible from the Web), you can use * as the domain. For example, this command allows all referring domains to access any object in the container `thiscontainer`:

```
$ swift post -r '.r:*' thiscontainer
```

Or again, using `curl`:

```
$ curl -H "X-Auth-Token: $TOKEN" -X POST -H "X-Container-Read: .r:*" \
  $STORAGE_URL/thiscontainer
```

Swift Authentication Systems

Two auth systems are distributed with every Swift installation: Keystone and TempAuth. However, these two are by no means the only auth systems that can be used with Swift. Other auth systems can be obtained from community open source projects, purchased from vendors, or created using custom middleware.

Keystone

Keystone is the OpenStack project that provides identity services for OpenStack components. As a result, Keystone is often the auth middleware of choice for projects that integrate with more than one OpenStack service, such as storing operating system images and snapshots. Swift has middleware (`swift.common.middleware.keystoneauth`) that allows it to authenticate against Keystone.

Setting up Keystone auth on Swift is fairly easy. Once a Keystone server is running, you should add a service endpoint for Swift. In the Swift proxy server configuration file *proxy-server.conf*, add the `authtoken` and `keystoneauth` middleware packages (in that order) to your pipeline.

For more information, please refer to the Keystone documentation on the `authtoken` middleware, to the Keystone Auth section of the Swift documentation (*http://bit.ly/keystone-auth*), and to the "Configuring Swift to use Keystone" webpage (*http://bit.ly/config-keys*).

TempAuth

Don't use TempAuth for production deployments!

TempAuth was originally designed to be used for testing Swift's auth middleware integration internally. It stores a list of usernames and passwords *in the clear* in the *proxy-server.conf* file, and is therefore not suitable for production deployments!

TempAuth is the other middleware auth system shipped with Swift. As already mentioned, it is intended for testing rather than production, but it is a complete auth system. TempAuth stores usernames, passwords, and group membership (particularly membership in the `.reseller_admin` group) in its middleware configuration section in the *proxy-server.conf* file, which is as insecure as it sounds. In addition to the security concern, this also means that whenever a user is added or a password is changed, the proxy server process must be restarted.

Although TempAuth is not suitable for production deployments, depending on your security considerations it might be sufficient for test clusters. Additionally, because it is a reference implementation of a fully functional (if poorly persisted) auth middleware, it has served as a template for the development of several other auth middleware packages.

TempAuth accepts usernames in the format `accountname:username`, so that the same Swift account (storage location) may be accessed by many users. For example, an account with a storage URL *https://example.swift.com/v1/AUTH_acct1* might be accessed by users `acct1:user1` and `acct1:user2`. These two users would have different passwords, different group memberships, and so forth.

Once it authenticates, TempAuth grants authorization access based on user type and groups. TempAuth has the concept of admin (account-level access) and non-admin (container-level access) users within an account.

The other way to gain access is through group permissions. TempAuth supports one privileged group: a user who is part of the `.reseller_admin` group can access any account.

You can learn more about TempAuth at Swift's overview page on the auth system (*http://bit.ly/authsystem*).

SWAuth

SWAuth (*http://bit.ly/gholt-auth*) is an auth middleware component for Swift that uses Swift itself to store account data. It has the advantages of not requiring the potentially complex deployment of another system (such as LDAP), and of having the authentication information stored in Swift's highly available infrastructure. It has the disadvantage of requiring a full Swift retrieval operation for each uncached auth operation, and there are certainly systems that are better optimized than Swift for the task of authenticating users.

SwiftStack allows you to configure and deploy SWAuth auth middleware through the Controller.

SwiftStack Authentication Systems

To best meet the needs of its varied users, SwiftStack created a custom auth system called SwiftStack Auth. Also, SwiftStack supports custom middleware for some of the most popular auth systems such as LDAP.

SwiftStack Auth

SwiftStack Auth (*http://bit.ly/ss-auth*), the default auth system in SwiftStack, provides an auth mechanism that is simple and fairly scalable (to the order of 25,000 users) to support a variety of uses. Although similar in structure to TempAuth, the SwiftStack auth system does not suffer from the drawbacks that make TempAuth unsuitable for production. SwiftStack Auth does not store passwords in clear text, and does not require a restart of the proxy servers whenever new users and accounts are added.

The SwiftStack Auth system is designed to be fast and simple. A flat file is deployed on each proxy node with hashed passwords, which the auth system periodically checks for changes. Due to this mechanism, a proxy restart is not required when users are added or removed. New users can be added via the SwiftStack Controller web interface. Alternatively, you can use the SwiftStack Controller's RESTful API to programmatically add and remove users, allowing integration between the Controller and other components of your system. SwiftStack Auth is a good choice for application development where it is relatively rare (no more than a couple of times per day, say) to alter passwords or add or remove users.

Unlike many auth systems, SwiftStack Auth supports immediate revocation of tokens. Most auth systems revoke access by refusing to issue new tokens, but existing tokens continue to work for the remainder of their lifetimes, which by default is 24 hours. SwiftStack Auth supports an administrative API call to revoke the token immediately. This token revocation functionality is also available for the SwiftStack LDAP and SwiftStack Active Directory implementations described next.

SwiftStack LDAP

LDAP (Lightweight Directory Access Protocol) is a well-known industry standard for enterprise-scale distributed authentication. If you have thousands of users, and especially if you want to integrate Swift with your organization's existing internal services, LDAP authentication is likely to be the best option.

SwiftStack offers LDAP authentication middleware that integrates with its SwiftStack Controller product. This middleware allows you to specify any of several ways to map a username (e.g., `bob`) to an LDAP *distinguished name* or *DN* such as `uid=bob,ou=Engineering,dc=example,dc=com`. In LDAP, distinguished names fill the role of primary keys in a database: lookups are done using the DN as a key. However, no one wants to log in using the full, overly verbose DN. Depending on your organization's LDAP schema, you might prefer to use a fixed template (conceptually, something like `uid=<...>,ou=Employees,dc=example,dc=com`), execute an LDAP search (find an entry using *LDAP attribute*-based criteria such as `userid=bob`), use LDAP PosixGroup or GroupOfNames membership as the LDAP-level authorization test, use attribute-based blacklists or whitelists, or another option.

See the "LDAP-based Authentication for SwiftStackAuth" webpage (*http://bit.ly/ssauth-ldap*) for information on authenticating with LDAP using SwiftStack.

SwiftStack Active Directory

SwiftStack also supports Microsoft's Active Directory (AD) for authentication. AD is a special-purpose database to manage large numbers of network-originating read and search operations. Data is stored in AD so that it can be seamlessly replicated; it is built on a hierarchical model and is very extensible. Many Microsoft products and end-user organizations store user contact data, printer queue information, and specific computer or network configuration data in AD.

AD relies heavily on DNS. Most administrators let AD manage and provide DNS services for all Windows computers. This facilitates the automatic registration of Windows computers that have recently started or joined the domain.

SwiftStack's AD authentication requires a Windows 2008 R2 or later implementation of AD. The AD auth module in SwiftStack is an optional add-on that you can enable for your cluster. When enabled in the Controller, you simply add your AD domain controller and other information to set up your AD integration.

For additional information on the SwiftStack AD add-on, contact a SwiftStack representative (*contact@swiftstack.com*) to request a copy of the SwiftStack Active Directory guide.

Conclusion

Auth is a complex topic. Or rather, auth comprises *many* complex topics.

We reviewed how, in the interest of providing a flexible and open storage platform, Swift has decided to implement auth services as middleware, rather than tying Swift to a single auth system. We saw authentication from the client's perspective: make an auth request and present your credentials, get a token in return, and use that token for storage requests. We discussed auth tokens, expiration times, and periodic re-authentication in more detail. We emphasized that a successful (Version 1) authentication request returns an auth token and the storage URL for the user's primary account.

We reminded you that Swift *users* are identities, and Swift *accounts* are storage areas, because that point bears repeating to clear up a common point of confusion.

We dove into the implementation details of how auth middleware is responsible for defining how authorization happens (via a callback stored in the `swift.authorize` key in the WSGI environment), even though authorization doesn't actually take place until the request is all the way through the middleware pipeline and in the core proxy server code. We further discussed delayed denial, which occurs when the core proxy server hopes to make a fast authorization decision but learns that it must query a container server in certain situations, such as in order to determine whether the incoming request is authorized at the container level.

Container-level access control allows you, as an account owner, to grant others the ability to read objects in a container within your account, to grant others the ability to write objects to a container within your account, or both. These privileges are granted on a per-container basis, meaning that you may grant the same user different privileges in different containers.

Account-level access control has three levels: read-only, read-write, and admin. Even read-only account access grants a user the privilege to read any object or (unprivileged) metadata in the account. Read-write access grants a user full control over data in the account, and admin access additionally grants control over account metadata, including privileged metadata such as the access control lists themselves. A user with admin access is an owner of the account, in every sense.

We finished the chapter with a quick review of some of the most popular authentication systems we've seen used with Swift. All of these make trade-offs among simplicity, scalability, and ease of integration. Different organizations will make different choices about which auth system is best.

We hope this provides a better understanding of how authentication, authorization, and access control work in Swift, and, most importantly, how they can best meet your particular needs.

CHAPTER 14

Cluster Tuning and Optimization

Hugo Kuo

When you first set up a cluster, the number of configuration settings and middleware options can seem a tad overwhelming. In this chapter, we'll cover options that new cluster operators might find useful to tune their clusters as well as optimize the cluster and user experience. Some adjustments might seem obvious right away, while others will become apparent after you have done some testing and benchmarking from Chapter 17. In addition to using existing middleware, you might find that custom middleware best fits your needs. More information about custom middleware can be found in Chapter 8.

Although most of the following settings are part of Swift, we point out some that are outside your cluster, but can have an impact on it.

Swift Settings

Tuning will have a dramatic impact on the performance of a Swift cluster. Numerous settings can be adjusted for the account, container, object, and proxy server processes to enhance your Swift cluster. Many can be found in the configuration files of the servers:

- Proxy: *proxy-server.conf*
- Account: *account-server.conf*
- Container: *container-server.conf*
- Object: *object-server.conf*

Here are some of the most common tuning settings for a cluster:

Workers

Worker processes are the ones carrying most of the weight in Swift. Each server hands over requests to worker processes, and each worker can handle multiple requests simultaneously using Eventlet, a multithreading library that provides high concurrency in Python. Eventlet creates and manages threads internally (green threads) instead of spawning operating-system threads, which require more resources.

Normally, each system creates one worker thread per CPU, and creates more worker threads if the system load requires it. You can change this through the `worker` configuration setting. A single worker can handle up to 1,024 requests simultaneously. So if you know that 10,000 simultaneous concurrent requests are expected to come in to your cluster, then you need at least 10 workers (10,000/1,024, rounded up to the nearest integer). Each server configuration file (*.conf*) allows a `workers` setting specific to that server (Table 14-1).

Table 14-1. Proxy, account, container, and object servers

Setting	Default	Purpose
`workers`	*auto* (one worker for each CPU core on the system)	Sets integer value for the number of workers created during system startup. Zero means no workers will be created at startup, although they will be started later when needed. Increasing the number of workers might reduce the chance that slow filesystem operations in one request will interfere with other requests. However, this might not be as efficient as tuning the `threads_per_disk` option (described in "Object workers and server threads per disk" on page 221.

Proxy server workers

The proxy server should have a lot of CPUs because its workload tends to be CPU-bound, as explained in "CPU" on page 164. The default number of workers, one per CPU core, is a good starting point.

Account and container workers

The account, container, and object server processes are not only juggling network traffic from the proxy, but accessing data on disk as well. Account and container server processes store and retrieve data in their SQLite databases. Therefore, each system should have enough workers so that your loadable filesystem operations—such as read and write—don't end up starving the Eventlet event loop.

This is because asynchronous network I/O works great, but asynchronous file I/O on pretty much every platform is terrible. So it's important to remember that a read or write system call on Linux can block.

The best `workers` setting will depend on your hardware and your network configuration. We won't give you specific numbers, because you should test your cluster as described in "Benchmarking Goals and Tools" on page 278 and base your setting on what's happening on the cluster.

A good starting point, however, is to run one or two processes per spindle or one per CPU core.

Object workers and server threads per disk

Object server processes, like the account and container server processes, are juggling network traffic from the proxy server processes as well as accessing data on disk. The data in this case, naturally, is the objects.

For object server processes, you want to be sensitive to the request latency of your clients as you put load into the cluster. If you have too few object server processes, and your disks are starting to get saturated, you can expect your clients to see inconsistent latency.

Let's say your client is trying to pull a 3 GB file out. If other people or other concurrent connections are working the disk pretty hard, some reads and writes will get blocked. This is because other connections in the same thread or worker as your large file stream will end up blocking the stream.

The older method of minimizing such contention was to configure a larger number of object workers. Since Swift 1.9, a more robust configuration has been available. Set the Object Server `threads-per-disk` option to a value of 3 or 4, maintaining the following constraint:

$$\text{object server workers} \times (1 + \text{threads-per-disk} \times \text{number of disks}) \leq 1000$$

Now do benchmarking to find out whether your settings give you the performance you need.

Chunk Size

When the proxy server receives a request, it reads data from the client in chunks. You want your chunk sizes to be large enough for your system calls into the kernel to get a decent amount of data back, while incurring as little overhead as possible.

The options you can tune are:

Client chunk size for the proxy server
: The amount of data the proxy server reads from and writes to the client at one time.

Object chunk size for the proxy server
: The amount of data that the proxy server reads from and writes to the account, container, and object servers. The objects are the important data to chunk.

Disk chunk size for the object server
: The amount of data that the object server reads from and writes to the disks on its node.

Network chunk size for the object server
: The amount of data that the object server reads from and writes to the proxy server.

On the proxy server, different client and object chunk sizes might be useful when your internal storage network is different from the public access network over which the proxy server communicates with clients. The traffic coming to the proxy server is not jumbo framed because it's coming in off the Internet, but you can bump up the object chunk size because it's on a nice fat LAN connection coming from the proxy server to the storage nodes.

Specifying a large chunk size on network connections allows the kernel to allocate large buffers, and is likely to be a more efficient use of network bandwidth, but if anything goes wrong with transmitting the large chunk, the client will need to retransmit a potentially large amount of data. This is appropriate in environments with minimal network contention and with clients and servers that have substantial memory available for buffers. Specifying a smaller chunk size makes the complementary trade-off, reducing the need for retransmission but with more overhead in network usage.

Although we're not going to give you any hard numbers, you can tune this and see how the CPU use of your proxy servers under a given load changes. If you drop the client chunk size down to something like 1024 bytes, or anything lower than the maximum transmission unit (MTU) of your jumbo frame network, you might see an increase in CPU use. If you are communicating with your clients over the Internet, data transmissions are already divided into units for transmission, so there's tuning to be done there as well.

So when should you use a larger chunk size? What are the trade-offs between small and large chunk sizes?

A decent rule of thumb is to start with a large size, and if that produces trouble, drop it down some. For example, a chunk size of 64 kilobytes is asking the kernel to send 64 K to Swift all at once, while the client might be trickling the data in or out more slowly than that. That means that a read system call will not be blocking because you're using nonblocking network I/O, but you can have higher latency between asking for that chunk and dealing with the chunk.

In some cases, a call could take so long that you might think there's a timeout or the client just went quiet on you. In fact, the client is just dribbling data in so slowly that the kernel's network buffer hasn't filled up in order to satisfy your read request. So you don't want to set the chunk size too high.

On the other hand, if you set it too low, you add more overhead for system calls going in and out of the kernel for each little chunk of data. That's the trade-off you need to negotiate.

Again, testing the size with your workload is really the way to determine the best chunk sizes for your cluster.

Settings for Background Daemons

In addition to the servers, Swift also runs background daemons—specifically auditors, replicators, updaters, and the reaper. These processes run where account, container, or object server processes are running. They are also discussed in Chapter 3.

When tuning Swift, it is important to know how these processes work and how they can be configured. One of the common concerns that Swift operators have when starting to use Swift is the amount of resources consumed by the background processes. When folks start up their Swift cluster and put a bunch of data in it, we often hear, "Oh my gosh, look at all of the disk I/O traffic—there's read I/O all over the place and there's only a little trickle of write I/O! What's going on here? I'm not even running swift-bench or any other benchmarking tool!"

What's happening is that the background daemons are doing their job.

However, if that level of background work is too high and you want to rein them in, here are some settings you should know about.

Auditors

Auditors are responsible for ensuring the integrity of the stored data. They constantly check it to catch bit rot and other ways that the data can go stale. Even though you will have three or more replicas of the data, you don't want to just let it sit unattended.

Although these processes are critical, they do create a load. The following settings can be used to rate-limit the auditing process, which will subsequently rate-limit its load on the I/O subsystem or CPU.

The account and container auditors run at intervals. As long-running processes, they sleep between their runs for a time determined by their `interval` settings (Table 14-2).

Table 14-2. Account and container auditors

Setting	Default	Purpose
`interval`	1800	Time in seconds to elapse before starting a new pass of the auditor.

For the object auditor, you can set three different intervals: `files_per_second`, `bytes_per_second`, and `zero-byte-files-per-second`.

Table 14-3. Object auditor

Option	Default	Purpose
`files_per_second`	20	Maximum files audited per second. Should be tuned according to individual system specs. Zero means unlimited.
`bytes_per_second`	10000000 (ten million)	Maximum bytes audited per second. Should be tuned according to individual system specs. Zero means unlimited.
`zero-byte-files-per-second`	50	This setting applies to zero-byte (empty) files.

Replicators

Replicators are the processes that carry out Swift's eventual consistency guarantee and synchronize missing data within the cluster.

Two primary replicator settings can be tuned: `concurrency` and `run-pause` (see Tables 14-4 and 14-5). `concurrency` is the number of simultaneous outstanding requests each replicator has. If that gets too high, you will see more rsync traffic and more request traffic as one server asks the other, "Hey, what version of this do you have?" The `run-pause` setting is the period of time that the replicator will sleep between its runs.

Table 14-4. Account and container replicators

Option	Default	Purpose
`concurrency`	8	Number of replication workers running simultaneously on the node.
`run_pause`	30	Time in seconds to wait between replication passes.

Table 14-5. Object replicator

Option	Default	Purpose
`concurrency`	1	Number of replication workers running simultaneously on the node.
`run_pause`	30	Time in seconds to wait between replication passes.

Reapers

When a user issues a delete, the request is recorded in the account so that no one can subsequently retrieve the data, but the delete is not carried out immediately. The account reaper comes through eventually and actually removes the objects in the containers within the account, then eventually removes the account record. The account reaper runs at intervals, sleeping between runs, and with each pass completes more of the deletion. The removal is done asynchronously because it can be an expensive operation, depending on the size of the data involved.

The two settings that can be adjusted for the account reaper are `concurrency` and `interval` (Table 14-6).

`concurrency` is the number of items to do in parallel. With higher `concurrency`, you're able to do more and get higher throughput, but at the same time you increase the load on the system. So if you want to lower the load, you can lower the `concurrency`.

However, there's a trade-off here. If you lower the `concurrency`, you'll raise the time it takes from start to finish to clean up a given workload. A lower `concurrency` might therefore require a higher `interval` to allow the reaper to finish its job.

Table 14-6. Account reaper

Option	Default	Purpose
`concurrency`	25	Number of reapers running simultaneously on the node.
`interval`	3600	Time in milliseconds to elapse before starting a new pass of the reaper.

Updaters

Updaters ensure that the listings in account and container databases are correct.

The container updater is responsible for keeping the container listings in the accounts up-to-date. Additionally, it updates the object count, container count, and bytes used in the account metadata.

The object updater has a similar responsibility for keeping the object listings in the containers correct. However, the object updater is running as a redundancy. The object server process has the primary responsibility of updating the object listing in the container. Should it fail to do so, the update is queued locally (as async pending), where the object updater will then attempt to update the container listing as well as the object count and bytes used in the container metadata.

For updaters, there are three variables that you can adjust: `interval`, `concurrency`, and `slowdown` (Tables 14-7 and 14-8).

The `concurrency` and `interval` settings for updaters behave like those for the account reaper. Concurrency is the number of items to do in parallel. With higher concurrency, you're able to do more and get higher throughput, but at the same time you get higher load. So if you want to lower the load, you can lower the concurrency, but you might then have to raise the interval.

The `slowdown` setting is another rate-limiting variable that defines how long to sleep between every update. This allows for a bit more fine-grained control for slowing down the updaters.

Table 14-7. Object updater

Option	Default	Purpose
`concurrency`	1	Number of updaters running simultaneously on the node.
`interval`	300	Time in milliseconds to elapse before starting a new pass of the updater.

Option	Default	Purpose
`slowdown`	0.01	Time in seconds to wait between updating objects.

Table 14-8. Container updater

Option	Default	Purpose
`concurrency`	4	Number of updaters running simultaneously on the node.
`interval`	300	Time in milliseconds to elapse before starting a new pass of the updater.
`slowdown`	0.01	Time in seconds to wait between updating objects.

Expirers

The object expirer, which runs as the `swift-object-expirer` daemon, offers the scheduled deletion of objects. The Swift client includes the `X-Delete-At` or `X-Delete-After` headers during an object `PUT` or `POST` and the cluster automatically quits serving that object at the specified time. The cluster shortly thereafter removes the object from the system.

Usually, just one instance of the `swift-object-expirer` daemon needs to run for the whole cluster. This isn't exactly automatic failover/high availability, but if this daemon doesn't run for a few hours it should not be any real issue. The objects that have expired but have not yet been deleted will return a `404 Not Found` response if someone tries to `GET` or `HEAD` them. They'll just be deleted a bit later when the daemon is restarted.

Two settings can be adjusted for the object expirer in its *object-expirer.conf* configuration file: `concurrency` and `processes` (Table 14-9).

Table 14-9. Object expirer

Option	Default	Purpose
`concurrency`	1	Increase this value to get more concurrency. A concurrency of 1 might not be enough to delete expiring objects in a timely fashion for a particular Swift cluster.
`processes`	1	It is possible to run multiple daemons to do different parts of the work if a single process with a concurrency of more than 1 is not enough (see the sample configuration file for details).

To run the object expirer as multiple processes, set `processes` to the desired number, either in the configuration file or on the command line. This internally divides the object expirer work into the number of parts you request. You now have to run one process for each part, starting it with a `process` option to specify the part of the work to be done by a process. So, for example, if you'd like to run three processes, set `processes` to 3 and run one process with a `process` option of 0, one process with a `process` option of 1, and one process with a `process` option of 2. If you ask for multiple processes, you must make sure to run one for each part of the work, or that part of the work will not be done. The `process` option can be specified either on the command line or in the configuration file.

Externally Managed Settings

Although many variables can be tuned in Swift to improve performance, some settings are in other programs outside Swift. Here we describe some useful tunings. Max connections setting for rsync:: This parameter allows you to specify the maximum number of simultaneous connections you will allow. Any clients connecting when the maximum has been reached will receive a message telling them to try later. The default is 0, which means no limit. A negative value disables the module. This setting might in some cases be a limiting factor on replication traffic.

Enabling jumbo frames
: This allows the cluster to get decent throughput with high-bandwidth network connections. Even on a 1-gigabit network, you're going to get higher throughput with jumbo frames. All of your networking equipment in the chain also needs to be aware of jumbo frames, be capable of handling them, and have them enabled in the configuration. The tools for testing that configuration is outside the scope of this book.

`ip_conntrack_max`
: If your server handles a lot of connections, and you're using iptables, or any modules that involve connection tracking such as the ip_conntrack iptables module, you will likely need to bump up `ip_conntrack_max` from the default value (which depends on the RAM size). Connection tracking limits the number of simultaneous connections your system can have, which can lead to a system log message of "ip_conntrack:table full, dropping packet."

Swift Middleware

Administrators can enable various middleware to add functionality and better tune their Swift clusters. Some middleware comes bundled with Swift (found in the *swift/common/middleware* directory), while custom middleware from third parties or created by you can be added as well. More information about custom middleware can be found in Chapter 8. We covered bundled middleware in greater detail in Chapter 7; in this chapter, we are highlighting the most useful ones for a new cluster operator. Some are essential middleware and some are less commonly enabled middleware that might be useful for your deployment.

Middleware Pipeline

The middleware pipeline, defined in *proxy-server.conf*, defines the order in which middleware will be applied. Many middleware components are order-sensitive, so it is often important to be aware of interactions between components.

However, deducing the ordering requirements from first principles is often difficult. To simplify this task, we offer the following example pipeline, which contains nearly all of the most popular middleware that ships with Swift. Erase any components that you don't use, keep the ordering for the ones you do use, and the following should serve you well:

```
[pipeline:main]
pipeline = catch_errors gatekeeper crossdomain healthcheck proxy-logging
    cache container_sync bulk formpost tempurl slo dlo ratelimit tempauth
    authtoken keystoneauth staticweb container-quotas account-quotas
    proxy-logging proxy-server
```

Note that the `proxy-logging` middleware is in the pipeline twice. The earlier instance allows logging of requests that are handled early in the pipeline but that don't reach the core proxy-server code, such as auth requests. The later instance allows the logging of requests that are generated from within the middleware pipeline, such as when a user's single request for a large object turns into several requests for segments.

Essential Middleware

In this section we single out some of the middleware that most commonly comes bundled with Swift that you should find helpful. Which pieces of middleware are essential to your cluster will depend greatly on your situation and might include custom middleware from third parties or created by you.

TempAuth

TempAuth is lightweight middleware that supports most authentication features, such as ACLs. We recommend using TempAuth to validate your new Swift cluster after deploying.

Don't Use TempAuth in Production

Remember, TempAuth is not suitable for production deployments, because it stores passwords in the clear and requires proxy restarts for every username or password change.

The syntax of TempAuth user options is:

```
user_$ACCOUNT_$USERNAME = $PASSWORD $Role1 $Role2 .. $RoleN
user_tenant1_user1 = password .admin .reseller_admin
```

KeystoneAuth

Swift is able to authenticate against OpenStack Keystone (*http://docs.openstack.org/developer/keystone*). Keystone is OpenStack's standard identity service, which makes it easy to integrate with other OpenStack services.

In order to use the `keystoneauth` middleware, the `authtoken` middleware will also need to be configured.

The `authtoken` middleware performs the authentication token validation, and retrieves actual user authentication information. It can be found in the python-keystoneclient distribution. The `keystoneauth` middleware performs authorization and maps the keystone roles to Swift's ACLs.

Recon

Various metrics and telemetry can be obtained from the account, container, and object server processes using the Swift Recon middleware and the `swift-recon` command. To enable this middleware, update your account, container, or object servers' pipelines to include `recon`, and add it to the correct filter in the server configuration file. An example follows:

```
[pipeline:main]
pipeline = recon object-server

[filter:recon]
use = egg:swift#recon
recon_cache_path = /var/cache/swift
```

TempURL

This allows the creation of URLs that provide temporary access to objects. Add TempURL to your pipeline if you need to share objects temporarily.

To create such temporary URLs, first an `X-Account-Meta-Temp-URL-Key` header must be set on the Swift account. Then generate an HMAC-SHA1 (RFC 2104) signature. This uses the TempURL key (set in the header) to cryptographically sign the following set of information: the resource URI, the permitted HTTP method (e.g., `GET` or `PUT`), and the expiration time of the temporary permission. None of those can be changed without invalidating the signature, which is what makes TempURL perform as advertised.

The `swift-temp-url` command, part of the Swift installation, can be used to generate a temporary URL. The usage is:

```
swift-temp-url <method> <seconds> <path> <key>
```

The parameters are:

`method`
: The allowed method, e.g., an HTTP verb such as `GET`.

`seconds`
: The number of seconds, starting from when the URL is generated, that the URL will accept requests sent to it.

`path`
: The full path to the resource (example: */v1/AUTH_account/c/o*)

`key`
: The `X-Account-Meta-Temp-URL-Key` for the account.

An example output is:

```
/v1/AUTH_account/c/o?temp_url_sig=34d49efc32fe6e3082e411eeeb85bd8a
    &temp_url_expires=1323482948
```

For more information on TempURL, see Chapter 7.

Container quotas and account quotas

The `container_quotas` middleware package implements simple quotas that can be imposed on Swift containers by a user who has permissions to set container metadata, most likely the account administrator. This can be useful for limiting the scope of containers that are delegated to nonadmin users or exposed to form post uploads. It can also just be a self-imposed sanity check to prevent a runaway process from using up disk space.

The `account_quotas` middleware package blocks write requests (`PUT`, `POST`) if a given account quota (in bytes) is exceeded. `DELETE` requests are still allowed.

Dynamic and Static Large Objects

Swift places a limit on the size of a single uploaded object; by default this is 5 GB. However, the download size of a single object is allowed to be virtually unlimited. This is thanks to the concept of *segmentation*. Objects larger than the default size can be broken into acceptable-sized segments that are uploaded with a special manifest file. Then when a download of the object is requested, Swift uses the manifest to concatenate the segments into the one large object and return it to the requester. This offers much greater upload speed with the possibility of parallel uploads of the segments.

The Static Large Objects (SLO) feature consults a user-defined manifest of the object segments, and uses the manifest when it is time to stitch the object back together.

We recommend including the SLO middleware in your pipeline, unless you are certain that users will never want an object larger than the cluster's maximum size.

The Dynamic Large Objects (DLO) feature is similar to SLO, but allows the set of segments to be defined by a container name and an object prefix, thus determining the names of segments dynamically instead of from the manifest. See Example 14-1.

Example 14-1. Upload of a Dynamic Large Object through a swift command

```
swift upload test_container -S 1073741824 large_file
```

For more about SLO and DLO, see Chapter 7.

Most Useful Middleware

Depending on the needs of your cluster, some of the following middleware might be very helpful.

Rate limiting

Rate limiting is performed on requests that result in database writes to the account and container SQLite databases. Rate limiting uses Memcache and is dependent on the proxy servers synchronizing their times very closely. The rate limits are limited by the accuracy of the proxy server clocks.

Cluster info

Swift, by default, provides clients with an interface providing details about the installation. For instance, a `GET` request to */info* will return configuration data in JSON format. For more about cluster info, see Chapter 7. You can disable the exposure of this information by setting `expose_info=false` in the proxy server configuration.

Bulk Operations

The Bulk Operations middleware package allows the sending of a single request to the proxy server to upload or delete many objects or containers. Bulk operations are a great way to upload the entire contents of a tar file, or to delete large numbers of objects from multiple containers. For more information about this middleware, refer to Chapter 7.

Other Middleware

These pieces of middleware are perhaps less commonly used, but if there is a need for them in your deployment, you will find them to be quite valuable.

Swift3

Swift3 middleware allows access to OpenStack Swift via the Amazon S3 API. Usually, we recommend developing applications using the Swift HTTP API and one of the language bindings that wrap it. But if you're working with third-party applications outside your control, you might need an alternative means of accessing the cluster. The Swift3 middleware, available through GitHub (*https://github.com/fujita/swift3*), implements Amazon's S3 API, allowing clients written for that specification to access a Swift cluster. Although developed and distributed independently of Swift proper, it is bundled with SwiftStack for convenience. Once enabled, your Swift containers will emulate Amazon S3 buckets.

Cross-domain policies

Cross-domain middleware is used to respond to requests for cross-domain policy information. A request to the */crossdomain.xml* path will generate a cross-domain policy document in XML. This allows web pages hosted elsewhere to use client-side technologies such as Flash, Java, and Silverlight to interact with the Swift API. You should use a policy appropriate to your site.

Name Check

The Name Check middleware package is a filter that disallows any paths that contain forbidden characters you specify or that exceed a defined length.

proxy-logging

This is logging middleware for the Swift proxy. It serves as both the default logging implementation and an example of how to plug in your own logging format or system. As in "Middleware Pipeline" on page 227, the `proxy-logging` middleware package is in the pipeline twice. The earlier instance allows logging of requests that are handled early in the pipeline but that don't reach the core proxy-server code, such as auth requests. The later instance allows the logging of requests that are generated from within the middleware pipeline, such as when a user's single request for a large object turns into several requests for segments.

CatchErrors

This provides high-level error handling and ensures that a transaction ID will be set for every request.

GateKeeper

This is required middleware that will be enabled by default for a cluster. It imposes restrictions on the headers that may be included with requests and responses. Request headers are filtered to remove headers that should never be generated by a client. Similarly, response headers are filtered to remove private headers that should never be passed to a client.

Container sync

Swift can mirror all the contents of a container to another container through background synchronization. The cluster has to be configured to allow sync requests between clusters. The configuration file is distributed to all proxy and container servers.

The SwiftStack Approach

SwiftStack makes it easy to configure different options and enable middleware. To manage and change tuning settings, a user can go to the cluster's Tune tab on the Controller. There the account, container, object, and proxy tuning settings can be adjusted. To enable and configure middleware, a user can go to the cluster's Middleware tab (Figure 14-1).

When running benchmarks, you can also visualize the bottlenecks with a comprehensive set of graphs and then make appropriate adjustments on the Swift tuning page. The SwiftStack Controller will then automatically push out the updated configuration settings and reload the Swift processes, all without any client downtime. This ensures that you are getting the most out of your hardware and that you are optimizing the performance for your needs.

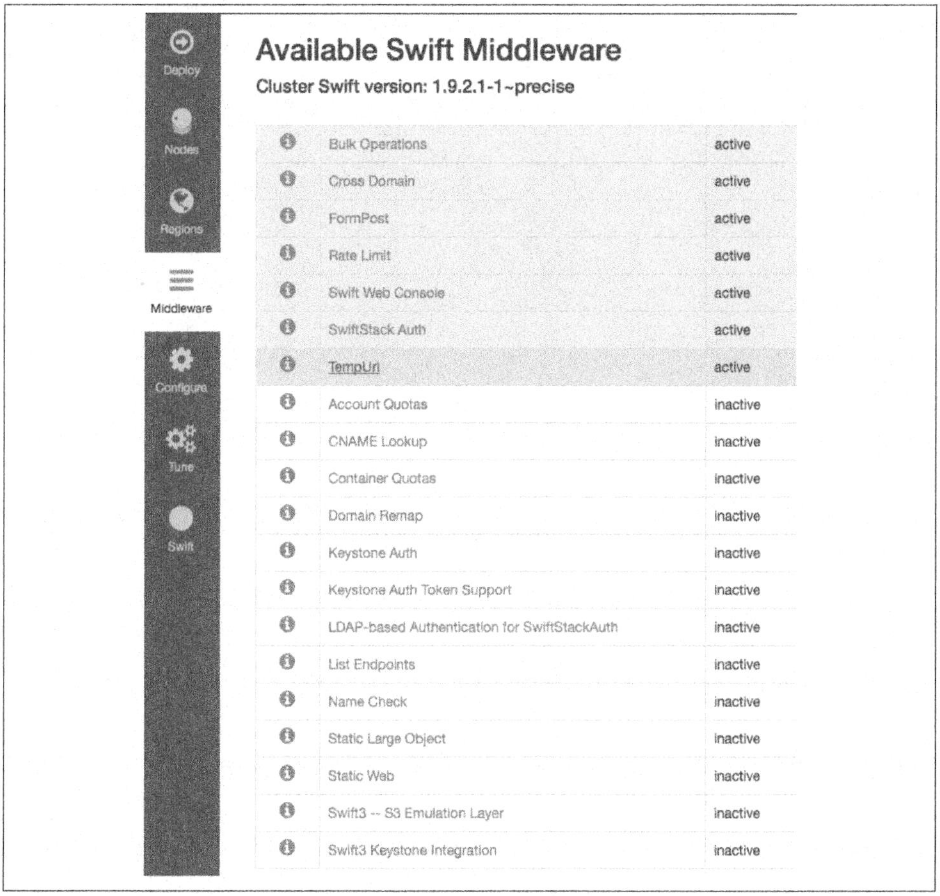

Figure 14-1. SwiftStack Middleware tab

Conclusion

Now you are aware of some key options for getting the best performance out of your cluster. In general, we've tried to give you a conceptual understanding of what the different tuning variables and useful middleware do so that you can experiment and determine what is best for you.

CHAPTER 15

Operating a Swift Cluster

Martin Lanner

In this chapter we move from installation to the everyday operations of a Swift cluster. We'll cover best practices for conducting day-to-day operational tasks, such as planning capacity additions and monitoring—whether you choose to do these in Swift or through SwiftStack. The recommendations and best practices in this chapter are based on our experiences building and operating both large and small clusters for a variety of workloads. By the end of this chapter, you'll have a good understanding of how to operate and monitor a Swift cluster and how SwiftStack automates many of these processes through the SwiftStack Controller.

Operational Considerations

Because Swift is a distributed system that is controlled by software, does not rely on RAID, and writes multiple copies of each object (file), operating a Swift cluster is fundamentally different from operating traditional storage systems such as storage area networks (SAN) or using network-attached storage (NAS) equipment.

When dealing with SANs and NASes, if a disk dies, the operator should make sure the bad disk is replaced right away to ensure that the RAID is rebuilt and is returned to full parity in the shortest time possible. With Swift, if a disk or even an entire node goes bad, it usually isn't a huge problem. The only time losing a drive or node can present issues is when a Swift cluster is small and very full. For example, if you have a three-node cluster that is 90% full, losing a few large disks or a node could cause problems because Swift might not have enough space to relocate data within the cluster.

How Swift Distributes Data

To understand how best to add and remove capacity in a Swift cluster, it is important to remember how Swift places data (discussed in more detail in "Locating the Data" on page 30).

Swift distributes data across disks in the cluster based on an as-unique-as-possible model. This data placement algorithm prefers locations that are in different regions, zones, nodes, and disks in order to minimize the risk of all replicas being lost. All data stored in Swift also has handoff locations defined, which are alternative data placement locations in the cluster, should one of the replicas not be available due to hardware or other failure.

When you add more capacity to a Swift cluster, data is redistributed evenly across cluster resources, including newly added drives. For instance, if the cluster is 80% full and you add a new node or a new rack without any data, the Swift cluster will reorganize itself so all drives will have a roughly equal percentage of data stored on them based on the disk weight. For a large cluster, this additional replication traffic might not be noticeable, but for a small cluster, the traffic needs to be managed to ensure it does not negatively affect performance of the cluster. It is therefore important to let the data flow into the new capacity you've added at a moderate rate, and not at the bottleneck rate of the network.

Keeping Track of the Rings and Builder Files

As we discussed earlier in the book (see Chapter 3), keeping the rings the same on all nodes is critical for Swift to work properly. Every time capacity is adjusted in a cluster, the rings will need to be updated on every node. With only a few nodes, the task of manually keeping the rings the same is manageable. However, with more than a handful of nodes, it can easily become a time-consuming task. All changes affecting Swift's rings will need to be kept track of and in sync.

Generating rings can be done from any server node with Swift installed. It is best, however, to dedicate one server as the one on which all ring generation is done. This server can be a node in the cluster or a standalone machine that does not participate in the cluster. For tracking, scalability, and backup reasons, keeping the builder files and rings on a dedicated, standalone machine is considered best practice. As rings are generated and updated through the lifecycle of a Swift cluster; the rings will then be distributed out to the Swift nodes every time they change.

Losing your builder files or rings would be a huge problem, so make sure you have them backed up properly.

Managing Capacity

Data is always growing and disk capacity is always increasing. Sometimes disks go bad and need to be replaced. When storage capacity is running low, new disks or nodes will need to be added, and occasionally nodes might need to be removed due to obsolescence or relocation of capacity to another cluster. These are all events that will trigger Swift ring changes. Capacity adjustments and ring changes go hand in hand and are integral parts of the lifecycle of a Swift cluster.

To keep track of the size of disks and to be able to gradually add or remove capacity in the cluster, we recommended that you create a convention for setting the disk weight. The *disk weight* is a number that defines the amount of data to be stored on a disk relative to other disks in the system. Although the disk weight is an arbitrary number, it is essential that the weight is kept to a sane, meaningful number and set in a consistent way throughout the cluster.

SwiftStack bases disk weight on the number of gigabytes per disk. For example, the disk weight of a 4 TB disk is 4,000. This helps make it clearer to an operator what the full size of the disk is. It also establishes a relative weighting system for the cluster, which is useful for capacity adjustments.

If you want to gradually increase the weight of a disk in the system, you can do so by setting the weight of a disk to a number lower than its relative full weight, as compared to other disks in the system. Hence, if you want to gradually add a 4 TB disk into the cluster, let's say by 25% of its full weight (4,000) at a time, then you would add it to the rings by a weight of 1,000 at a time. As discussed earlier, this would require the rings to be pushed four times (4×1,000) to reach the disk's full weight in the system. In between the rings being pushed to the cluster, it is prudent to wait until the cluster has rebalanced itself based on its latest rings. After rebalancing has happened, the next incremental push can take place.

So why do we have to do all this tedious work to add or remove new disks in the cluster? Why not just add a disk in with 100% of its weight? The reason for gradually adding or removing disks is that you don't want to overwhelm the cluster, which can negatively affect the experience of end users. When adjusting capacity, the replicators and auditors will be working harder, thus using more CPU, and the network traffic between nodes will increase as data is relocated between nodes to balance the cluster.

For example, maybe you have a 1 PB cluster that is starting to get full and you have just purchased and installed equipment with another 1 PB of storage. Let's say your existing 1 PB is 90% full. If you were to add the new 1 PB immediately, what will happen as soon as you push the new rings out is that half of the existing data will start flowing onto the disks in the new 1 PB of equipment, in an attempt to rebalance the cluster to make every drive in the system become approximately 45% full (half of 90%). That's 450 TB of data that needs to move, and if unleashed all at one time, it could saturate the network links in the cluster and hurt availability for end users.

As you are probably figuring out, capacity management can be tricky. It is important to do it carefully and with a plan. In the next few sections we will go over examples of how capacity adjustments can be made. At the end of this section of the chapter, we will outline how capacity adjustments are handled when using the SwiftStack Controller.

What to Avoid

Just as with any other storage device or system, completely filling up a Swift cluster should be avoided. Full disks, nodes, zones, and regions can be challenging and time-consuming to deal with.

At the end of this chapter we will cover some of the monitoring integration procedures we see commonly used to ensure that disks and clusters don't fill up.

The only real way out of a full cluster is to add more capacity. Adding a few extra drives, if you have empty drive bays, is fast and can alleviate the immediate problem of a full cluster. However, adding new nodes can take a long time, especially if you don't have spare, unused nodes sitting around in inventory. Procuring new hardware can sometimes take weeks, and if the cluster is already getting very full and more data is continuously being added, the cluster will reject new data when it fills up. The existing data itself will be safe, but the cluster might become become slow as it traverses handoff locations attempting to find a place to put incoming data.

Adding Capacity

Based on the convention mentioned earlier of assigning a sensible weight to disks, throughout this chapter we will be using a full disk weight of 1,000, which corresponds to a 1 TB disk, for all disks. In the first example that follows, we start with one node with three disks in it, already provisioned. This is a single-node cluster. From there we will be adding capacity to our cluster by performing the following tasks:

- Existing cluster: initial ring on node
  - Adding disks immediately
  - Adding disks gradually
- Adding nodes
  - Adding a node immediately
  - Adding a node gradually

To make capacity adjustments, we will use the `swift-ring-builder` program. If you recall, we used it in Chapter 9 to build our first Swift cluster. It is used for all additions and removals of disks and nodes. `swift-ring-builder` is used with all the rings, but in this chapter, because we will mainly be focusing on adding object capacity, we will predominantly use the `object.builder` subcommand. Of course, if you were to add account or container capacity, you would use the `account.builder` or `container.builder` command instead.

Existing Cluster: Initial Ring on Node

Starting off, we have one node in our cluster. The following `swift-ring-builder object.builder` command shows our original, single-node cluster, including three disks (Swift devices) with a perfectly balanced object ring.

Lines in output have been broken over multiple lines to fit the book's page size. The "Devices" line is a long heading, and it is followed by three lines, one for each device.

```
root@swift01:/etc/swift# swift-ring-builder object.builder
object.builder, build version 3
1024 partitions, 3.000000 replicas, 1 regions, 1 zones, 3 devices, 0.00
balance
The minimum number of hours before a partition can be reassigned is 1
Devices:    id  region  zone      ip address  port  replication ip
replication port      name weight  partitions balance meta
             0       1     1       127.0.0.1  6000       127.0.0.1
  6000      n1d0 1000.00       1024    0.00
             1       1     1       127.0.0.1  6000       127.0.0.1
  6000      n1d1 1000.00       1024    0.00
             2       1     1       127.0.0.1  6000       127.0.0.1
  6000      n1d2 1000.00       1024    0.00
```

Adding disks immediately

To add devices to the ring, we will need to use the `swift-ring-builder` command to specify the *name* of the new disk. In the following command, we add a device named `n1d3` (short for node 1; device 3), with a weight of 1,000:

```
root@swift01:/etc/swift# swift-ring-builder object.builder add
r1z1-127.0.0.1:6000/n1d3 1000
Device d3r1z1-127.0.0.1:6000R127.0.0.1:6000/n1d3 with 1000.0 weight got id 3
```

If we run the `swift-ring-builder` command again without arguments making a request, you will see that device 3 is now listed in the last row at the bottom. Also, note that the balance of the disk is –100.00 before we rebalance the cluster with the new disk:

```
root@swift01:/etc/swift# swift-ring-builder object.builder
object.builder, build version 4
1024 partitions, 3.000000 replicas, 1 regions, 1 zones, 4 devices, 100.00
balance
The minimum number of hours before a partition can be reassigned is 1
Devices:    id  region  zone      ip address  port  replication ip
replication port      name weight  partitions balance meta
```

```
             0        1     1         127.0.0.1  6000         127.0.0.1
6000         n1d0 1000.00       1024    33.33
             1        1     1         127.0.0.1  6000         127.0.0.1
6000         n1d1 1000.00       1024    33.33
             2        1     1         127.0.0.1  6000         127.0.0.1
6000         n1d2 1000.00       1024    33.33
             3        1     1         127.0.0.1  6000         127.0.0.1
6000         n1d3 1000.00              0 -100.00
```

Now it's time to rebalance the object ring to assign partitions to the device. Rebalancing can be done by issuing the following command:

```
root@swift01:/etc/swift# swift-ring-builder object.builder rebalance
Reassigned 768 (75.00%) partitions. Balance is now 0.00.
```

After rebalancing, if you rerun the `swift-ring-builder object.builder` command, you should see something similar to:

```
root@swift01:/etc/swift# swift-ring-builder object.builder
object.builder, build version 5
1024 partitions, 3.000000 replicas, 1 regions, 1 zones, 4 devices, 0.00
balance
The minimum number of hours before a partition can be reassigned is 1
Devices:    id  region  zone      ip address  port  replication ip
replication port       name weight  partitions balance meta
             0        1     1         127.0.0.1  6000         127.0.0.1
  6000       n1d0 1000.00          768     0.00
             1        1     1         127.0.0.1  6000         127.0.0.1
  6000       n1d1 1000.00          768     0.00
             2        1     1         127.0.0.1  6000         127.0.0.1
  6000       n1d2 1000.00          768     0.00
             3        1     1         127.0.0.1  6000         127.0.0.1
  6000       n1d3 1000.00          768     0.00
```

Notice how the partitions are now evenly spread across all the devices and the balance is 0.00.

Adding disks gradually

After adding one disk immediately, as in our earlier example, the `swift01` node and its object ring now have four disks, mapped to devices 0-3. In the following output you can see that we have added a fifth disk, device 4 (`d4`). Our previous operation added a disk with 100% of its capacity. The next step will be to add a disk to a node with a weight of 100, or 10% of its total capacity weight of 1,000 (1 TB). You can see that partitions have also been assigned to the disk. The final columns show that the partitions roughly correspond to 10%, compared to the other drives with a total weight of 1,000.

```
root@swift01:/etc/swift# swift-ring-builder object.builder
object.builder, build version 5
1024 partitions, 3.000000 replicas, 1 regions, 1 zones, 5 devices, 1.24
balance
The minimum number of hours before a partition can be reassigned is 1
```

```
Devices:    id  region  zone      ip address  port  replication ip
replication port       name weight  partitions balance meta
             0       1     2        127.0.0.1  6000        127.0.0.1
  6000       n1d0 1000.00        750     0.10
             1       1     2        127.0.0.1  6000        127.0.0.1
  6000       n1d1 1000.00        749    -0.04
             2       1     2        127.0.0.1  6000        127.0.0.1
  6000       n1d2 1000.00        749    -0.04
             3       1     2        127.0.0.1  6000        127.0.0.1
  6000       n1d3 1000.00        750     0.10
             4       1     2        127.0.0.1  6000        127.0.0.1
  6000       n1d4  100.00         74    -1.24
```

The distribution of partitions across disks nicely illustrates how Swift uses partitions to distribute data across the cluster and how disks can be of different sizes, allowing Swift to proportionally fill up disks based on their size and the number of partitions on each disk.

Subsequently, if you later want to increase the weight of the fifth disk (ID 4, `n1d4`) on node 1 in the system from 100 to 500, you would run the following command:

```
root@swift01:/etc/swift# swift-ring-builder object.builder set_weight d4 500
d4r1z2-127.0.0.1:6000R127.0.0.1:6000/n1d4_"" weight set to 500.0
```

After you run the `set_weight` command, if you look in the weight column, you will see that weight of d4 has now been increased to 500.0:

```
root@swift01:/etc/swift# swift-ring-builder object.builder
object.builder, build version 8
1024 partitions, 3.000000 replicas, 1 regions, 1 zones, 5 devices, 78.32
balance
The minimum number of hours before a partition can be reassigned is 1
Devices:    id  region  zone      ip address  port  replication ip
replication port       name weight  partitions balance meta
             0       1     2        127.0.0.1  6000        127.0.0.1
  6000       n1d0 1000.00        750     9.86
             1       1     2        127.0.0.1  6000        127.0.0.1
  6000       n1d1 1000.00        749     9.72
             2       1     2        127.0.0.1  6000        127.0.0.1
  6000       n1d2 1000.00        749     9.72
             3       1     2        127.0.0.1  6000        127.0.0.1
  6000       n1d3 1000.00        750     9.86
             4       1     2        127.0.0.1  6000        127.0.0.1
  6000       n1d4  500.00         74   -78.32
```

However, due to the `min_part_hours` limit described in "The create command" on page 129, it might not be possible to rebalance the cluster immediately. If so, you will see a message similar to this:

```
root@swift01:/etc/swift# swift-ring-builder object.builder rebalance
No partitions could be reassigned.
Either none need to be or none can be due to min_part_hours [1].
```

If you wait a bit and later run `swift-ring-builder` again, you will see that `d4` has new partitions on it and that the balance is very close to 0, which is a good sign:

```
root@swift01:/etc/swift# swift-ring-builder object.builder
object.builder, build version 8
1024 partitions, 3.000000 replicas, 1 regions, 1 zones, 5 devices, 0.20
balance
The minimum number of hours before a partition can be reassigned is 1
Devices:    id  region  zone      ip address  port  replication ip
replication port       name weight  partitions balance meta
             0       1     1       127.0.0.1  6000        127.0.0.1
  6000       n1d0 1000.00        683     0.05
             1       1     1       127.0.0.1  6000        127.0.0.1
  6000       n1d1 1000.00        683     0.05
             2       1     1       127.0.0.1  6000        127.0.0.1
  6000       n1d2 1000.00        682    -0.10
             3       1     1       127.0.0.1  6000        127.0.0.1
  6000       n1d3 1000.00        682    -0.10
             4       1     1       127.0.0.1  6000        127.0.0.1
  6000       n1d4  500.00        342     0.20
```

To ensure the new disk's capacity is fully used, you would need to repeat the steps just shown until `d4` reaches a weight of 1,000, or 100%, of its capacity. At this point, finally, the ring is balanced and has an equal amount of partitions across all the 1 TB disks in the node:

```
root@swift01:/etc/swift# swift-ring-builder object.builder
object.builder, build version 10
1024 partitions, 3.000000 replicas, 1 regions, 1 zones, 5 devices, 0.10
balance
The minimum number of hours before a partition can be reassigned is 1
Devices:    id  region  zone      ip address  port  replication ip
replication port       name weight  partitions balance meta
             0       1     1       127.0.0.1  6000        127.0.0.1
  6000       n1d0 1000.00        615     0.10
             1       1     1       127.0.0.1  6000        127.0.0.1
  6000       n1d1 1000.00        615     0.10
             2       1     1       127.0.0.1  6000        127.0.0.1
  6000       n1d2 1000.00        614    -0.07
             3       1     1       127.0.0.1  6000        127.0.0.1
  6000       n1d3 1000.00        614    -0.07
             4       1     1       127.0.0.1  6000        127.0.0.1
  6000       n1d4 1000.00        614    -0.07
```

Adding Nodes

Adding nodes is essentially the same process as adding disks, except because disks are now added to the cluster through another node, the IP addresses will be different. To illustrate how we go about adding a node, we will start with the same example. Again, let's use the `swift-ring-builder object.builder` command to take a look at our starting point: a single node cluster with three disks.

```
root@swift01:/etc/swift# swift-ring-builder object.builder
object.builder, build version 3
1024 partitions, 3.000000 replicas, 1 regions, 1 zones, 3 devices, 0.00
balance
The minimum number of hours before a partition can be reassigned is 1
Devices:    id  region  zone      ip address  port  replication ip
replication port      name weight  partitions balance meta
             0       1     1      192.168.1.1  6000      192.168.1.1
  6000       n1d0 1000.00       1024     0.00
             1       1     1      192.168.1.1  6000      192.168.1.1
  6000       n1d1 1000.00       1024     0.00
             2       1     1      192.168.1.1  6000      192.168.1.1
  6000       n1d2 1000.00       1024     0.00
```

Adding a node immediately

Just as before, adding nodes can be done in two ways: immediately or gradually. We will start by adding them immediately. However, it is worth reiterating that adding nodes immediately, especially if you are adding relatively large amounts of capacity, might trigger a significant amount of data to be moved from existing nodes and disks to the newly added ones, with negative impacts on cluster performance and thus the experience of the end users.

Therefore, if you are planning on adding nodes with many terabytes of new disks, consider adding the nodes gradually. There is no hard-and-fast rule for when to add capacity immediately or gradually, but as a general guideline, if you are increasing cluster capacity by *more* than 20%, you should probably consider doing it gradually. Conversely, if you are adding *less* than 20% of capacity, adding a node (or nodes) immediately is usually safe.

In the following example we now have two nodes:

- 192.168.1.1 (original node)
- 192.168.1.2 (new node)

You already know how to use the `swift-ring-builder object.builder add` command. The following example starts after we have already run that command to add the new node and the disks in it as devices. To make it clear which node contains the disks, we have named the new disks `n2d0` through `n2d2`. As you can see in the last three lines of the following output (devices 3-5), the weight, partitions, and balance columns have been added but have yet to be balanced in the cluster:

```
root@swift01:/etc/swift# swift-ring-builder object.builder
object.builder, build version 6
1024 partitions, 3.000000 replicas, 1 regions, 1 zones, 6 devices, 100.00
balance
The minimum number of hours before a partition can be reassigned is 1
Devices:    id  region  zone      ip address  port  replication ip
```

```
replication port      name weight  partitions balance meta
             0       1     1      192.168.1.1  6000      192.168.1.1
  6000       n1d0 1000.00       1024  100.00
             1       1     1      192.168.1.1  6000      192.168.1.1
  6000       n1d1 1000.00       1024  100.00
             2       1     1      192.168.1.1  6000      192.168.1.1
  6000       n1d2 1000.00       1024  100.00
             3       1     1      192.168.1.2  6000      192.168.1.2
  6000       n2d0 1000.00          0 -100.00
             4       1     1      192.168.1.2  6000      192.168.1.2
  6000       n2d1 1000.00          0 -100.00
             5       1     1      192.168.1.2  6000      192.168.1.2
  6000       n2d2 1000.00          0 -100.00
```

Now let's go ahead and start rebalancing the cluster, effectively reassigning partitions to the new disks in the second node, by running the `rebalance` command:

```
root@swift01:/etc/swift# swift-ring-builder object.builder rebalance
Reassigned 1024 (100.00%) partitions. Balance is now 37.70.
```

Balance of 37.70 indicates you should push this ring, wait at least 1 hour, and rebalance/repush.

In this case, we are doubling the capacity of the cluster by adding three more disks to the existing three. With more disk capacity added, Swift can't safely redistribute all the partitions at once across the cluster, so we end up with a partial rebalance on the first rebalance try. Therefore, to fully balance the cluster, it will be necessary to perform another rebalance, pushing out the rings again:

```
root@swift01:/etc/swift# swift-ring-builder object.builder
object.builder, build version 7
1024 partitions, 3.000000 replicas, 1 regions, 1 zones, 6 devices, 37.70 balance
The minimum number of hours before a partition can be reassigned is 1
Devices:    id  region  zone      ip address  port  replication ip  replication
port       name weight  partitions balance meta
             0       1     1      192.168.1.1  6000      192.168.1.1
6000       n1d0 1000.00       669    30.66
             1       1     1      192.168.1.1  6000      192.168.1.1
6000       n1d1 1000.00       705    37.70
             2       1     1      192.168.1.1  6000      192.168.1.1
6000       n1d2 1000.00       674    31.64
             3       1     1      192.168.1.2  6000      192.168.1.2
6000       n2d0 1000.00       341   -33.40
             4       1     1      192.168.1.2  6000      192.168.1.2
6000       n2d1 1000.00       341   -33.40
             5       1     1      192.168.1.2  6000      192.168.1.2
6000       n2d2 1000.00       342   -33.20
```

Now that we have the object ring rebalanced with the three new disks, it's also necessary to distribute the rings to all nodes in the system. Remember, all the nodes *must* have the same rings, or Swift won't operate correctly.

After having given the cluster an hour or more (as suggested earlier) to replicate data to the new partitions on the new disks, it's time to try another rebalance of the object ring. So we repeat the `swift-ring-builder object.builder rebalance` step:

```
root@swift01:/etc/swift# swift-ring-builder object.builder rebalance
Reassigned 512 (50.00%) partitions. Balance is now 0.20.
```

The line of output gives us what we need, and looking at the builder file for the object ring, it should now be similar to:

```
root@swift01:/etc/swift# swift-ring-builder object.builder
object.builder, build version 8
1024 partitions, 3.000000 replicas, 1 regions, 1 zones, 6 devices, 0.20 balance
The minimum number of hours before a partition can be reassigned is 1
Devices:    id  region  zone      ip address  port  replication ip  replication
port        name weight  partitions balance meta
             0       1     1       192.168.1.1  6000      192.168.1.1
6000        n1d0 1000.00        512     0.00
             1       1     1       192.168.1.1  6000      192.168.1.1
6000        n1d1 1000.00        512     0.00
             2       1     1       192.168.1.1  6000      192.168.1.1
6000        n1d2 1000.00        512     0.00
             3       1     1       192.168.1.2  6000      192.168.1.2
6000        n2d0 1000.00        512     0.00
             4       1     1       192.168.1.2  6000      192.168.1.2
6000        n2d1 1000.00        511    -0.20
             5       1     1       192.168.1.2  6000      192.168.1.2
6000        n2d2 1000.00        513     0.20
```

Don't forget that we're still not 100% ready. You still need to distribute the new rings to all the nodes. Once you have the new object ring (in this example) distributed to both nodes, your small cluster should be balancing itself within a matter of hours. In larger clusters, the redistribution of data in the cluster can take longer. If you're curious about the process and like to see what's going on under the hood, you can always run the Swift logs on your nodes through the `tail` command to watch the replicator, auditor, and other processes do their work.

Adding a node gradually

By now this should all seem very familiar to you. Adding capacity, whether nodes or just single disks, is very similar. Following the previous examples, we will add capacity by adding a new node gradually. Again, adding nodes gradually is typically the recommended way to add capacity to a cluster in production, because if too much of the cluster's resources, CPU, RAM, input/output operations per second (IOPS), or networking get tied up in trying to replicate data as fast as possible to the new disks, users might experience a performance slowdown.

In our first round of adding the new node and its new disks to the cluster, we will add 10% of the capacity of devices 3, 4, and 5:

```
root@swift01:/etc/swift# swift-ring-builder object.builder
object.builder, build version 6
1024 partitions, 3.000000 replicas, 1 regions, 1 zones, 6 devices, 267.38 balance
The minimum number of hours before a partition can be reassigned is 1
Devices:    id  region  zone      ip address  port  replication ip  replication
port        name weight  partitions balance meta
             0       1     1       192.168.1.1  6000      192.168.1.1
6000        n1d0 1000.00        683  -26.63
             1       1     1       192.168.1.1  6000      192.168.1.1
6000        n1d1 1000.00        683  -26.63
             2       1     1       192.168.1.1  6000      192.168.1.1
6000        n1d2 1000.00        682  -26.74
             3       1     1       192.168.1.2  6000      192.168.1.2
6000        n2d0  100.00        342  267.38
             4       1     1       192.168.1.2  6000      192.168.1.2
6000        n2d1  100.00        341  266.31
             5       1     1       192.168.1.2  6000      192.168.1.2
6000        n2d2  100.00        341  266.31
```

The next step is to distribute the rings to all the nodes and wait for the replicators to move data around to the new disks and settle down. Then we go ahead and add another 10% of the capacity of devices 3, 4, and 5, for a total of 20% (or weight 200):

```
root@swift01:/etc/swift# swift-ring-builder object.builder
object.builder, build version 10
1024 partitions, 3.000000 replicas, 1 regions, 1 zones, 6 devices, 100.39 balance
The minimum number of hours before a partition can be reassigned is 1
Devices:    id  region  zone      ip address  port  replication ip  replication
port        name weight  partitions balance meta
             0       1     1       192.168.1.1  6000      192.168.1.1
6000        n1d0 1000.00        683  -19.96
             1       1     1       192.168.1.1  6000      192.168.1.1
6000        n1d1 1000.00        683  -19.96
             2       1     1       192.168.1.1  6000      192.168.1.1
6000        n1d2 1000.00        682  -20.08
             3       1     1       192.168.1.2  6000      192.168.1.2
6000        n2d0  200.00        342  100.39
             4       1     1       192.168.1.2  6000      192.168.1.2
6000        n2d1  200.00        341   99.80
             5       1     1       192.168.1.2  6000      192.168.1.2
6000        n2d2  200.00        341   99.80
```

Again, we distribute the new rings to all nodes. We repeat this process until eventually, we apply the full weight (1,000) to use 100% of the new disks' capacity in the cluster:

```
root@swift01:/etc/swift# swift-ring-builder object.builder
object.builder, build version 14
```

```
1024 partitions, 3.000000 replicas, 1 regions, 1 zones, 6 devices, 0.20 balance
The minimum number of hours before a partition can be reassigned is 1
Devices:    id  region  zone      ip address  port  replication ip  replication
port      name weight  partitions balance meta
             0       1     1      192.168.1.1  6000      192.168.1.1
6000      n1d0 1000.00        512    0.00
             1       1     1      192.168.1.1  6000      192.168.1.1
6000      n1d1 1000.00        512    0.00
             2       1     1      192.168.1.1  6000      192.168.1.1
6000      n1d2 1000.00        512    0.00
             3       1     1      192.168.1.2  6000      192.168.1.2
6000      n2d0 1000.00        513    0.20
             4       1     1      192.168.1.2  6000      192.168.1.2
6000      n2d1 1000.00        511   -0.20
             5       1     1      192.168.1.2  6000      192.168.1.2
6000      n2d2 1000.00        512    0.00
```

Then we do our final distribution of the rings.

Of course, this full process will need to be done every time capacity is added to a cluster.

Removing Capacity

Capacity removal is the opposite of adding capacity. It can be done either immediately or gradually, just as when adding capacity. In this section, we will demonstrate how to remove an entire node from the cluster.

There are many reasons why you would remove capacity, including:

- You simply don't need the capacity you currently have in the cluster anymore.
- Planned obsolescence: A node is being replaced by another node with newer and better hardware.
- The disks in a node are being upgraded with larger disks in order to increase cluster capacity, while still maintaining the same physical hardware footprint.

One critical thing you need to consider when removing capacity from a cluster is how much capacity you will have left once capacity has been removed. If you accidentally remove too much capacity, so that the remaining disks in the cluster are entirely full, you will create problems, as described in "What to Avoid" on page 238. This will make it hard to operate the cluster until you have added additional capacity again. Always keep this in mind when you are removing capacity, as not only could you end up creating a lot of extra work for yourself, but you can also risk severe problems with the end-user experience trying to use the cluster.

With that warning out of the way, let's continue learning how to remove by capacity. These are the steps we will go through:

- Removing nodes
- Removing disks
  — Removing disks immediately
  — Removing disks gradually

Removing Nodes

In this example, the initial object ring consists of a total of six disks in two different nodes, with three disks in each node:

```
root@swift01:/etc/swift# swift-ring-builder object.builder
object.builder, build version 14
1024 partitions, 3.000000 replicas, 1 regions, 1 zones, 6 devices, 0.20 balance
The minimum number of hours before a partition can be reassigned is 1
Devices:    id  region  zone      ip address  port  replication ip  replication
port      name weight  partitions balance meta
             0       1     1       192.168.1.1  6000      192.168.1.1
6000      n1d0 1000.00        512     0.00
             1       1     1       192.168.1.1  6000      192.168.1.1
6000      n1d1 1000.00        512     0.00
             2       1     1       192.168.1.1  6000      192.168.1.1
6000      n1d2 1000.00        512     0.00
             3       1     1       192.168.1.2  6000      192.168.1.2
6000      n2d0 1000.00        513     0.20
             4       1     1       192.168.1.2  6000      192.168.1.2
6000      n2d1 1000.00        511    -0.20
             5       1     1       192.168.1.2  6000      192.168.1.2
6000      n2d2 1000.00        512     0.00
```

Removing a node is really the same as removing all disks on it. Hence, to remove node 2 (192.168.1.2), we will need to remove all disks on it from the ring. Disks can be removed one by one, using the `swift-ring-builder object.builder remove` command. Note that the `remove` command takes the device ID as the parameter indicating which disk (device) to remove:

```
root@swift01:/etc/swift# swift-ring-builder object.builder remove d3
d3r1z1-192.168.1.2:6000R192.168.1.2:6000/n2d0_"" marked for removal and will be
removed next rebalance.

root@swift01:/etc/swift# swift-ring-builder object.builder remove d4
d4r1z1-192.168.1.2:6000R192.168.1.2:6000/n2d1_"" marked for removal and will be
removed next rebalance.

root@swift01:/etc/swift# swift-ring-builder object.builder remove d5
d5r1z1-192.168.1.2:6000R192.168.1.2:6000/n2d2_"" marked for removal and will be
removed next rebalance.
```

As usual, once the ring builder commands have been issued, it's time to rebalance the ring:

```
root@swift01:/etc/swift# swift-ring-builder object.builder rebalance
Reassigned 1024 (100.00%) partitions. Balance is now 0.00.
root@swift01:/etc/swift# swift-ring-builder object.builder
object.builder, build version 18
1024 partitions, 3.000000 replicas, 1 regions, 1 zones, 3 devices, 0.00 balance
The minimum number of hours before a partition can be reassigned is 1
Devices:    id  region  zone      ip address  port  replication ip  replication
port        name weight  partitions balance meta
             0       1     1      192.168.1.1  6000      192.168.1.1
6000        n1d0 1000.00       1024     0.00
             1       1     1      192.168.1.1  6000      192.168.1.1
6000        n1d1 1000.00       1024     0.00
             2       1     1      192.168.1.1  6000      192.168.1.1
6000        n1d2 1000.00       1024     0.00
```

If everything looks good, we need to distribute the rings to all the nodes in the cluster. Obviously, since no devices are left on node 2 anymore, updating the rings on node 2 isn't strictly necessary. However, if your reason for removing the disks in node 2 is to upgrade the node from the 1 TB disks it was using to 3 TB disks, you could still update the rings on node 2 in order to make sure it has the latest rings for the cluster. On the other hand, if your intention is to not use node 2 again, you could skip updating the rings on it and simply turn the node off.

Removing Disks

In the next two examples we are starting with a single node that has four disks in the object ring, device IDs 0-3:

```
object.builder, build version 20
1024 partitions, 3.000000 replicas, 1 regions, 1 zones, 4 devices, 0.00 balance
The minimum number of hours before a partition can be reassigned is 1
Devices:    id  region  zone      ip address  port  replication ip  replication
port        name weight  partitions balance meta
             0       1     1      192.168.1.1  6000      192.168.1.1
6000        n1d0 1000.00        768     0.00
             1       1     1      192.168.1.1  6000      192.168.1.1
6000        n1d1 1000.00        768     0.00
             2       1     1      192.168.1.1  6000      192.168.1.1
6000        n1d2 1000.00        768     0.00
             3       1     1      192.168.1.1  6000      192.168.1.1
6000        n1d3 1000.00        768     0.00
```

Removing disks immediately

To remove device d3, type in the following command:

```
root@swift01:/etc/swift# swift-ring-builder object.builder remove d3
d3r1z1-192.168.1.1:6000R192.168.1.1:6000/n1d3_"" marked for removal and will be
removed next rebalance.
```

Inspecting the object ring, it should now have only three devices left in it:

```
root@swift01:/etc/swift# swift-ring-builder object.builder
object.builder, build version 22
1024 partitions, 3.000000 replicas, 1 regions, 1 zones, 3 devices, 0.00 balance
The minimum number of hours before a partition can be reassigned is 1
Devices:    id  region  zone      ip address  port  replication ip  replication
port       name weight  partitions balance meta
             0       1     1       192.168.1.1  6000      192.168.1.1
6000       n1d0 1000.00        1024     0.00
             1       1     1       192.168.1.1  6000      192.168.1.1
6000       n1d1 1000.00        1024     0.00
             2       1     1       192.168.1.1  6000      192.168.1.1
6000       n1d2 1000.00        1024     0.00
```

Go ahead and push the new object ring out to your node. Once the new ring has been applied, the auditors and replicators will move data around to ensure that three replicas of every object are stored on the remaining disks in the cluster. In this particular example, because of the as-unique-as-possible principle of Swift, each of the three disks in our single-node cluster will hold one copy of each object.

Removing disks gradually

In our final capacity adjustment example, we will perform a gradual disk removal. We will begin by setting the weight to 500, reducing the capacity of device 3 by 50%, which will drain data off the disk and move it to other disks in the system. To do so, use the following command to reduce the weight of d3 to 500 (half its original weight of 1,000):

```
root@swift01:/etc/swift# swift-ring-builder object.builder set_weight d3 500
d3r1z1-127.0.0.1:6000R127.0.0.1:6000/n1d3_"" weight set to 500.0
```

Running the `swift-ring-builder object.builder` command should display something like:

```
object.builder, build version 27
1024 partitions, 3.000000 replicas, 1 regions, 1 zones, 4 devices, 1.22 balance
The minimum number of hours before a partition can be reassigned is 1
Devices:    id  region  zone      ip address  port  replication ip  replication
port       name weight  partitions balance meta
             0       1     1       192.168.1.1  6000      192.168.1.1
6000       n1d0 1000.00          881    0.37
             1       1     1       192.168.1.1  6000      192.168.1.1
6000       n1d1 1000.00          867   -1.22
             2       1     1       192.168.1.1  6000      192.168.1.1
6000       n1d2 1000.00          881    0.37
             3       1     1       192.168.1.1  6000      192.168.1.1
6000       n1d3  500.00          443    0.94
```

Rebalance and push the new object ring to the cluster and wait for the replicators to do their job. When the data has been redistributed to the other drives, repeat the `set_weight` command to lower the weight of device 3 to 0. The `object.builder` command should then show a ring like this:

```
object.builder, build version 30
1024 partitions, 3.000000 replicas, 1 regions, 1 zones, 4 devices, 0.00 balance
The minimum number of hours before a partition can be reassigned is 1
Devices:    id  region  zone      ip address  port  replication ip  replication
port      name weight  partitions balance meta
             0       1     1      192.168.1.1  6000      192.168.1.1
6000      n1d0 1000.00        1024    0.00
             1       1     1      192.168.1.1  6000      192.168.1.1
6000      n1d1 1000.00        1024    0.00
             2       1     1      192.168.1.1  6000      192.168.1.1
6000      n1d2 1000.00        1024    0.00
             3       1     1      192.168.1.1  6000      192.168.1.1
6000      n1d3    0.00           0    0.00
```

To apply the changes, distribute the newly created object ring and let the cluster do its job.

Finally, remove the device from the ring completely using the `remove` command. At this point there should be no data left on the disk, as all of it has been moved to other object disks:

```
root@swift01:/etc/swift# swift-ring-builder object.builder remove d3
d3r1z1-192.168.1.1:6000R192.168.1.1:6000/n1d3_"" marked for removal and will be
removed next rebalance.
```

Run the `swift-ring-builder object.builder rebalance` command and push out the object ring, which now doesn't include the d3 disk.

Managing Capacity Additions with SwiftStack

SwiftStack lets you effortlessly manage your cluster and its rings in a seamless and structured way, without all the pitfalls of manual ring management.

As you have probably come to appreciate by this point, doing capacity adjustments manually can be tedious and prone to human error. If you make mistakes, you can misconfigure your cluster and it can start misbehaving. It is one thing to stand up a cluster the first time and make the occasional capacity addition or removal. System administrators with relatively little Linux and Swift experience can typically read tutorials, copy and paste, and get a Swift cluster up and running at a basic level. But that will go only so far.

Consequently, automating capacity adjustments is an obvious choice for anything more than just a few Swift nodes. After all, Swift is intended to scale out to tens, maybe hundreds or thousands of nodes. Additionally, beyond the original setup of a Swift cluster, managing a cluster on a daily basis and through its lifecycle, including capacity adjustments, troubleshooting, middleware configuration, planned hardware obsolescence, institutional memory, and operator turnover, is not a trivial task. At SwiftStack, we have built a lot of our Swift tooling and system lifecycle processes around what has been covered in this chapter.

In the following sections, we will revisit capacity adjustments, this time seeing how the SwiftStack Controller manages adding and removing drives and nodes.

Adding Capacity

When you add new capacity to a SwiftStack cluster, such as additional disk drives, the SwiftStack Controller automates the process by:

1. Detecting new devices that are added to a node
2. Labeling drives with a unique label, so they can be mounted, unmounted, and re-mounted without losing their identity in the process
3. Mounting the drives
4. Formatting the drives with the XFS filesystem
5. Adding the drives to the ring
6. Deploying the new ring to all cluster nodes

Although the SwiftStack Controller automates the process of adding additional capacity, the operator still needs to manage and plan for capacity additions, and pay attention to how full existing drives are. A good rule of thumb is to keep at least 10-20% free on all drives to keep enough headroom for future capacity needs and provide ample time to order and install additional drives or nodes as capacity requirements increase.

During capacity adjustments, it's important to note that other configuration changes that require a configuration push will interrupt an ongoing gradual add or remove cycle and set it back one cycle. This is in itself not a problem, but it means that making other cluster configuration changes while a capacity adjustment is in progress will cause the capacity adjustment to take longer to complete than it otherwise would.

Adding Drives

To add additional drives to an existing node in a SwiftStack cluster, install the physical drives in the node and follow these steps:

1. In the SwiftStack Controller, go to Configure Cluster and choose Edit for the node to which you have added the drives. Note that the SwiftStack Controller will automatically detect additional drives in the cluster.

2. Add drives on the node to your cluster through either the Add Gradually or Add Now button.
3. Select Change.
4. Lastly, use the Deploy Config to Cluster button to apply the changes.

With SwiftStack, you can automatically add additional capacity, such as new drives, into your existing cluster with two different options: Add Gradually and Add Now. With gradual capacity additions, the SwiftStack Controller will slowly increment the weights on each new device, rebalance the rings, and safely distribute them out to all the nodes. The SwiftStack Controller will also track information about replication activity so it knows when to do the next increment. On the node monitoring page, you can track the percent complete for each device.

When you select Add Now, the SwiftStack Controller adds the new cluster resources immediately, which will result in instant replication traffic between the nodes to evenly redistribute the data across the cluster as fast as possible. Immediately adding drives is a valid method when you have a new cluster, need to add capacity quickly, or are adding only a few disks or nodes to a relatively large cluster with much more capacity than what you are adding.

To determine whether Add Gradually or Add Now is most appropriate, use the following guidelines as a starting point:

- If you're adding more than 20% capacity is, Add Gradually is probably most appropriate.
- If you're adding less than 20% capacity, Add Now might be more appropriate.

This, however, varies based on:

- The actual size of the cluster
- The percentage added
- The cluster workload

For a cluster with more than a few dozen drives, it's usually acceptable to use the Add Now feature. When adding a new node, however, it might be more appropriate to Add Gradually.

Adding a Node

To add a new node to an existing SwiftStack cluster, install the SwiftStack Node software on the node as described in the latter half of Chapter 10.

To determine whether you should Add Gradually or Add Immediately and for a reminder about how you can monitor the process, see "Adding Drives" on page 252.

The SwiftStack Controller will add the newly available capacity to the cluster.

Removing Capacity

SwiftStack also makes it easy to remove capacity from a cluster, which you'll need to do when you want to upgrade to larger drives, swap out older drives, or replace a whole node. The process for removing capacity is similar to adding capacity. But instead of Add Gradually, you can Remove Gradually and then wait until all data has been removed from the disk(s) or node(s) so you can remove them from the cluster.

Don't forget to deploy the new configurations to the cluster.

Removing a Node

The following procedures can be used when it is necessary to remove a node from a cluster. You might need to remove a node when upgrading hardware; when you've experienced hardware failure; or when you're conducting operational and failure testing of a SwiftStack cluster. When conducting operational and failure testing, these procedures will enable you to safely simulate node and disk failures without potentially damaging the hardware by physically removing disks or forcing servers to shut down through a hard power-off event.

To safely remove a node from a SwiftStack cluster, do the following:

1. Gracefully shut down the node by issuing `sudo shutdown -h now`. The node will shut down and the SwiftStack Controller will show the node as unreachable.

   When a node is down, Swift assumes that the disks are still healthy and that the data on those disks is recoverable. Consequently, if the node is powered back on, Swift will simply bring the node back into the cluster and will start syncing any new data to the node.

2. Delete the node from the SwiftStack Controller's GUI. When the node is deleted from the controller, a ring push will be initiated, which will completely remove the node from the cluster.

Removing a Disk

There are times when you will need to remove a disk. For example, if a disk has failed or is having issues, or if you want to replace a disk with a larger disk to increase capacity, you'll need to remove it. As you already know, disks can be removed in two ways: now (immediately) or gradually (incrementally). Here is what happens behind the scenes in each of the scenarios:

- If a disk is removed using the Remove Now button, it is immediately removed from the cluster and the data remains on the disk. As always when using the SwiftStack Controller, the removal or addition of capacity will trigger new rings to be built and a configuration push to be initiated.
- If a disk is removed through Remove Gradually, data will be slowly removed from the drive and transferred to other disks in the cluster. The cluster will try to remove 25 GB per hour from the disk. Thus, removing data completely from a drive with 2 TB of data on it will take approximately 80 hours, or close to 3.5 days. However, if the cluster is under heavy load or busy with other processes, it might drain less than 25 GB of data per hour, which would make the total removal process slower. In the meantime, every hour there's a new ring pushed to the cluster, which triggers a rebalancing of the disks in the cluster.

If for any reason a configuration push cannot be completed and the ring cannot be updated, the gradual removal of data will be interrupted. For example, if a node goes down and is not repaired and reinstated or removed from the cluster, the ring updating cannot continue until the cluster is healthy again. The gradual removal of data will continue once a new ring can be pushed to the cluster.

To immediately remove a disk in the SwiftStack Controller, follow these instructions:

1. Go to the node from which you want to remove the disk.
2. Click Manage.
3. Find the disk you want to remove; for example, `sde`.
4. From the dropdown menu, select Remove Now. The disk will be instantly deleted from the cluster and a configuration push will be initiated to rebalance the cluster.

To remove a disk gradually, in the SwiftStack Controller, follow these instructions:

1. Go to the node from which you want to remove the disk.
2. Click Manage.
3. Find the disk you want to remove; for example, `sde`.
4. From the dropdown menu, select Remove Gradually.

After removing a disk from a node, if you later want to reuse the disk in the cluster, you should ensure that the data on the disk is removed so that it looks like a new disk to Swift. One way of removing all data is to simply format the disk.

Monitoring Your Cluster

A Swift cluster has many moving parts with many daemons running in a distributed, shared-nothing fashion across nodes, all working together. It is therefore important to be able to tell what's going on inside the cluster when diagnosing issues and performance or planning capacity changes. Thus, monitoring your Swift cluster infrastructure becomes important. Most organizations have their favorite monitoring tools. Luckily, because Swift runs on top of Linux, almost all the common monitoring tools out there are relatively easy to integrate into your Swift environment.

As has been noted earlier, hardware failures in a Swift cluster are usually not as critical as they tend to be in traditional storage systems. Still, you are surely going to want to have some kind of monitoring set up. When hard drives or servers fail, which they will, you are going to want to know about it. Perhaps more important, although not directly part of Swift itself, all networking and load-balancing equipment supporting access to the Swift cluster and replication links between nodes need to be monitored.

Swift-Specific Metrics: What to Look For

When analyzing Swift monitoring data, the following are the key metrics to keep an eye on:

Async pendings
: An async pending is a file created when an object is uploaded while there is contention during an update to a container listing record. If the upload backs up or the container servers gets busy, the operation will throw an error and the Object Server will write to disk a record that says, "Hey, this container needs to be updated to increment this number of bytes by one object." That file on disk that needs to be written later is called an async pending. These are normal in a Swift cluster. It's not a crime to have async pendings on your disk, but what you need to watch for is whether they're accumulating. *That's* a problem.

  What is important to track here is the number of async pendings over time. If you're seeing your rate of generation go way up in comparison to the rate at which they're serviced, that would be something to look into. Perhaps there's too much contention and the account/container records need to be distributed across more or higher-performing media.

CPU use
: Load in general isn't an interesting metric, but one basic machine stat that *is* important is CPU utilization. Proxy servers in particular are prone to becoming CPU-bound and causing bottlenecks in your throughput. This would surface if you underprovisioned your proxy server or a heavy workload comes its way. Another way it could surface is with a large number of requests per second that add up to relatively low volumes of data transfer (for example, lots of `HEAD`s, `PUT`s, or `GET`s for small

objects). If you have a workload like that, then you'll get a pretty good number of requests per second and your proxy server would be CPU-bound. So watching CPU utilization with proxy servers is particularly important.

The same goes for storage nodes' CPU use, but it's generally less of an issue because they'll generally get I/O-bound before they get CPU-bound. The possible exception might be an SSD-backed account/container server where your I/O capacity and latencies are so good that your CPU has a chance of becoming bottlenecked.

I/O use
: Another useful metric is I/O utilization. These statistics can be tracked per drive, but rolling them up into a node and cluster view can be really handy. When you have per-drive stats, you'll be able to see any hotspots that show up. This might happen if you have requests that are piling up on a particular account or container. In this case, you will see a huge number of concurrent `PUT`s to objects within the same container in the per-disk I/O.

Relocation activity
: If you see spikes, that could indicate that a drive is having trouble.

Timing statistics
: Timing stats are reported for each request. Each part of the request is broken down very granularly so you can pinpoint where issues arise, if they do. You can see if the request involved an account, container, or object. You can see the differences between the proxy server handling the request and the Account/Container/Object Server handling the request. Each request also gets broken down by the verb (`GET`/`HEAD`/`PUT`), so you can get a lot of information out of what each service is seeing.

As a Swift operator, even if you have very little knowledge about what specific clients are experiencing, all these metrics can give you a window into the latency they might be subject to and any problems they might be encountering. You can see whether clients are getting a lot of 404 errors or whether all of a sudden 500 errors pop up. If you use a monitoring system that can alert you to these kinds of problems, it will help you detect problems early, so you can address them within the Swift cluster before clients start experiencing issues.

You really want to catch any problem before your clients experience it. All of these internal metrics enable operators to gauge how clients experience the Swift cluster.

Monitoring and Logging Tools

Some of the most frequently used monitoring and logging systems with Swift are:

- Monitoring
  - Nagios

- Zabbix
  - Ganglia
  - Zenoss
- Logging
  - Elasticsearch (Logstash, Kibana)
  - Splunk

There are surely others, too. The point here is that whatever your organization is already using or is familiar with it, will likely work well to keep track of your Swift environment. Of course, the ultimate choice of what monitoring tool or tools to use, and how they alert an operator, is up to each operations team. Setting up some form of monitoring is critical, though, because you really want to know if and when problems occur.

SwiftStack Tools

If you are using SwiftStack, you can get lots of cluster and node statistics from the SwiftStack Controller. Additionally, on nodes installed with the SwiftStack management agent, you also get Swift-specific Nagios plug-ins on every node. Although the SwiftStack Controller provides extensive monitoring and reporting, you might want to consider integrating Swift with other upstream monitoring and alerting systems. Other monitoring tools might be able to detect anomalies that the SwiftStack system won't report on or can't specifically pinpoint in your environment.

The Nagios plug-ins installed on each individual SwiftStack node provide the following Swift-specific information:

- Unmounted SwiftStack devices
- Drive capacity use
- Background Swift daemons
- Most recent Swift backend daemon sweep time

Using the SwiftStack Controller, you can also configure syslogging to the logging facility of your choice and redirect events to your logging tool. This is as easy as specifying the facility in the Controller configuration and providing the location of the logging server.

Lastly, if you use a monitoring tool that can receive SNMP traps, that's also an option.

Cluster-level metrics

The SwiftStack Controller highlights the following top-level metrics in the Controller console for each cluster:

Cluster CPU use
: The percentage of time that a node is using the CPU or performing disk I/O. CPU utilization is provided both for the overall cluster and for individual nodes. High rates (e.g., above 80%) are generally bad. If your CPU use is high, processes might have a harder time getting resources. This means that processes on the node will start to slow down and that it might be time to add additional nodes to the cluster.

Cluster proxy throughput
: The aggregate throughput for all inbound and outbound traffic, displayed in bytes per second. This will indicate network bottlenecks.

Average node memory use
: The memory usage for all nodes in your cluster. Memory is displayed as used, buffered, cached, or free.

Total cluster disk I/O
: Measures the total number of input/output operations per second (IOPS) on disks for the overall cluster and for individual nodes. Disk I/O is shown for both read IOPS and write IOPS. Note that because Swift constantly guards against bit rot, the cluster will continuously read some amount of data.

Top 5 Least Free Disks
: The fullest disks in the cluster. Swift distributes data across the cluster evenly, so how full your disks are will correspond to how full the overall cluster is and when you should consider adding additional capacity.

The SwiftStack Controller also makes available several other monitoring graphs for your cluster, which you can use when tuning or troubleshooting your SwiftStack cluster. For the overall cluster, these graphs include:

- Total Cluster Interface Bandwidth
- StatsD Statistics Per Node
- Average OpenVPN Traffic
- Top 4 Average Node Process Groups by RSS
- object-updater sweep Timing and Count
- object-replicator.partition.update Req Timing and Count
- Proxy Req Timing and Count
- account-replicator replication Timing and Count

Node-level metrics

For each node, the following monitoring graphs are available:

- Total node disk I/O
- Per-disk read throughput
- Per-disk write throughput
- Per-disk read IOPS
- Per-disk write IOPS
- Node proxy server throughput
- CPU utilization (all CPUs)
- Per processes group CPU usage
- Account processes CPU usage
- Container processes CPU usage
- Object processes CPU usage
- Memory utilization
- Node interface bandwidth
- StatsD statistics
- OpenVPN traffic
- Top 4 node process groups by RSS
- Object replicator operations
- Object-updater sweep timing and count
- object-replicator.partition.update req timing and count
- Proxy req timing and count
- account-replicator replication timing and count

These metrics and graphics are available under the "View all" graphs for this cluster menu.

Operating with SwiftStack

We have looked at several scenarios for adding and removing capacity and we have covered the best monitoring practices.

At this point, you should have a good understanding how Swift works and can and should be maintained, managed, and monitored.

Perhaps the greatest lesson is that although Swift is based on and relies on many common Linux packages and system administrator best practices, Swift at scale isn't necessarily easy to manage and maintain. There are many server and procedural processes to keep track of to make Swift run smoothly. At SwiftStack, we built the SwiftStack Controller to streamline the day-to-day tasks involved in running a Swift cluster. Using the SwiftStack Controller makes it significantly easier, less risky, and more cost effective to run Swift clusters. Some of the highlights of the Swift Controller are:

- SwiftStack makes the process of adding and removing capacity easy and highly automated.
- The SwiftStack Controller tracks not only server-level metrics such as CPU utilization, load, memory consumption, and disk usage, but also hundreds of Swift-specific metrics to understand what the different daemons are doing on each server. This helps the operator answer questions such as, "What's the volume of object replication on node8?", "How long is it taking?", "Are there errors? If so, when did they happen?"
- The SwiftStack Controller collects and stores monitoring data for over 500 metrics for each node in your SwiftStack cluster. A subset of these are reported in the SwiftStack Controller so you can get a bird's eye view of your cluster performance, with options to drill down into specific metrics for tuning and troubleshooting.
- SwiftStack Nodes include StatsD, a simple statistics daemon. To avoid the problems inherent with middleware-based monitoring and after-the-fact log processing, StatsD metrics are integrated into Swift itself. With StatsD, metrics are sent in real-time from the nodes to the SwiftStack Controller. The overhead of sending a metric is extremely low: a one-UDP packet transmission.

Conclusion

This chapter covered how to best manage capacity in your Swift cluster both through Swift and SwiftStack; options for monitoring a cluster to prevent problems for your clients or with your data; and how to use SwiftStack tools and metrics to manage and maintain a cluster. In upcoming chapters we'll move to failure handling, testing, and benchmarking and tuning.

PART V

Debugging and Troubleshooting

Swift is very resilient, handling disk and node failures gracefully. But it also offers several tools for figuring out what to do when something goes wrong, or achieving the performance you need.

CHAPTER 16

Hardware Failures and Recovery

Martin Lanner

All clusters occasionally experience a hardware failure. Hardware failures can come in many forms: whole drives can become unresponsive, a power supply to a node can fail, a switch can break and affect a single node or an entire rack, or a power outage can take out racks or an entire region.

Fortunately, Swift was designed to withstand hardware failures, both small and large. Drives, nodes, or even whole racks can fail, and a Swift cluster can continue to operate without impact to the durability and availability of the data.

By default, Swift places data in cluster locations that are as unique as possible, preferring locations that are in different regions, zones, nodes, and disks. This makes it easier to deploy small clusters and provides great durability when the cluster experiences a hardware failure. All data stored in Swift also has several "handoff" locations defined, which are alternative data placement locations in the cluster should one of the three replicas not be available due to a hardware failure or unavailability.

It is important to note that drives in a Swift cluster are not mirrored and are not configured with RAID. This means that when there is a hardware failure, such as a drive failure, the entire cluster participates in the replication of the data to handoff locations. There are no RAID rebuilds, which could cripple the performance of the cluster.

Handling a Failed Drive

A drive failure in Swift is not an emergency. Should an individual drive in a cluster fail, the following happens automatically, without any intervention by the operator:

1. Using built-in checks, Swift detects that a disk has been error limited, meaning it can't be written to or read from, and marks the disk as failed.

2. A drive failure triggers replication. The monitoring system in use, the SwiftStack Controller, or both alert the operator of the drive failure by indicating that there is a missing device.

Note that when a drive fails, it becomes unmounted, which indicates to Swift that the drive has failed. Then, the replicators for all the affected objects on different servers detect that one of the object replicas is unavailable due to the drive failure. At this point replication to the handoff node is triggered. In other words, when your drive becomes unmounted, its data suddenly has only two replicas in the cluster, but replicators immediately get to work to restore a third object during the replication pass.

So once again there are three replicas in the cluster. Also, unlike RAID systems, Swift doesn't need any rebuild time when a failed drive is replaced. Because the entire cluster participates in the replication of data that was stored on the failed drive, the cluster quickly replicates the data that was stored on the failed drive to handoff locations in the cluster, always ensuring that the replica count is maintained.

Depending on how you have deployed Swift, the procedure for handling drive failures might differ somewhat. If you are using SwiftStack, the Controller provides built-in alerts and simple tools to help you replace a disk. If you have built your cluster by hand or through some configuration management tool and integrated it all with your monitoring system of choice, your workflow might be a little different. However, in general terms, these are the steps you should follow:

1. Acknowledge the alert. To acknowledge and archive an alert in the SwiftStack Controller, click Acknowledge Alert. That alert is then removed from the count of alerts that appear on the top of the page. To acknowledge and archive all alerts, click Archive All Alerts.
2. Remove the failed drive from the ring, either using the process we learned in the previous chapter, or if you're using the SwiftStack Controller, simply by selecting the Remove Now or Remove Gradually options described in "Removing Capacity" on page 254. If the disk is exhibiting patterns of "dying," but seems to still be somewhat operational, you can try to gradually remove it. If, on the other hand, the disk has completely failed, you should just remove it immediately. Either way, the action you take will start removing the disk from the cluster.
3. Replace the failed drive in the physical node. A failed drive can normally be replaced during regularly scheduled maintenance periods. In other words, drive failures in Swift are not critical events. As a matter of fact, operators of large Swift clusters typically don't go out and physically replace dead drives more than every two weeks, maybe even less frequently. Remember, the data on the drive has already been recreated in handoff locations elsewhere in the cluster, always ensuring that the defined number of replicas exist.
4. Format and add the replacement drive in Controller.

5. The replacement drive is folded into the cluster (see the "Adding Capacity" on page 252) and the cluster redistributes data in an even manner across cluster resources.

Should a drive failure happen during an upload, the following happens. When an object `PUT` comes in (an upload), the proxy server tries to stream that object out to three storage servers. Let's say this object is destined for a currently failed drive. When the node with the failed drive tries to write the object, it reports an error stating that the drive is failed. The proxy server receives that information and selects a handoff location, which is determined by the ring. The ring determines the next handoff locations for every single object. The proxy server simply takes the next handoff location for this particular object and tries to send the replica of the object there instead. That way the cluster still has three replicas and the client sees a success.

Handling a Full Drive

You should be prepared to handle full drives, which can happen if a cluster has not added enough capacity to keep up with data growth. As Swift distributes data across the cluster evenly, the fullest disks correspond to how full the overall cluster is, and this determines when you should consider adding additional capacity. Again, this is where monitoring capacity is useful, particularly the Top 5 Least Free Disks setting.

When new devices are added to the ring, the Swift replicator processes will distribute data from the full drives to the newly added capacity.

Handling Sector or Partial Drive Failure (a.k.a. Bit Rot)

In a Swift cluster, auditing processes run continuously to ensure that all data is always available. It does this by traversing the cluster and running checks for each object on a given node to detect corruption, which is done in three different ways:

- The auditing process conducts a quick pass to check for zero-byte files. Leaving a zero-byte file is how the XFS filesystem notifies the operator that it has detected corruption.
- A slower-moving process recalculates each object's checksum and compares it to what Swift has for it on record. If the file is determined to be corrupt, it is moved to a quarantined location. Replication is triggered and a fresh copy of the file is replicated, replacing the corrupted copy.
- Finally, as a stopgap, if the file is requested and a yet-to-be-detected corrupt file is returned to the client, Swift recalculates the checksum as the file is being streamed to the client. If the checksum fails, the object is moved to the quarantine location. The client can then compare the checksum and refetch the object.

Should any of these processes turn up a bad file, Swift automatically quarantines the specific objects and replicates the objects to handoff locations.

Handling Unreachable Nodes

If an entire node becomes unreachable due to a power failure, networking issue, or motherboard failure, you should get an alert from your monitoring system that something is amiss with your cluster. Swift itself continuously monitors whether nodes are available in the cluster by detecting connection timeouts (0.5 seconds long) and node timeouts (10 seconds long). Should a node be unavailable within these timeouts, Swift will treat the node as unreachable.

When a node is unreachable, Swift assumes that the data is still available on the node but temporarily not accessible. This differs from drive failures in that Swift will not automatically attempt to replicate data to handoff locations, because the failure is very likely caused by a networking issue, a failed power supply, or some other reason the node is temporarily inaccessible. Even if a node cannot be reached, the data is most likely still intact on the drives in the unavailable node. Rather than taking immediate action and removing the node and all its drives from the cluster (ring), potentially triggering a large amount of replication, it might be simpler to fix whatever is wrong with the node and reconnect it to the cluster. While the node is down, any new writes coming in to the cluster will continue to be written using three replicas, using handoff locations until the node comes back up.

A consistent naming and mapping convention for all your Swift nodes and drives is a good strategy for keeping your cluster healthy and making it easier to manage and maintain the cluster. For example, SwiftStack uniquely IDs every drive in the system so that you can keep track of where each drive is expected to be mapped back into the Swift ring. It is best to avoid relying on the `/dev/sd_x_` location of drives. Using direct `/dev/sd_x_` mappings often becomes problematic because when there are hardware changes, the system might change the `/dev/` location of each drive.

When there is a node failure, it is typically considered more critical than a drive failure. One of the reasons it is more critical is that nodes include several disks, comprising a much larger amount of overall capacity. Hence, when you lose a node, you tend to lose much more storage capacity at once. Also, if you do need to remove the node, you will see an increase in replication in the cluster, which might affect its overall performance. Therefore, when node failure occurs, an operator should take rapid action to ensure that the desired availability level for the cluster is maintained.

The recommended procedure for handling unreachable nodes is:

1. Acknowledge the alert from your monitoring system. If you are using SwiftStack, you can acknowledge and archive an alert by clicking on Acknowledge Alert.

2. Do *not* make any other cluster configuration changes while you have a node down. It's important to not introduce other configuration changes in the cluster when dealing with hardware failures as that might introduce additional variables could affect the operation of your cluster.
3. Check network connectivity to the node. If you have out-of-band (OoB) management, such as IMPI, DRAC or iLO, on the problematic node, investigate whether you can reach the node via your OoB network interface. If not, maybe a switch is down or the node's motherboard has severe problems. In most cases, though, we find that networking issues are the cause of nodes becoming unreachable. If you can get to the node via OoB management and everything generally looks fine on the node, start checking switches, cables, networking cards, etc. to ensure they work as they should. If a networking issue is indeed the root cause, the node can be reconnected with the cluster without any special procedures. Once the node is reachable again, Swift's consistency processes will ensure that data on all nodes in the cluster is rebalanced and distributed evenly. Should the root cause be faulty hardware on the node itself, proceed to the next section on handling a failed node. Otherwise, proceed to the next step.
4. Reconnect the node to the cluster. Swift's auditing process automatically ensures that any changes to the data on the node during the time it was down will be updated.

Handling a Failed Node

What happens if you know the unresponsive system is never going to come back online? Say the motherboard burns out, the power supply fails and fries and corrupts most of the drives, or a forklift rams the node and completely destroys it. What does Swift do? What do you as an operator need to do?

As mentioned earlier, what Swift *won't* do is replicate all the data that's on that node (or zone/region) to handoff locations. What Swift *will* do is mark that node as failed and not attempt to upload any new data to it. All new, incoming data will be sent to handoff locations to ensure that the cluster will still have three good replicas.

The logic behind not initiating replication is that a node failure is much more likely to be caused by specific, transitory events than by system catastrophes such as fire or water damage. Given this, Swift assumes that events related to nodes are transitory and all the drives are not physically destroyed. Initiating replication on an entire node, zone, or region is a high-cost operation and should only be initiated when you know that the data on the disks truly is irrecoverable.

To permanently remove a node using SwiftStack to initiate replication:

1. Acknowledge the alert, if using the SwiftStack Controller.

2. Do *not* make any configuration changes to the cluster.
3. If the node needs to be replaced or repaired over an extended period of time, remove the node from the ring and make sure the new ring is distributed out to all nodes. To carry out this step, you can use the command-line procedures from Chapter 15 or, if you are using the SwiftStack Controller, remove all drives for the failed node through the Remove Now option. Either one of the procedures will generate a new ring without the disks in the failed node and push it out to the operational nodes. This ensures that the cluster re-creates a third copy and moves data from handoff locations to the primary locations, all according to the new ring.

   Performing a node removal will result in increased replication traffic on your cluster, which might affect performance during replication. If you have many, many nodes in the cluster, however, the performance degradation might not be noticeable to users.
4. To restore the same capacity you had before the node failure, replace the failed node in the data center with a new node and go through the steps of adding a node to a cluster.

Node Failure Case Study

Assume you have a cluster with six nodes. You've created three zones in the cluster, with two nodes in each zone. All nodes are identical and have the same number of disks. What this means is that the as-unique-as-possible algorithm will, for every object written, place a copy of the object in zones 1, 2, and 3. You can't specify which node in each zone the object will be put on, but you do know that the data will be evenly distributed between the nodes.

Now, imagine the cluster is 60% full. That means that on average all drives will be roughly 60% full. If your drives are 1 TB drives, each drive will have approximately 600 GB of data on it.

What if node 2 in zone 1 suddenly becomes unavailable? What's the problem? Because you know your environment and your cluster well, you quickly figure out that the node is completely dead and determine that it probably won't be possible to repair it within a reasonable amount of time, because the hardware is old and getting spare parts will take at least a few days. You might think that in order to avoid running the cluster in a non-optimal, degraded state, it would be best to remove the node immediately.

But wait—that's going to present a problem! With the current setup, because the cluster is 60% full, if node 2 in zone 1 is removed, data from that node will be replicated to node 1 in zone 1. After all, the cluster was set up using three zones on purpose to ensure that data is spread out in the cluster in a manner as durable and available as possible. The problem you're facing now is that removing node 2 from the ring will force all its data to disks in node 1, but there isn't enough space on node 1 because the disks are already 60% full. Adding 600 GB of data to a 1 TB disk that already has 600 GB of data on it won't work.

Swift will work around this issue by moving data to handoff locations in other zones once node 1 gets full. However, the plan to remove the node from the ring goes directly against our better judgment and knowledge: one should never fill up nodes or disks. If you later add a replacement node back into zone 1, Swift will eventually balance everything by itself, but it will take time and it will degrade performance while the replicators are working hard to solve the problem.

So what have we learned? The design of your cluster matters—sometimes *a lot*—and using most of the available space in the cluster might have huge ramifications. In the case we just looked at, acting too fast without first thinking through the problem might cause bigger problems than your current situation. Even if a node is down, data typically has not been destroyed. The alternative—to operate with only two available copies of an object for some time—might be a smaller problem than aggressively trying to fix the issue to ensure you have three available replicas. After all, all new objects being written will still be written in threes.

There isn't necessarily a right or wrong answer here, other than possibly to add new capacity now. However, that isn't always viable or realistic. In either case, if you can't add more capacity to zone 1, the cluster will be operating in a non-optimal state. But unlike with a RAID array, your data isn't at risk if you do nothing. Taking your time to ponder the situation and the right tactic to take is a luxury that Swift affords you.

Conclusion

Hardware failures in a Swift cluster are usually not critical or time-sensitive events. A complete node failure is a larger concern than disk failures. Disk failures in Swift do not require personnel to rush to the data center to swap drives. Swift is designed to work around hardware failures and does so beautifully. However, it is important that Swift operators understand how Swift handles failures, as it helps operations to run smoothly and ensures that no hasty, misdirected actions are taken.

CHAPTER 17
Benchmarking

Martin Lanner
Darrell Bishop

The two previous chapters covered various operational considerations and best practices, as well as how to handle hardware failures and recovery. Of course, when you have a Swift cluster running, or maybe even before you do, you will inevitably ask: "How will this cluster perform?"

After all, you don't want to buy and put something in production that can't meet the needs of your applications and users. Hardware, size, services tiering, use case, and tuning all greatly affect how a Swift cluster performs.

That said, performance questions and concerns usually stem from the experience of having bought a storage system that doesn't live up to expectations, which often results in having to upgrade the storage platform for a considerable cost. On top of that, when it comes to upgrading SAN and NAS systems, it usually also involves forklift upgrades from the old system to the new system, which in turn comes at considerable additional labor cost and frequently requires some amount of system downtime. This is not the case with Swift, an important factor to keep in mind. Compared with traditional storage, a Swift cluster is very adaptable and can be easily expanded or reconfigured to provide better performance if needed, all without requiring forklift upgrades or any downtime.

Because object storage platforms in general work in a very different manner from traditional storage platforms, including scaling *out* instead of scaling *up*, and can run on a large variety of hardware without highly specialized components, it becomes harder to provide a simple and authoritative answer to the question, "How will this cluster perform?" No one wants the answer, "It depends ..." However, without specific inputs about a fair number of things, such as detailed hardware configuration, number of nodes, number of disks, network capacity, user concurrency, and object sizes, it is quite hard to provide even an approximate number for sizing a cluster.

So the more you know about the expected use of your cluster, the easier it will be to provide performance estimates and size a cluster appropriately. This process isn't necessarily much different from traditional storage, except that:

- Sizing traditional storage typically needs fewer inputs to get a reasonable estimate.
- Most system administrators have a better understanding of traditional storage, simply because the administrators have worked with it for a long time.
- The variety of hardware and configuration options of traditional storage are generally fewer and scale to a limited degree. Object storage typically scales out linearly and can hence provide completely different metrics.
- Input/output per second (IOPs) isn't necessarily the best metric to use to measure the performance of a Swift cluster. Requests per second can many times be a much more useful metric.

Because the variety and sizes of hardware are mostly static in traditional storage, such as with SANs and NASes, and because that storage is limited in its ability to scale out, deriving performance numbers is relatively easy. For example, most product lines of SANs and NASes come in a handful, or even fewer, models. If you have a SAN product with three different models, those models usually have distinctive features that customers need or want. In most cases, a missing feature automatically disqualifies one or two models immediately, leaving you with a limited choice of what model(s) to get.

Let's call the models "Small," "Medium," and "Large." If you've already decided that you cannot use the Small model, your choice is now between Medium and Large. Before you make up your mind about which model to get, you typically do some performance-related due diligence on the two remaining models to ensure that you get what you need now and for the foreseeable future.

To find out what the performance characteristics of the two SAN models are, all one usually needs to do is look at the specifications sheets provided by the vendor. Or, if those numbers aren't readily available, it's still fairly easy to get benchmark numbers gathered by people who have run benchmarks against those particular models.

Given that a SAN typically only scales to some N number of drives, relies on a controller card with some limited throughput, and has a fixed CPU and RAM, there will usually be an identifiable bottleneck in the system that will constrain it. So in our example, because the configuration of those two models are likely somewhat static, all that needs to be done to find the maximum throughput is to execute a few benchmark runs against the particular models of the SAN and increase the load until the maximum throughput is found.

With Swift and object storage in general, calculating performance numbers and giving a simple answer to "What hardware should I get and how will this cluster perform?" is usually not quite as straightforward. But, given enough information about the environment, it's definitely possible to make good hardware and cluster architecture recommendations, from which one can subsequently estimate performance.

Evaluating Performance

Evaluating storage performance has traditionally been done by measuring how many IOPS a disk or a system can sustain. Thus, one of the most commonly asked questions when it comes to performance of Swift is, "How many IOPS can Swift provide?" That's a question that is impossible to answer without more information about the specific system. The best one can do is to form some hypotheses.

IOPS can definitely be an interesting metric, but because Swift is accessed through an HTTP API, IOPS might not be as important a metric as it is for SANs or NASes. For Swift, in many cases, requests per second might be a more interesting and useful metric than IOPS. And that is why most benchmarking suites for object storage tend to report on requests per second rather than IOPS.

As you know, Swift doesn't rely on any type of RAID. Therefore, because every object disk in the system is available to read and write to individually, if you have 100 7,200-RPM SATA disks in your cluster and each disk can provide an average of 100 IOPS, the total theoretical cluster IOPS would be:

100 disks * 100 IOPS/disk = 10,000 total IOPS

Granted, that's just a theoretical number and should be taken with a grain of salt because there are many things going on in a Swift cluster and all the IOPS will not be available to users at any given time. Still, as you can imagine, simply adding up the IOPS of all disks in the system isn't necessarily the most helpful metric you can get.

Performance Metrics, Benchmarking, and Testing

Even though performance metrics of an object store oftentimes cannot be compared one-to-one to SANs and NASes, and object store configurations can vary greatly, this is not to say that Swift clusters cannot and should not be benchmarked and tested for performance during a variety of situations and states. On the contrary, before deploying a storage cluster into production, it is prudent to test it thoroughly to ensure that it operates and performs as expected. The most common categories of testing are:

- Functional testing with the Swift API
- Operational testing
- Failure scenario testing
- Benchmarking

Because we've already covered functional Swift testing in Chapter 5, capacity adjustments in Chapter 15, and failure handling in Chapter 16, you should already be quite familiar with operations related to those topics. Therefore, we won't cover those kinds of operations in detail in this chapter. However, it is important to understand how Swift performs even under non-optimal circumstances. So, given what you learned in earlier chapters about managing capacity and failure handling, we encourage you to intentionally introduce failures while you are doing benchmark testing.

At the risk of stating the obvious, we advise that before you start benchmarking with various intentionally introduced, controlled failures, you *always* perform the same benchmark under "perfect" conditions. For example, if you want to see how performance is affected when a disk is dead, first run a benchmark with all disks in a healthy condition, then run the same benchmark with one or more disks unmounted. Similarly, if you want to understand the impact of a node going offline, first run a benchmark with all nodes online, then run the same benchmark with a node turned off, simulating a node failure.

Now that you understand some of the basics of Swift benchmarking and the major differences between object storage and traditional storage platforms, and how to interpret and think about benchmarking between them, we'll spend the rest of this chapter providing an overview of the benchmarking process and common benchmarking tools that can be used to test Swift, such as ssbench and swift-bench. Then we will go into more detail about how to actually run benchmarks and discuss some typical test cases.

Remember, each environment and workload is unique, though, so although we provide general guidance on benchmarking in this chapter, an individual test plan should be developed for a particular deployment. Our goal in this chapter is to give you the information you need to create an appropriate customized plan for testing and benchmarking.

Preparing Your Cluster for Benchmarking

When doing benchmarking it's critical that the cluster is operating properly, or you might end up getting misleading results. Consequently, before you start the benchmarking process you should ensure that your cluster is healthy. Some of the items you should check are:

Networking
: Check all cables, NICs, switch settings, and network speeds between all nodes using IPerf. Also, test performance from clients to proxies and from proxies to storage nodes.

Storage
: To get predictable and repeatable results, remove all data from disks in the cluster before starting benchmarking. To do so, run each of the following commands as

root on each storage node, then proceed to the next command. If you are using SwiftStack, you also need to first shut down the SwiftStack agent, `ssnoded`, or it will automatically try to restart the Swift daemons. The `swift-init all stop` command stops the Swift daemon on the node where you run it. If you do not do this, Swift's replication service will prevent you from deleting all data.

These steps will delete *all* data within the Swift cluster! Do *not* do this if there is valuable data stored in the cluster.

```
stop ssnoded   # Required only on SwiftStack Nodes
swift-init all stop
rm -rf /disk/mount/*/*
swift-init all start
start ssnoded  # Required only on SwiftStack Nodes
```

Disks
: Before running the benchmark tool, make sure that no disks in any of the Swift rings are unmounted.

Swift health
: Make sure all your Swift daemons are running and that the nodes are in good health. On SwiftStack Nodes, you can get a quick health check by running `sudo ssdiag` on every node, making sure no potential problems are reported. Confirm Swift connectivity and basic operation by storing and retrieving a few objects using any Swift client.

Pitfalls and Mistakes to Avoid

Being a good systems administrator you've gone through the checklist for things to do before benchmarking a cluster, as noted in the section above. Still, the first few results come back not looking at all like what you had expected. Following is a short list of some common issues we've seen during benchmarking. Any of these things, among many others, can interfere with benchmarking, including:

- Not using jumbo frames when you thought you were. As explained in "Externally Managed Settings" on page 227, jumbo frames are a valuable feature but require extensive network and system configuration.
- Mismatched configuration between network interfaces and switch ports for link speed, port bonding, and other settings.
- Misconfigured Ethernet driver settings (review `ethtool` output and configuration).

- Misconfigured kernel tunables (e.g., setting `net.netfilter.nf_conntrack_max` too low will result in packet loss).
- Having disks that were supposed to be in the account/container rings or the object ring but were not.
- Scalability problems in the authentication layer. If authentication caching has not been enabled or has been misconfigured, it can manifest as bizarre benchmark results.
- Misconfigured or overly aggressive Swift tunables. For example, if you have enabled the object-server thread pool feature of Swift, the product of `thread-count`, `disks-per-storage-node`, and `object-server-workers` should be kept below 1,000, because once it goes above that, you will start getting declining returns:

$$\text{thread-count} \times \text{disks-per-storage-node} \times \text{object-server-workers} \leq 1000$$

As you can tell, some of the above issues can easily go beyond one person's expertise and control. For example, it's relatively common that the Swift sysadmin isn't a networking expert and relies on a team of network admins. Being a studious person, the Swift operator might read that one can gain some performance by using jumbo frames on the nodes. Therefore, all relevant NICs on the nodes were configured with an MTU of 9,000. However, the network team might not have been told that all switches also have to be configured with jumbo frames and suddenly strange behavior crops up, making benchmarking results disappointing or difficult to understand.

Benchmarking Goals and Tools

Benchmarking helps you determine whether the cluster is sized, configured, and tuned well for the desired workload. It can also tell you whether the hardware is capable of handling your expected workload. The goal is to test performance before putting the cluster in production so you can be sure that your cluster will hold up as expected.

Several benchmarking tools can be used with Swift. The two most commonly used and easily available are swift-bench and ssbench. swift-bench is older, being originally part of the Swift code repository. It has since been split out into a separate repository. SwiftStack continues to package and distribute swift-bench.

A newer and more comprehensive test suite is ssbench, which provides more detailed output. swift-bench is good for basic benchmarking and testing, but if you want to do more interesting benchmarking that better matches what you might see in real-world usage of a Swift cluster, ssbench is a better choice.

The basic operation of both ssbench and swift-bench is to request basic operations (create, delete, etc.) of many objects of various sizes on the servers you specify. You can control how many clients are simulated, how big the requests are, and a few other options. Both tools report your cluster's performance at the end.

Other benchmarking tools can also be used, including:

- COSBench by Intel (*http://bit.ly/ic-cosbench*)
- getput by HP
- Commercial benchmarking tools, such as Loadrunner

Later in this chapter, we will review how to use ssbench and swift-bench.

Don't Get Greedy

When conducting benchmarking, it is tempting to overload the system, either with too many concurrent requests or files that are too large. Resist this impulse and start very small. Model tests might seem boring and it might feel like you're wasting your time. On the flip side, if you start with tests that are too challenging, you might end up being confused or disappointed by the results when in fact it might be that you have thrown in too many parameters and created an unlikely or unrealistic scenario.

Before designing your test scenario, it's helpful to try to figure out what you expect to see and what metrics you will look at during the benchmark run. For example, if your load balancer in front of the cluster only has a 1 Gbps NIC for incoming client traffic and one 1 Gbps NIC for traffic going to the Swift proxy nodes, you might want to test how long it takes to transfer one hundred 1 GB files (a total of 100 GB) of data to the cluster.

Obviously, if you launch your scenario with a concurrency of 100 users, meaning 100 users are trying to each simultaneously upload a 1 GB file, there's not enough bandwidth to the cluster to handle such a sudden influx of data. On the other hand, if you have only one client (user) trying to upload the one hundred 1 GB files, one after another, there will be less networking and CPU pressure on the proxy nodes. One user is a better first test.

Also, it's important to remember that if your load balancer's client-facing NIC is 1 Gbps, and you have, say, three proxy nodes, the load balancer's cluster-facing 1 Gbps NIC will be able to serve only around 333 Mbps to each of the proxy nodes, and will not even be able to take advantage of the full 1 Gbps outward-facing NIC on the proxy nodes.

Clearly, there are a lot of things to keep in mind when constructing a scenario and trying to figure out what the result will be. For that reason alone, start small and incrementally increase the load until you start seeing bottlenecks.

Once you're ready to run the scenario, start with one client and no concurrency. Keep an eye on the Swift logs (*/var/log/swift/all.log*). If you notice anything unexpected, stop and investigate. With only one client so far, you will have an easier time diagnosing anything unusual.

If the benchmark results make sense and the system metrics are in line with expectations, proceed to crank up the client concurrency. But again, don't get greedy; step up the load in small increments.

Bottlenecks

One of the purposes of benchmarking is to identify bottlenecks, given a particular load. A Swift cluster will perform only as well as its "weakest link." The extremes are obvious. If you have two proxy servers and 100 storage nodes, your proxy servers will choke your performance. But benchmarking can reveal bottlenecks that are not obvious from educated guesses. You can use the following system metrics to identify bottlenecks in your Swift cluster:

Load balancer throughput
: Make sure your load balancer isn't choking your Swift cluster. Benchmark directly against the proxy servers before benchmarking through any load balancer. You can tell ssbench-worker to balance the load across multiple proxy servers by specifying one storage URL with one storage URL per proxy server with `-S`.

SSL termination
: Make sure SSL termination isn't choking your cluster. Benchmark directly against proxy servers using HTTP to establish a baseline before benchmarking through any SSL termination. Use hardware SSL acceleration. With modern server CPUs supporting encryption-accelerating instructions (e.g., Intel's AES-NI), this is easier than ever. Just make sure your SSL terminating software is taking advantage of it.

CPU utilization
: If a subset of CPU cores are saturated, consider increasing the relevant Swift server worker count to spread CPU load more evenly. If all cores are saturated on a proxy, consider adding more proxies. If CPU is saturated on storage nodes, consider reducing the worker count or provisioning your nodes with more powerful CPUs or fewer disks per chassis.

Network bandwidth
: Although network saturation is more likely to be an issue for the load balancer or proxy servers, be sure to monitor the storage nodes as well. For example, if you have 10 G NICs on the cluster-facing interface on the proxy servers, and only 1 G NICs on the object servers, the object server network connections could be your limiting factor while your proxy tier still has bandwidth to spare.

Memory thrashing
: If the number of partitions is high relative to the amount of RAM in the storage nodes, contention for memory between buffer cache and inode cache can be a

problem. You can get information on kernel cache structures using `slabtop -sc -o`. In the SwiftStack Controller, the "XFS Inode Reads" graph displays the XFS inode fetch rate (fetches per second) and the inode cache hit percentage (higher is better). A poor inode cache hit percentage can be a sign of memory thrashing.

Disk I/O
: For small-object workloads, the spindles of a small- or medium-size cluster can get overwhelmed. Keep an eye on `iostat -x -m -d` output for high `await` and `%util` values. If the workload saturates the available IOPS of a large percentage of your disks, you need to add more disks.

If you have a specific latency target in mind that your cluster must meet, you can adjust the concurrency and check the latency columns in the ssbench report to verify the effects of concurrency on latency and adjust concurrency accordingly.

If you want to check that all requests were successful during a benchmarking run, ssbench will report retries and errors per operation type. You can also search the Swift logs (*/var/log/swift/all.log* on SwiftStack Nodes) for the word "ERROR."

Under heavy load, some requests from the proxy to backend nodes might fail and handoff locations might get used. You can find evidence of this in the Swift logs.

Not all "Handoff requested" log messages are the same. Storing new objects at handoff locations is not ideal, and you can use benchmarking to find the threshold of load at which handoffs start showing up. However, it is perfectly normal for a `GET` or `HEAD` to an account, container, or object that really doesn't exist to look into handoff locations. This is done in case an earlier partial `PUT` failure left objects at a handoff location. This type of handoff will happen regardless of load and does not represent a problem of any kind. So just be careful when analyzing Swift logs for handoff location usage.

Benchmarking with ssbench

The following sections explain how to use ssbench. We'll follow that with a similar description for swift-bench, and then show some important benchmarks you should run before deploying your cluster.

Installing ssbench

Install ssbench on your benchmarking servers. The latest version and installation instructions are always available at the project's GitHub site (*https://github.com/swiftstack/ssbench*).

A Basic ssbench Run

ssbench comes with a few simple sample scenario files. After you have installed ssbench, you can find them in */usr/local/share/ssbench/scenarios/*. To run one of the sample scenarios, enter a command such as:

```
ssbench-master run-scenario \
-A http://<cluster-api-ip>/auth/v1.0 -U <username> -K <key> \
-f /usr/local/share/ssbench/scenarios/very_small.scenario \
-u 4 --workers 2
```

ssbench scenario files are simple JSON files. A scenario file like the *very_small.scenario* above will typically include:

Name
: A human-readable, friendly name for the scenario.

Sizes
: Specifies one or more specific file sizes or ranges. For example, you could specify one size named `tiny` and one size named `small`, using the file size parameters `size_min` and `size_max` to give boundaries of the minimum and maximum sizes in bytes for each file size.

Initial files
: Initial files are the number of files (per the file size definition used in `sizes`) to load into the cluster before the actual benchmark run starts.

Operation count
: The operation count provides the total number of files that will be run against the cluster during the benchmark run, not counting the initial files.

CRUD profile
: CRUD profiles determine the distribution of Creates (`PUT`), Reads (`GET`), Updates (`POST`) and Deletes (`DELETE`) that will be performed using the operation count. It's often easiest to think about CRUD profiles as percentages. For example, if you have an operation count of 10,000, you could specify a CRUD profile of `[70,15,10,5]`, which would translate into 7,000 `PUT`s, 1,500 `READ`s, 1,000 `POST`s and 500 `DELETE`s. You can even have multiple CRUD profiles in one scenario file, applied to different file sizes.

User count
: The user count is the number of concurrent users trying to perform operations during the benchmark run.

In the example ssbench run above, we run *very_small.scenario*, taking the contents of the scenario file and running it against the cluster API (`-A` *http://<cluster-api-ip>/auth/v1.0*), using a Swift account (`-U <username>`) and its API key (`-K <key>`). The `-f` specifies the scenario file. Additionally, we use two command-line arguments to override the default values of two settings. Using the `-u flag`, we override the default value for the concurrency and set it to 4. Then using the --workers flag we set the number of ssbench-worker processes to 2.

The worker count should be roughly equal to the number of CPU cores in your benchmarking machine. You can experiment by raising and lowering the number of workers to see what happens to the request latencies and the number of requests per second that ssbench can generate.

Defining Use Cases

There are many use cases for Swift, and Swift will perform differently based on the workload and use case. This is true whether you use ssbench, swift-bench, or any other benchmarking suite. Getting a well-defined use case will help you create good benchmarking scenarios. With ssbench it's easy to convert a use case and create scenario files that match the use case well. Therefore, you should use different scenario files in order to best simulate the load the cluster will be under given your specific use cases. Some common use cases are:

- Backups
- Applications running directly against Swift
- Media serving (photos, audio, video, etc.)
- Serving web content directly (using the Static Web middleware) or acting as a CDN origin server
- Mail or log archiving
- Sync and share applications

As outlined earlier, in ssbench scenario files, you can specify multiple "size categories," or file size ranges. These are useful when trying to simulate a mixture of usage patterns.

For example, if you want to test the expected performance of your Swift cluster when it is used mainly for backups, but sometimes for file sharing, you could create one size category representative of the backup size range and two size categories for file-sharing sizes (perhaps a small range for images and a large one for video files). You would weight the CRUD profile for the backup size category heavily toward Create because backups are more often written than read.

You would give the file-sharing size categories a more even spread of CRUD operations. In this manner, you can see the effect the two different workloads have on each other and how each workload affects the latency of requests.

For a more detailed discussion of CRUD profiles see the section called "Defining the Scenario File" on page 286 later in this chapter.

How ssbench Works

ssbench performs the following steps during a benchmark run:

1. Use the authentication process to retrieve a token and a storage URL. If the retrieved token becomes invalid during a run, the ssbench-workers will authenticate again and start using the new token. If you want to bypass the authentication system and use a specific storage URL, you can specify the storage URL with the `-S` command-line argument and the token with `-T`. When this is done, the benchmark run will start failing if the supplied token becomes invalid.
2. Generate containers for use during the benchmark to spread container update load. The default is 100 containers.
3. Upload initial objects based on the `initial_files` in the scenario file.
4. Start generating request "jobs," which are dispatched round robin across all the participating ssbench-worker processes.
5. Collect result statistics for each request from the workers and efficiently spool the results directly to disk.
6. Clean up populated objects in the cluster. Use the `-k` option to keep populated objects instead of deleting them.
7. Generate a report from the data file and print it to STDOUT.

Measuring Basic Performance

As we explained in "Don't Get Greedy" on page 279, measuring basic performance and establishing a baseline is an important task when starting to benchmark a cluster. To start off, establish a baseline for proxy server performance by measuring the performance of a single proxy server node. To test a single proxy server node with ssbench, you can:

1. Get an auth token using the `python-swiftclient` command-line interface:

   ```
   $ swift -A $AUTH_URL -U $USERNAME -K $PASSWORD stat -v
   ...
       Auth Token: AUTH_tk98924ccc3f414b9fb6f652ab81c11782
   ...
   $ export TOKEN=AUTH_tk98924ccc3f414b9fb6f652ab81c11782
   ```

2. Invoke `ssbench-master` using the token and a storage URL pointing to the single proxy server you want to test:

```
$ ssbench-master run-scenario -f scenarios/very_small.scenario --workers 1
-S http://$PROXY_IP/v1/$ACCOUNT -T $TOKEN
```

To isolate the performance of requests per second, use a scenario specifying zero-byte objects. Start with a client concurrency of 1 and perform a benchmark run lasting at least 15 minutes (use the `--run-seconds` argument to `ssbench-master run-scenario`).

Then double the client concurrency, and repeat. Do this until the CPU cores of the one proxy server are saturated. You can perform this test for reads only, writes only, or arbitrarily, mixed workloads.

If you have trouble saturating the proxy server's CPU cores, you might need to add more benchmark horsepower. Consider running more ssbench-worker processes, either on the same benchmark server or on additional benchmark servers. Alternatively, you might need to adjust your Swift configuration, by increasing the number of proxy-server workers or other cluster settings.

A small object read-only workload should have no trouble saturating a proxy CPU, because data will be serviced entirely from the buffer cache. However, a small object write workload can exhaust your cluster's aggregate IOPS capacity if the cluster has too few disks.

Watch the output of `iostat -x -m -d 15` on your storage nodes. If the `await` (milliseconds) and `%util` columns are high, you might be limited by your disks instead of by the proxy server. Another bottleneck can be the container server. If you have a proxy server CPU to spare, and the cluster's disks are not fully saturated, but you can't get more requests per second, you might need to spread the benchmark run across more containers or upgrade your container servers to use SSD media.

To isolate throughput performance, use a scenario specifying objects in the hundreds of megabytes. For this test, you must make sure your total network interface bandwidth between the benchmark servers and the single proxy server is greater than the bandwidth of the proxy server (double is a good rule of thumb). For example, if the proxy server has a single 1 Gbps NIC for client traffic and one additional 1 Gbps NIC for cluster traffic, you would want at least 2 Gbps of benchmark server capacity (perhaps two servers each with a 1 Gbps NIC or a single benchmark server with a 10 Gbps NIC). If the proxy server has a single 10 Gbps NIC for both client requests and cluster traffic, you might need only one benchmark server with a single 10 Gbps NIC, as the proxy servers' traffic would be split between the client-facing and cluster-facing networks. With a throughput performance test, you want to see saturated proxy server network interfaces with CPU to spare.

Taking ssbench Further

You can and should take advantage of ssbench's more advanced features.

- Generate an ssbench test profile, a so-called scenario file, or use the sample files provided by SwiftStack. Creating your own scenario files is easy: just edit one of the existing scenarios, which are in JSON, and save your custom scenario to a new file. Watch out for trailing commas and other tricky JSON syntax. SwiftStack can provide you with a ZIP file that includes a variety of scenario templates. To get the template files, please contact SwiftStack Support at *support@swiftstack.com*.
- Run ssbench in multiserver mode, using more than one benchmarking node to generate requests. If you have anything but a small cluster, you probably will need more than a single benchmarking node.
- ssbench will store its result statistics (*.stat* file) under */tmp/ssbench-results/* by default. You can generate reports from the data files in this directory using the `ssbench-master report-scenario` command.
- Check the cluster resource utilization using your monitoring suite or through the SwiftStack Controller.
- For individual and real-time monitoring of each Swift node, you can use tools such as `htop`, `iftop`, `iostat`, `vmstat`, and `collectl`.

Defining the Scenario File

To define a scenario file, you can create a file named anything you want. SwiftStack recommends naming the scenario file with a human-readable description indicating the key elements of what the scenario file includes. Doing so will make it easier to distinguish between various benchmark runs, of which you will likely have many. A scenario file could include things such as purpose, concurrency, operation count, and CRUD profile. For example, scenario file names could look something like:

- *uc1-backup-large.scenario* for Use Case 1, backups, large files
- *uc2-photo-app-medium.scenario* for Use Case 2, photo sharing app, medium-size files
- *1MB-C-c500-o100000.scenario* for 1 MB files, Create, 500 users, 100,000 files
- *2GB-R-c10-o20.scenario* for 2 GB files, Read, 10 users, 20 files

Elements of the scenario file

Earlier, we covered the fundamental pieces of a scenario file. Here we will explore the elements of scenario files a bit deeper. The most important part of a scenario file is the definition of one or more "size categories," each of which might have a CRUD profile. A CRUD profile simply defines the relative probability that an operation will be a Create,

Read, Update, or Delete. There is a global, top-level CRUD profile for each scenario, but it can be overridden by individual size categories.

Real-world workloads are likely to involve multiple object types, often of different sizes. The size categories in the ssbench scenario file allow you to model these. Size category names can be anything, but reports will look best with short names. You should also choose names that match the use case you're exploring with the benchmark (e.g., "videos" or "vm_images").

Each size category specifies a minimum and maximum size (in bytes) and an optional CRUD profile. As the test generates objects to send, each object's size will be randomly chosen between the minimum and maximum sizes. The test will also generate a combination of Create, Read, Update, and Delete requests matching the CRUD profile.

Thus, a CRUD profile of `[3, 4, 2, 2]` would lead to a test containing 27% Create, 36% Read, 18% Update, and 18% Delete requests. As noted earlier, depending on your scenario, it might help to treat the CRUD profile numbers as percentages. For example, the CRUD profile could be `[50, 30, 15, 5]`, representing 50%, 30%, 15%, and 5% respectively, adding up to 100%.

If you want a size category with a single object size, just set the minimum and maximum values to the same number. If a size category does not specify a CRUD profile, ssbench will use the scenario's top-level CRUD profile for that size category.

Example 17-1 is an example of a scenario in JSON format specifying three size categories. Each has a name by which you can refer to it, followed by the minimum size of the file to be created and the maximum size. The first two size categories have their own CRUD profiles; the "small" size category will use the top-level CRUD profile. The scenario also contains three initial file sizes and ends with a top-level CRUD profile.

Example 17-1. Simple scenario file

```
"sizes": [{
  "name": "zero",
  "size_min": 0,
  "size_max": 0,
  "crud_profile": [60, 15, 20, 5]
}, {
  "name": "tiny",
  "size_min": 4096,
  "size_max": 8192,
  "crud_profile": [10, 80, 9, 1]
}, {
  "name": "small",
  "size_min": 20000,
  "size_max": 40000
}],
"initial_files": {
  "zero": 300,
```

```
    "tiny": 100,
    "small": 10
  },
  "crud_profile": [10, 75, 15, 0],
```

Near the end of the scenario file, just above the global CRUD profile, you will notice the `initial_files` stanza. Initial files can be defined for each size category included in a scenario. The parameter represents the number of files that will be loaded into the cluster per size category before the benchmark run kicks off. Why is this important? Well, if you have defined a CRUD profile that includes reads, updates, or deletes, you have to have something to read from, update, or delete. Thus, if you don't have "initial files" loaded in the cluster when the benchmark kicks off, if the first few CRUD operations happen to be reads, updates, or deletes, your benchmark run will get errors if there are no objects in the cluster to perform those operations on.

Running a benchmark test and viewing the output

For each operation of the benchmark run, a size category is first chosen based on the relative counts for each size category in the `initial_files` dictionary. This probability for each size category appears under the "% Ops" column in the report. Then an operation type is chosen based on that size category's CRUD profile.

If size categories have different CRUD profiles, the overall CRUD profile of the benchmark run will be a weighted average of the values in the "% Ops" column and the CRUD profile of each size category. This weighted average CRUD profile is included in the report on the "CRUD weighted average" line.

For the scenario file in Example 17-1, you would see the derived weighted CRUD profile in the report:

```
% Ops     C   R   U   D       Size Range       Size Name
 73%    % 60  15  20   5        0 B            zero
 24%    % 10  80   9   1        4 kB -    8 kB  tiny
  2%    % 10  75  15   0       20 kB -   40 kB  small
---------------------------------------------------------------------
          47  32  17   4      CRUD weighted average
```

So regardless of size, you would expect about 47% of the operations during the benchmark run to be Create, 32% to be Read, 17% to be Update, and 4% to be Delete. You would also expect about 73% (300 / 410 × 100) of the operations to be zero bytes.

Useful ssbench options

You can tell ssbench to perform a set number of Swift requests (using the `operation_count` setting) or run for a set length of time (using the `run_seconds` setting).

To collect resource utilization, we recommend you run benchmarks for at least 15 minutes. That way it will be easier to view charts in your stats-gathering application, or in the SwiftStack Controller.

The `user_count` scenario file setting determines the number of concurrent requests, which simulate that same number of clients performing operations in parallel as fast as they can. Remember that it is best to start this at 1 and increase it only after a successful run.

For a comprehensive list of ssbench scenario file settings, see the ssbench page on Github. Many scenario file settings may be overridden on the `ssbench-master run-scenario` command line. For a list of command-line options with which you may override scenario file values, see either the ssbench page on Github or the usage message:

```
ssbench-master run-scenario -h
```

The ssbench-worker

The ssbench workers perform operations against the Swift cluster and report the results to the controlling `ssbench-master`. The `ssbench-master` process efficiently spools results directly to disk. After a benchmark run, the raw results file is read, compressed, and used to generate a final report. A single ssbench-worker process cannot use more than one CPU core. Assuming the network interface of the benchmark server is not already saturated, more load may be generated by running up to one ssbench-worker process per CPU core.

For high-throughput testing, it is often necessary to use many benchmark servers, especially if they have only 1 Gbps NICs. This is described in the next section.

Before trusting the benchmark results, you should determine the limits of the benchmark servers themselves. You can do this by adding the `--noop` command-line flag to `ssbench-master run-scenario`. The scenario run and jobs will be sent to and from the ssbench-worker processes, but nothing will actually talk to the Swift cluster. This test tells you the maximum requests per second your specific benchmark setup is capable of. If you want to generate more requests per second against an actual cluster, you will need to add more benchmark nodes or use the `--batch-size` flag on both the `ssbench-master` and `ssbench-worker` command lines.

Ways to Start ssbench-worker

There are two ways to start an ssbench run. The first method is easier: just supply `--workers=N` on the `ssbench-master` command line to automatically start and use *N* ssbench-worker processes. The workers all run on the same server as the master and are stopped automatically after the benchmark run completes. For example:

```
ssbench-master run-scenario -f very_small.scenario -u 4 -c 80 -o 500
--workers 2
```

The second method is to manually start one or more ssbench-worker processes by specifying the `--zmq-host` option with the hostname of the server on which you will run `ssbench-master run-scenario`. You can use multiple servers this way.

For example, to run a benchmark with 400 concurrent connections, using four ssbench-worker processes spread across two benchmark servers, enter commands similar to these:

```
bench-host-01$ ssbench-worker -c 100 --zmq-host bench-host-01 1 &
bench-host-01$ ssbench-worker -c 100 --zmq-host bench-host-01 2 &

bench-host-02$ ssbench-worker -c 100 --zmq-host bench-host-01 3 &
bench-host-02$ ssbench-worker -c 100 --zmq-host bench-host-01 4 &

bench-host-01$ ssbench-master run-scenario -f scenarios/very_small.scenario
-u 400 -o 40000
```

The `-c` option sets the size of the worker's connection pool, which limits the number of concurrent requests the worker can handle. The default value is 64, but here we allow 100 concurrent requests on each of the four workers. The sum of all workers' `-c` values must not be greater than the user count specified by the scenario or the `-u` command-line option to `ssbench-master`. Setting the total ssbench-worker concurrency value higher than necessary can lead to resource problems, so try to keep them close, as in the previous example.

After using the second method, you can kill all ssbench-worker processes, even those on other benchmark servers, by running:

```
ssbench-master kill-workers
```

Benchmarking with swift-bench

The swift-bench tool was originally in the Swift repository but now has its own repository (*https://github.com/openstack/swift-bench*). This benchmark tool is good for generating a single type of load at a time (e.g., only `PUT`s and then only `GET`s) and calculating a total average rate of requests per second per operation. The workload may be spread across multiple benchmark servers. swift-bench allows you to specify a particular workload for each operation type. The following settings and associated switches control the benchmark run:

Total client concurrency (`-c`)
: When multiple `swift-bench-client` processes are running, this value is "split up" across the clients. You can also specify a different concurrency value for the `PUT`, `GET`, and `DELETE` stages.

Size of objects (`-s`)
: This can be a single value, in bytes, or a range if you also supply the `-l` option. When both `-l` and `-s` are specified, each object's size in bytes is randomly chosen from the range between the `-l` and `-s` numbers.

Number of objects (`-n`)
: The number of uniquely named objects to upload during the `PUT` stage. This is analogous to the ssbench "Create" operation (not "Update").

Number of GETs (`-g`)
: The number of download operations to issue during the `GET` stage.

Number of containers (`-C`)
: The number of containers across which objects should be distributed. This can prevent the container server from being a bottleneck.

The command-line switches provided with `swift-bench` expose only a subset of its functionality. More advanced functionality is accessible only through a configuration file.

Preparation

All the benchmarking preparations that we discussed as part of the ssbench setup also apply to swift-bench, or any other benchmarking tool for that matter. That said, as a quick reminder, make sure that your network and the CPU of the machines that are running the benchmark are not limiting your results, or you could be testing something other than what your cluster can do. So, while you are running the benchmarks, you need to make sure that the systems on which you are running the benchmarking are not being limited by the hardware of the benchmark machine itself. If there's a bottleneck, you want it to be in the Swift cluster, not in your benchmarking setup.

How swift-bench Works

Every swift-bench run performs the following steps:

1. Create containers for benchmark data.
2. Upload the specified number of objects, reporting the average rate as it goes, as well as the final average rate for `PUT` operations per second.

3. Download a random object the specified number of times, reporting the average rate as it goes, as well as the final average rate for `GET` operations per second.
4. Delete all uploaded objects, reporting the average rate as it goes and the final rate of `DELETE` operations per second.
5. Delete the containers created in step 1.

Number of Containers

By default, swift-bench uses only 20 containers, which might cause a bottleneck in the container server during `PUT`s and `DELETE`s. When you `PUT` an object, the three object servers each write their replica to disk. When that happens, the object servers will try to update the container servers so the container servers can maintain an accurate count of both objects and the sum of all of their sizes. Therefore, an object `PUT` also includes a container update as part of the request. If you are using only a few containers, the container server might become the limiting factor. Unless you are trying to benchmark the container servers, be sure to use enough containers to spread the load around.

Testing High Concurrency (-c, -b)

`swift-bench` will put as much load against the cluster as it can. In other words, it will go as fast as it can, given the limitations of the concurrency that you specify. This is because `swift-bench` uses Eventlet under the hood just like Swift does. Therefore, `swift-bench` does an extremely good job of managing a large number of concurrent network connections even though it's a single process. This means that a single `swift-bench` instance can generate a considerable amount of load on a Swift cluster.

To simulate the load of hundreds or possibly thousands of clients, crank up the concurrency:

```
$ swift-bench -c 100
```

To increase the concurrency even further, SwiftStack added the ability to run `swift-bench` in a client-server mode. This allows a benchmark run to use multiple servers. Each client will listen for benchmarking commands from the "driver" and report back results. This allows you to use one `swift-bench` invocation to see the results of multiple benchmarking clients. Run a separate command-line tool called `swift-bench-client`, which is the client, and tell `swift-bench` about all the clients using the `-b` command-line option. swift-bench will carve up the load, send it out, and aggregate the results that come back.

There are some limitations to this client-server approach. There is no coordination between the clients, so one client could finish with its portion of the `PUT`s and start on its `GET`s while other clients are still performing uploads. When you distribute a workload that way, it's not directly comparable to a single swift-bench client running the same specified load.

Generally, you will want to run multiple `swift-bench-client` processes on separate machines so you can get enough benchmark client bandwidth to match the bandwidth of your proxy servers. Make sure that nothing on your client side where you're trying to generate the load, such as the available networking speed, is unrealistically limiting the load that goes into the cluster. If you have two proxies with one 10 Gbps NIC each and benchmark servers with 1 Gbps NICs, you would need 20 to 30 benchmark servers to stress the throughput of your proxy servers. Two or three 10 Gbps boxes running swift-bench is fine. In that case, you can start up a couple of `swift-bench-client` processes on each machine to make sure that you're using more than one CPU core per benchmark server.

Testing Latency

Consider a benchmark with a concurrency of something small; for example, two:

```
$ swift-bench -c 2
```

The rate will be dominated by the latency of each request because it's only doing up to two requests in parallel. That makes this test run particularly sensitive to the request latency. Therefore, if you're trying to target benchmarking request latency, don't set your concurrency low.

If you are interested in your cluster's request latency, ssbench can deliver much better reports than swift-bench because ssbench natively tracks and stores the request latency for every single request.

Object Size (-s, -l)

The `-s` value is the size, in bytes, of each object to upload. This allows you to see how your cluster performs with various object sizes. For example, you could know what it would do with 100 MB objects coming in. Obviously, your requests per second will diminish depending on how much bandwidth you've got available.

If you also specify the `-l` option, each object will have a size, in bytes, between the lower bound of the `-l` value and the upper bound of the `-s` value.

A neat thing to try is to set the value to 0 bytes. This way you can stress out your proxy servers to see how many requests per second they can field.

Even zero-byte objects can saturate your storage node disks' IOPS capacity because a zero-byte PUT still results in disk I/O. If you are trying to stress your proxy tier, but you don't have enough disks, you will saturate your disk IOPS first. So, as mentioned earlier, keep an eye on system metrics as you benchmark so you can identify bottlenecks. If the bottleneck is not where you want it, you might not be stressing the part of the system you intend to test.

Number of Objects (-n)

The -n value is the number of objects to be uploaded into the cluster during the PUT stage. This value, along with the size of the objects being put in, have an impact on how much storage the benchmark run will consume in the cluster. So if you're just playing around with swift-bench on a small virtual machine, you won't want to go too crazy or you will fill up the little toy disks attached to the virtual machine.

Number of GETs (-g)

The -g is the number of times that GET requests will be made for objects. The value of -g is completely independent of the number of objects (-n). Usually the number of GETs is greater than the number of PUTs, because GET operations consume less cluster resources and therefore usually have a higher request-per-second rate.

Don't Delete Option (-x)

The -x flag prevents swift-bench from cleaning up the containers it created and the objects it uploaded into them during the benchmark run. This is useful if you want to fill up a cluster with data for other testing purposes.

There was a bug with -x in previous versions of swift-bench, so make sure you are running a recent version.

Creating a Configuration File

Create a configuration file with the following lines, updated for your environment and account settings. In the file shown, the first three settings are the authorization URL, user name, and key described in "Authentication credentials" on page 198. Be sure to create enough containers to support the workload you are testing. Unlike AWS S3, Swift likes to use a lot of containers.

```
[bench]
auth = http://swift.example.com/auth/v1.0
```

```
user = benchmark-test-user
key = benchmark-password
num_containers = 100
```

Sample swift-bench Run

A sample small swift-bench run, with a concurrency of 20, 10-byte objects, uploading 100 objects, then downloading 200 objects, might look like this:

```
$ swift-bench -c 20 -s 10 -n 100 -g 200 /etc/swift/swift-bench.conf
swift-bench 2014-02-28 16:32:54,546 INFO Auth version: 1.0
swift-bench 2014-02-28 16:32:56,056 INFO Auth version: 1.0
swift-bench 2014-02-28 16:32:58,348 INFO 100 PUTS **FINAL** [0 failures],
54.6/s
swift-bench 2014-02-28 16:32:58,348 INFO Auth version: 1.0
swift-bench 2014-02-28 16:32:59,789 INFO 200 GETS **FINAL** [0 failures],
264.0/s
swift-bench 2014-02-28 16:32:59,789 INFO Auth version: 1.0
swift-bench 2014-02-28 16:33:01,282 INFO 100 DEL **FINAL** [0 failures],
93.2/s
swift-bench 2014-02-28 16:33:01,282 INFO Auth version: 1.0
```

Running a Distributed swift-bench

To generate the load required to benchmark a Swift cluster, it's not unrealistic to need a lot of clients on each machine and to use multiple machines to run the benchmarking.

To do so, swift-bench includes a client called `swift-bench-client`, which you run with two required positional arguments, *ip* and *port*. The first argument should be one of the IP addresses on a network interface on the client benchmark server to which the `swift-bench` master process can route packets. The second argument can be any unused port on the client benchmark server, as long as no firewall blocks it.

For example, to spread a swift-bench run across four clients on two benchmark servers:

```
bench-host-01$ swift-bench-client 192.168.100.2 7000
bench-host-01$ swift-bench-client 192.168.100.2 7001

bench-host-02$ swift-bench-client 192.168.100.3 7000
bench-host-02$ swift-bench-client 192.168.100.3 7001

bench-host-03$ swift-bench -b 192.168.100.2:7000 -b 192.168.100.2:7001 -b
192.168.100.3:7000 -b 192.168.100.3:7001 -c 100 -s 100 -n 1000 -g 10000
```

Sample swift-bench Configuration

For reference, an example swift-bench configuration file (*http://bit.ly/conf-sample*) is available on GitHub. This configuration file can serve as a starting point for your benchmarking runs. The current contents are:

```
[bench]
# auth = http://localhost:8080/auth/v1.0
# user = test:tester
# key = testing
# auth_version = 1.0
# log-level = INFO
# timeout = 10

# You can configure PUT, GET, and DELETE concurrency independently or set all
# three with "concurrency"
# put_concurrency = 10
# get_concurrency = 10
# del_concurrency = 10
# concurrency =

# A space-sep list of files whose contents will be read and randomly chosen
# as the body (object contents) for each PUT.
# object_sources =

# If object_sources is not set and lower_object_size != upper_object_size,
# each PUT will randomly select an object size between the two values.  Units
# are bytes.
# lower_object_size = 10
# upper_object_size = 10
# If object_sources is not set and lower_object_size == upper_object_size,
# every object PUT will contain this many bytes.
# object_size = 1

# num_objects = 1000
# num_gets = 10000
# num_containers = 20
# The base name for created containers.
# container_name = (randomly-chosen uuid4)

# Should swift-bench benchmark DELETEing the created objects and then delete
# all created containers?
# delete = yes

# Without use_proxy, swift-bench will talk directly to the backend Swift
# servers.  Doing that will require "url", "account", and at least one
# "devices" entry.
# use_proxy = yes

# If use_proxy = yes, this will override any returned X-Storage-Url returned
# by authentication (the account name will still be extracted from
# X-Storage-Url though and may NOT be set with the "account" conf var).  If
# use_proxy = no, this setting is required and used as the X-Storage-Url when
# deleting containers and as a source for IP and port for back-end Swift
server
# connections.  The IP and port specified in this setting must have local
# storage access to every device specified in "devices".
# url =
```

```
# Only used (and required) when use_proxy = no.
# account =

# A space-sep list of devices names; only relevant (and required) when
# use_proxy = no.
# devices = sdb1
```

Statistics Tools

If you've been running some benchmarks against Swift, you will likely have come to appreciate the information that the benchmarking tool provides you and it might already have answered most of the questions about how well your cluster performs under various use cases. Benchmarking alone provides great information and insight into what clients will experience and what your Swift cluster is capable of. However, combined with other tools, such as the ones listed below, you can get even more information and further test the impact of tuning or architectural changes:

iPerf
: Measures raw network throughput between two NICs

httperf
: A tool for measuring web server performance

htop
: An interactive process viewer for Linux

iostat
: Reports CPU statistics and input/output statistics for devices, partitions, and network filesystems

vmstat
: Reports information about processes, memory, paging, block I/O, traps, and CPU activity

ifstat
: Reports network interfaces bandwidth, similar to vmstat/iostat for other system counters

The reason these tools (and others) can many times be incredibly useful is that they can help you verify and troubleshoot conditions that you encounter during your benchmarking. Benchmarking suites typically won't be able to pinpoint where a bottleneck exists or why; they will only identify that it exists. So, to truly understand what your cluster is doing and how all the different parts of it play a role in the performance you ultimately can get out of it, using and understanding metrics of system tools outside what the benchmarking suites provide is always a good idea.

Conclusion

In this chapter, you learned how to test and benchmark your Swift cluster. Going through operational and failure testing as part of benchmarking is a great way to learn how Swift works under various conditions. Failure testing in conjunction with benchmarking also helps you trust Swift. As you see things continuing to work despite failures, you gain an appreciation for how Swift works around and through failures.

Benchmarking tools can help you determine the limitations of your deployment and correct for these limitations, if need be. Operational testing, including failure testing, and benchmarking can be fun and are critical processes to help you understand your cluster's performance and its bottlenecks. Benchmarking is a great way to learn how your cluster will respond to your intended workload(s). So, you should always do some benchmarking before you put a cluster into production. And don't forget: always scale up your benchmarking from very low numbers and increase them incrementally. That will help you better understand the benchmarking tool you're using and how your cluster is working.

A Swift Afterword

Thanks for spending some time with OpenStack Swift. We hope it's been helpful and informative. Before wrapping up, we wish you all the best in your work with Swift, and invite your feedback.

To close, we'd like to reflect on some of our recent experiences working with Swift and try to look ahead. Much of this will echo what we've been saying throughout the book, but we hope that this will reassure you that by choosing Swift you're positioning yourself —and your organization—on the right side of history (at least as far as object storage goes).

Over the past few years, we've had the privilege of working with hundreds of architects, operators, and deployers of private cloud-storage infrastructure. We observed three noteworthy trends: (1) a pervasive transition to object-based storage, (2) a strong desire to use open source software, and (3) the adoption of OpenStack Swift as the standard for object storage.

The Transition to Object Storage

In 2013, adoption of public object-storage services continued at an ever-accelerating rate. In April, Amazon announced that 1 trillion objects had been uploaded to S3 in the prior 10 months. For a bit of context, it took six years for the first 1 trillion objects to be uploaded. By some estimates, S3 generated several hundred millions of dollars of revenue for Amazon in 2013—and grew over 100% annually. HP, IBM, Google, Microsoft, Rackspace, and Oracle also grew or launched their public object-storage offerings.

Much of this amazing growth is fueled by the numerous web, mobile, and software-as-a-service (SaaS) applications that depend on object storage. For these applications, the performance, scale, and durability of object storage is essential. Traditional filesystem technologies cannot provide the dramatic increase of scale that these applications require. Arrays do not meet the price-per-capacity needs either. Object storage is quite simply the natural storage platform for applications being built today.

Companies looking to store vast amounts of archival data are also benefiting from the cost advantages of object storage. Even major tape vendors are now promoting object-based technologies to meet the needs of increased scale and to lower the cost of long-term archives.

Why Being Open Matters

OpenStack Swift is open source software. To understand why this matters for storage architects and operators, let's look back at what happened to the rest of the infrastructure stack. Previously dismissed by their proprietary competitors as "immature," open source operating systems, middleware, application frameworks, and databases are now standards in enterprise and web infrastructure. The open source model has so completely and fundamentally transformed the infrastructure tier in the data center that very few proprietary infrastructure platform technologies still have a sustainable competitive advantage.

That same transformation is now changing the storage tier, one organization at a time. Vendors of proprietary storage technology often claim that open source cannot produce enterprise-grade storage solutions. However, when done the right way (open code, flexible design, large community), open source platforms not only produce enterprise-grade storage solutions, they provide ones that are the clear winner over locked-in, failure-vulnerable systems. Today, using open source platforms is an irreversible change in enterprise architectures.

It is important to remember that using an open source storage engine does not preclude working with commercial vendors in the OpenStack ecosystem. Jonathan Bryce, executive director of the OpenStack Foundation, explained it this way at the November 2013 OpenStack Summit.

> Cutting edge technology from an open source project is being used by some of the biggest companies in the world. How do they get a comfort level deploying this technology? Partners and support from the community, like SwiftStack and others in the ecosystem that have helped Enterprises meet their business needs.

The Swift ecosystem is very active with great development velocity and real diversity. Swift is much larger than what any single storage company could build. Over 166 developers have contributed to the OpenStack Swift codebase. The Havana release of Swift, which included support for global clusters, had top contributors (by patch count) from five different companies: SwiftStack, Rackspace, Red Hat, eNovance, and IBM. With the recent Icehouse release, Intel, Red Hat, and SwiftStack all worked on storage policies for Swift. It's this ecosystem, in large part, that is driving enterprises to adopt Swift for their production object-storage needs and this ecosystem that will be the reason why Swift continues to succeed.

The Object-Storage Standard

The Swift API is increasingly becoming the API of choice. Terri McClure, senior analyst at Enterprise Strategy Group, notes, "The Swift API has been adopted by or is on the roadmap for most vendors as an object-storage interface, enabling those vendors to serve public, private, and hybrid cloud deployments without concerns about users making proprietary API investments." Naturally, the biggest cloud operators have APIs that developers use so applications can write to those storage clouds. EMC, Oracle, and Red Hat are a few of the largest vendors who announced support for the Swift API in 2013. This allows their users to integrate with public clouds that run Swift, and leverage private clouds riding the popularity of Swift in private deployments.

We predict that the future will further cement Swift as the standard for object storage.

Now It's Your Turn

Now it's your turn—in two ways. First, it's your turn to start applying and working with Swift, SwiftStack, and anything else that you're integrating with. We hope that this process will be satisfying and fulfilling. There's a great community of Swift operators and developers you can turn to for help. And we're always happy to hear from you (*contact@swiftstack.com*).

Second, it's your turn—if you wish—to share with us your comments, feedback, and suggestions. We're planning to produce a second edition of this book and we're very interested in your sense of what we need to correct or add. Thanks, in advance, for helping us create a resource that will serve you better. You can share comments and feedback by visiting this book's website (*http://swiftstack.com/book/*).

Thanks and we look forward to hearing from you, working with you, or just seeing you around.

Index

Symbols

A

We'd like to hear your suggestions for improving our indexes. Send email to index@oreilly.com.

B

C

D

E

F

G

H

I

J

K

L

M

N

O

P

Q

R

S

T

U

V

W

X

Z

About the Author

Joe Arnold is the co-founder and CEO of SwiftStack, a leading provider of object storage software. An innovator in cloud-computing infrastructure, Joe has been examining, addressing, and building solutions that help move today's cloud reality forward when it comes to speed, scale, and power. He built one of the first widely-used cloud platforms-as-a-service (PaaS) on top of Amazon Web Services at Engine Yard, and managed the first public OpenStack launch of Swift after its release as an open source project. He has subsequently deployed multiple large-scale cloud storage systems. While at Engine Yard, he additionally oversaw the development of their Ruby on Rails deployment platform (AppCloud), and managed the open source efforts of Rails 3, JRuby, and Rubinius. Joe has been active in the OpenStack community since 2010. He has also authored a popular book on yo-yo techniques called *From Beginner to Spinner*.

Colophon

The animal on the cover of *OpenStack Swift* is a swallow (of the *Hirundinidae* or *Pseudochelidoninae* families). These designations include the barn swallow and the martin, which are the most commonly recognized types of swallows. Despite their small wings and little feet, swallows have strong powers of flight, partly thanks to their distinctive square or forked tails.

These agile birds live all over the world except for the coldest, most remote regions. The common swallow is in almost perpetual migration, and the cliff swallow is renowned for its annual return to the San Juan Capistrano Mission in California (approximately halfway between L.A. and San Diego). Other common hangouts for this bird family include Canada, New Zealand, and Argentina; Antarctica is the only continent they do not visit. African swallows have the greatest species diversity, but they are less migratory than their European and North American counterparts (and as far as we know, no types of swallows carry coconuts with them as they migrate).

The swallows' pointed wings allow them to glide and increase their stamina in the air, as well as giving them agility to catch insects. Along with flying skills and expressive calls, a long tail may help the males of the species attract females. Swallows remain monogamous once they mate. Overall, gender differences are subtle and usually come down to coloring.

Swallows can be very territorial, especially around nesting areas, which are large communal roosts. They may even attack people who get too close during the breeding season. However, there is a generally symbiotic relationship between swallows and humans, largely because they consume a lot of insects. A "flight" or "sweep" of swallows was long considered to bring good luck to sailors, and historian Pliny the Elder records that they were used as messenger birds to report the winners of horse races. Saint Francis of Assisi is said to have preached to swallows in the woods, after which they bowed their heads, and he found them disarmingly charming and beautiful.

Many of the animals on O'Reilly covers are endangered; all of them are important to the world. To learn more about how you can help, go to *animals.oreilly.com*.

The cover image is from Wood's *Illustrated Natural History*. The cover fonts are URW Typewriter and Guardian Sans. The text font is Adobe Minion Pro; the heading font is Adobe Myriad Condensed; and the code font is Dalton Maag's Ubuntu Mono.